WOMEN AND
JEWISH DIVORCE:
THE REBELLIOUS WIFE,
THE AGUNAH AND THE RIGHT OF
WOMEN TO INITIATE DIVORCE
IN JEWISH LAW,
A HALAKHIC SOLUTION

WOMEN AND JEWISH DIVORCE:
THE REBELLIOUS WIFE, THE AGUNAH AND THE RIGHT OF WOMEN TO INITIATE DIVORCE IN JEWISH LAW, A HALAKHIC SOLUTION

by

Shlomo Riskin

Ktav Publishing House, Inc.
Hoboken, NJ
5788/1989

Library of Congress Cataloging-in-Publication Data

Riskin, Shlomo.
    Women and Jewish divorce.
      p. cm.
    Bibliography: p.
    Includes index.
    ISBN 0–88125–122–4 : $17.95. ISBN 0–88125–132–1 (pbk.) : $11.95
    1. Divorce (Jewish law)—History. 2. Husband and Wife (Jewish—History.
3. Agunah—History. 4. Rabbinical literature—History and criticism. I. Title.
LAW <General Risk 1988>
296.1′8—dc19   88–8854
                                                     CIP

DEDICATION

To my beloved parents,

Harry and Rose Riskin,

*who have always encouraged
me even when I rebelled
against their wishes,
and to my beloved
parents-in-law,*

David and Charlotte Pollins,

*who provided for me the
very antithesis of a rebellious wife*

TABLE OF CONTENTS

INTRODUCTION

The halakhic history of *moredet,* the rebellious wife, provides a fascinating glimpse at the development of Jewish law and the forces behind it. In Mishnaic and early Talmudic times, a *moredet* was a woman who denied her husband sexual relations as punishment for some offense he had committed against her—real or imagined. Since she wished to remain his wife, the earliest halakhic approach was to legislate successively harsher decrees against her, designed to coerce her into resuming marital relations.

In Biblical times, a man could divorce his wife at will; a woman could not initiate divorce proceedings. This was not as unjust as it first appears. Acutely aware of the socioeconomic liabilities incumbent upon a divorcee, most women preferred methods other than divorce to achieve their purpose. As Resh Lakish, a first-generation Palestinian Amora (ca. 230 C.E.) observed, "A woman would rather live with grief than live alone" (bKid 41a).

Perhaps because of this consideration, the rabbis of the Mishnaic period sought to protect a woman from being divorced against her will. The *ketubah,* or marriage contract (which some think to be Biblical in origin and at the very latest was instituted by Rabbi Shimon ben Shetach ca. 40 B.C.E.), made it impossible for a husband to divorce his wife without giving her a substantial sum of money, at least enough for two years' sustenance. Moreover, a physical or occupational problem with the husband was sufficient grounds for the court to force him to divorce his wife if she so wished. In order further to protect the wife's position Rabbenu Gershom in Northern

Germany (ca. 960 C.E.–1028 C.E.) enacted a decree which made it impossible for a husband to divorce his wife against her will.

But what about the woman who "merely" found her husband distasteful, though she had no legally justifiable grounds for divorce? Here the Talmudic sages found themselves in a dilemma. Historically, Halakhah had sought to preserve the institutions of marriage and family at almost all costs. Divorce is sanctioned only as the final option. "Even the altar of the Holy Temple sheds tears over him who divorces his first wife" (bGit 90b). Clearly, a woman's petition for the rabbinical court to grant her a divorce because of subjective considerations was viewed with caution. Consideration for the woman dictated that a means be found to extricate her from an intolerable position. Yet the possibility existed that she had "cast her eyes on another man" (mNed 11:12), in which case the court would disallow the divorce in order to preserve the family. (It should be noted that no such dilemma arose in the case of the husband's seeking a divorce for purely subjective reasons. Before Rabbenu Gershom's circumscribing polygamy, a man could "cast his eye on another woman" and marry her, without dissolving his original family.) The legal authorities are divided over this issue, presumably on the basis of the relative importance they placed on each factor: the feelings of the woman or the stability of the family.

The Jerusalem Talmud and ancient marriage contracts found in the Cairo Genizah seem to prove that in early Amoriac times (third and fourth centuries of the common era) the dilemma was resolved in favor of the woman's feelings. A stipulation in the *ketubah* ensured that if either party found the other distasteful, the court could impose a divorce. That such stipulations were used we see from the fact that in Babylonia in later Amoraic times, the Mishnaic term *moredet* was expanded to include a woman who sought a divorce on the basis of the claim "[my husband] is distasteful to me." In such a case, the Rabbis forced her husband to grant her a divorce after twelve months if she still desired it, although the woman forfeited any alimony provided in her marriage contract. Later, the Geonim (ca. 800–1000 C.E.) went a step further by eliminating the twelve-month waiting period and reinstituting the alimony payment. These measures were promoted by their fears that a frustrated or destitute woman might turn to conversion or prostitution. The scholars Alfasi (1013–1103 C.E.) and Maimonides (1135–1204 C.E.), representing the early Sages of North Africa and Spain, and Rabbenu Shmuel ben Meir (ca. 1080/85–1174 C.E.), an early Sage of France, likewise followed the Gaonic precedent of coercing the husband to grant a divorce, although different traditions existed regarding monetary compensation.

The entire picture changed radically in later generations, due largely to the halakhic views of one individual—the younger brother of Rabbenu Shmuel ben Meir, Rabbenu Tam (1100–1171 C.E.). His chief concern was to preserve the institution of marriage and minimize the number of divorces. Insisting that there was no Talmudic precedent for coercing a husband to divorce his wife on the basis of her subjective claim that he was repulsive to her, he rejected the earlier Gaonic decrees. So overwhelming was his personality, and so cogent his legal reasoning, that his ruling influenced all subsequent halakhic authorities. From his time onward, the tide turned in the other direction, and the position of earlier authorities such as Alfasi and Maimonides was rejected. To this day the law is such that a woman who finds her husband distasteful has no legal recourse and must remain tied to a husband she abhors.

In this work I hope to demonstrate that Rabbenu Tam's reading of the Talmudic texts, notwithstanding its universal acceptance by successive generations of scholars and final incorporation into the codes, was indeed a minority opinion, and that there is no reason not to restore the means—accepted by the Geonim, and the early authorities of North Africa, Spain, and France—of enabling the woman to free herself from an intolerable marriage. It is the burden of this work to prove that there are sufficient legal grounds to do so, and it is up to the contemporary halakhic community to grant the woman her proper due.

ACKNOWLEDGEMENTS

I am most grateful to a number of most unique individuals to whom I owe a great deal in the preparation of this volume.

First and foremost to my most revered Rebbe and teacher Ha-Rav Joseph B. Soloveitchik, in whose shiur I was privileged to sit and from whose waters I was so privileged to drink for seven of my most formative years of Torah study.

It was Professor Meyer Simcha Feldblum with whom I studied at the Bernard Revel Graduate School of Yeshiva University, who first suggested the topic of this study and who directed my original research.

Prof. Larry Schiffman helped me organize my material and was an invaluable help in shepherding me through the complex requirements for a doctoral degree from New York University. He is therefore in many ways responsible for this finished product.

Karen Cohen Toso helped turn rabbinic language into more or less readable prose.

Professor Yaakov Elman not only read the manuscript and made many helpful suggestions but also painstakingly checked each of the footnotes and verified their accuracy.

And of course my beloved congregants of Lincoln Square Synagogue and the city of Efrat provided the necessary impetus to making my Torah a "Torat Chaim" which attempts never to lose contact with human needs and contemporary issues.

I would also like to take this opportunity to thank the family of HaRav Bezalel Zolty z.t.l., for permission to publish the important *responsum* reproduced in chapter VII.

Most of all I must give thanks to the Almighty for granting me the opportunity to labor in His vineyard.

WOMEN AND
JEWISH DIVORCE:
THE REBELLIOUS WIFE,
THE AGUNAH AND THE RIGHT OF
WOMEN TO INITIATE DIVORCE
IN JEWISH LAW,
A HALAKHIC SOLUTION

CHAPTER I
MOREDET IN THE TANNAITIC PERIOD

In order properly to evaluate the halakhic development of the treatment accorded a "rebellious wife," it is necessary to analyze the Tannaitic sources which deal with the problem. The term *moredet* first appears in the Mishnah, but it is not precisely defined. Is a rebellious wife a woman who refuses to cook dinner for her husband? One who refuses him marital relations? Or one who refuses to remain married to a husband she no longer loves, and demands a divorce despite his objections? Clearly, the legal definition of *moredet* will have far-reaching ramifications for the institution of marriage, the rabbinic role in stabilizing the marital relationship, women's rights, and even the possibility of a woman suing for divorce. In order to arrive at this definition, we must first understand the relevant mishnas in their entirety, and thereby begin to clarify the original intent of the term *moredet*.

MISHNAH

המורדת על בעלה, פוחתין לה מכתובתה שבעה דינרין בשבת
ר' יהודה אומר: שבעה טרפעקין
עד מתי הוא פוחת? עד כנגד כתובתה
ר' יוסי אומר: לעולם הוא פוחת והולך שמא תפול לה ירושה ממקום אחר, גובה הימנה.
וכן המורד על אשתו, מוסיפין על כתובה שלשה דינרין בשבת
ר' יהודה אומר: שלשה טרפעיקין[1]

If a wife rebels against her husband, the [lump-sum] alimony pro-

3

vided for by her marriage contract is to be reduced by seven *dinarim* each week [of her refusal].

R. Yehudah says: seven *quinarii*.

For how long do the reductions continue? Until the entire alimony has been depleted.

R. Yose says: Reductions continue to be made [even after the alimony has been depleted], since she may receive an inheritance from another source from which her husband [can] continue to collect.

Likewise, if a husband rebels against his wife, an addition of three *dinarim* a week is to be made to the alimony provided for by her marriage contract.

R. Yehudah says: three *quinarii* [1½ *dinarim*].[2]

PENALTY FOR REBELLION

This mishnah ordains that a rebellious wife has the amount of alimony provided for in her marriage contract (in case of divorce by her husband) reduced each week, in a gradual but steady fashion. If the average marriage contract provided for payment of two hundred *zuzim* (*dinarim*),[3] it would take approximately seven months, according to the anonymous opinion (*Tanna Kamma*) stated in the mishnah—and fourteen months according to R. Yehudah—for the entire alimony to be forfeited. The first view limits the reduction to the alimony mentioned in the *ketubah* itself, although he probably includes the additions and marriage gifts generally included within the marriage document, whereas R. Yose extends the reductions to include even an unanticipated inheritance which may fall to the wife at a later time. The dispute in this mishnah emanates from the fourth generation of Tannaim, students of R. Akiba, who lived during the first half of the second century C.E., although the original law was probably much earlier.[4]

DEFINITION

It is not clear from the mishnah what a wife must do (or refuse to do) in order to be called *moredet,* although it seems she must fail to fulfill some particular responsibility. Reinforcing this view is the wording of the text of mKet 5:5, which delineates certain wifely obligations.

אלו מלאכות שהאשה עושה לבעלה: טוחנת ואופה ומכבסת; מבשלת, ומניקה את בנה
מצעת לו את המטה ועושה בצמר, הכניסה לו שפחה אחת — לא טוחנת, ולא אופה ולא
מכבסת; שתים — אינה מבשלה ואינה מניקה את בנה; שלש — אינה מצעת לו את
המטה ואינה עושה בצמר; ארבעה — יושבת בקתדרא
רבי אליעזר אומר: אפילו הכניסה לו מאה שפחות. כופה לעשות בצמר, שהבטלה מביאה
לידי זימה.
רבן שמעון בן גמליאל אומר: אף המדיר את אשתו מלעשות מלאכה — יוציא ויתן
כתובתה, שהבטלה מביאה לידי שעמום.[5]

These are the household duties a wife does for her husband: she grinds, bakes, and washes; she cooks and nurses her child; she makes his bed and spins wool. If [she brought into the marriage] one maid, she need not grind, bake, or wash; [if she brought into the marriage] two [maids], she need not cook or suckle her child; [if with] three [maids], she not need need not make his bed or spin wool; [and if she brought] four [maids], she sits on her throne. R. Eliezer says: Even if she brings in one hundred maids, he must force her to spin wool, for inactivity leads to lewdness. Rabban Shimon ben Gamliel says: If a husband makes a vow to keep his wife from performing any tasks, he must grant her a divorce and give her the alimony provided for by the marriage contract, for inactivity leads to boredom.

Since household tasks are the only wifely obligations explicitly discussed in this mishnah, and since, even according to R. Eliezer, she is required at the very least to spin wool, logic might dictate that the "rebellious wife" mentioned in our original mishnah is a woman who refuses to perform these tasks.[6] As an added support for this interpretation, it can be noted that the reduction of the alimony by seven *dinarim* each week may well be based on the fact that there are seven types of household duties delineated by the mishnah.[7]

The difficulty with this interpretation lies in the precise nature of the work the wife is obligated to perform. Is the wife obligated to perform these tasks, in return for which the husband is obligated to support her, or is the husband obligated to support his wife, in return for which the wife must perform the household duties? If the first is correct, the woman is forbidden to enter a marriage with the stipulation, "Do not support me and I will not perform the household tasks for you," since their performance is seen as a primary responsibility. If the latter reasoning is correct, such a stipulation would be permissible, since the only concern is for an equitable economic arrangement convenient to the wife. First-generation Amoraim were divided on this issue, with the Babylonian Rav giving the woman the option of forgoing support in return for which she is freed from her household obligations,[8] while the Palestinian Resh Lakish denied her the right to make such a stipulation. If the wife might indeed forgo the husband's support and not perform her household duties (because they were not considered her primary marital obligation), it would be highly improbable that the term "rebellious wife" in our mishnah refers to that woman who refuses to perform her household duties.

Alternatively, a *moredet* may be defined as a woman who refuses to have sexual relations with her husband. Indeed, the mishnah immediately preceding the one which discusses *moredet* speaks about sexual responsibility, albeit that of the husband to the wife.

המדיר את אשתו מתמשיש המטה — בית שמאי אומרים שתי שבתות, בית הלל אומרים שבת אחת. התלמידים יוצאין לתלמוד תורה שלא ברשות — שלושים יום. הפועלים — שבת אחת.

העונה האמורה בתורה: הטיילין — בכל יום. הפועלים — שתים בשבת; החמרים — אחת בשבת; הגמלים — אחת לשלשים יום; הספנים — אחת לששה חדשים; דברי רבי אליעזר.[9]

If a man makes a vow that he will not engage in sexual relations with his wife,

The House of Shammai says: he may do so for [only] two weeks.
The House of Hillel says: he may do so for [only] one week.

Students are permitted to leave [their homes] in order to study Torah without the permission [of their wives] for [a maximum of] thirty days.
Workmen [are permitted to leave their homes for the sake of

employment without the permission of their wives for a maximum of] one week.

[The minimum number of times] an individual is Biblically obligated to engage in sexual relations with his wife:
> one who is at leisure—once a day;
> workmen—twice a week;
> donkey—drivers [who travel near their homes]—once a week;
> camel—drivers [who travel far distances]—once in thirty days;
> sailors—once in six months. These are the words of R. Eliezer.

Clearly, the context of the mishnah is decisive. The preceding mishnah delineates the sexual obligations of the husband to the wife; it is logical to assume that a *moredet* is a wife who refuses to fulfill her sexual obligations to her husband. The problem with this interpretation is that the mishnah we examined earlier speaks of the wife's marital obligations only in terms of her household tasks. It is possible that the mishnah concerning household tasks and our mishnah of *moredet* originally formed a single unit which dealt with both the wife's obligations to her husband and the penalty for her refusal to fulfill them. Later 5:6 was inserted, since the conclusion of 5:5 deals with the husband's vow that his wife not work, and 5:6 deals with his vow not to have sexual relations with her. This subsequent insertion of 5:6, which is tangential to the entire issue of the wife's work obligations, may be responsible for the confusion concerning the definition of a *moredet*. Moreover, although the Bible enjoins a husband to provide his wife with sexual gratification, there is no explicit biblical command for the wife to provide her husband with sexual satisfaction.[10]

Before we can even suggest that a *moredet* is a woman who refuses to have sexual relations with her husband, we must determine the exact nature of a wife's marital responsibility. According to Rav Kahana (apparently the first-generation Amora) such responsibility, does exist. Based upon her marital agreement, it is the moral foundation of her marital obligation.

דאמר רב כהנא: תשמישי עליך, כופין אותה ומשמשתו דשעבודי משעבדת ליה; הנאת תשמישך עלי אסור, שאין מאכילין לו לאדם דבר האסור לו.[11]

> Since Rav Kahana said: If a wife vows "pleasure from sex with me is
> forbidden to you [her husband]," she is forced and he has relations
> with her, for she is obligated to him [and she has no right to cancel
> her obligation]; [however,] if she vows "the pleasure of having sexual
> relations with you [her husband] is forbidden to me" [and therefore
> makes the vow on herself and not him], he is prohibited from having
> sexual relations with her, since we may never feed an individual a
> food which is prohibited to him. [However, he may then cancel the
> vow, which is his Biblical right, in accordance with Numbers 30:9].

The majority of Talmudic commentaries agree with the view of
Rav Kahana that the wife is obligated to provide her husband with
sexual relations.[12] They derive this obligation from the *mutual*
nature of the responsibility that both partners assume at the time of
the marriage.

ועוד תדע לך שהרי האשה אינה מצווה ב„עונה" ואפילו הכי באוסרת הנאתה על בעלה
לא חייל נדרה כלל ואין צריך להפר מהאי טעמא, דשעבודי משעבדה ליה.

> And further know that although a woman is not explicitly [Biblically]
> directed to provide her husband with sexual relations; nevertheless, if
> she takes a vow prohibiting her husband from deriving sexual plea-
> sure from her, the vow does not take effect at all. The husband need
> not [even] rescind the vow, since she is obligated [to submit] to him.[13]

If, indeed, a woman is obligated to sexually gratify her husband,
why is it that the Bible only specifies the obligations of a man to his
wife? Perhaps it is to ensure that the husband—who was seen as the
aggressive partner in initiating the marriage[14]—not take advantage
of his privilege, and that he behave with restraint and sensitivity.[15]
The Bible impresses upon a man the fact that he must view sex as not
only his own privilege but his wife's as well.

Having ascertained that a woman is obligated to have sexual
relations with her husband, it seems clear that in the context of this
mishnah, a *moredet* may be either a woman who refuses her husband
sexual gratification (in accordance with 5:6) or one who refuses to
fulfill her household duties (in accordance with 5:5). The Amoraim

entertain both possibilities. The majority of Talmudic commentaries grant the wife the option of refusing her husband's support, and thereby freeing herself from her work obligations; at the same time, they maintain that a wife is responsible to engage in sexual relations with her husband. It seems clear that the Rabbis understood the *moredet* of our mishnah to be that wife who rebels against her mandated sexual responsibility.

MOTIVATION

Having determined the nature of the wife's rebellion, it remains for us to examine her motivation. Assuming that a woman is termed *moredet* because of her refusal to have sexual relations with her husband, can we understand what prompts her refusal? Does she find him repulsive and through this behavior seeks a divorce, or is her refusal a means by which to gain certain concessions from a husband whom she fundamentally loves and to whom she wishes to remain married?

As stated earlier, the Mishnah recognizes the possibility that a woman may find it impossible to continue living with her husband, and may appeal to the court for a divorce. In such instances, not only did the Rabbis force the husband to grant the divorce, they also ensured that the woman would receive her full alimony. However, in any case, objective factors had to support the wife's claim.

ט. האיש שנולדו לו מומין. אין כופין אותו להוציא. אמר רבן שמעון בן גמליאל במה דברים אמורים במומין הקטנים אבל במומין הגדולים כופין אותו להוציא.
י. ואלו כופין אותו להוציא: מוכה שחין ובעל פוליפוס והמקמץ והמצרף נחושת והבורסי — בין שהיו בם עד שלא נשאו ובין מנשאו נולדו.
ועל כולן אמר רבי מאיר: אף על פי שהתנה עמה יכולה היא שתאמר: סבורה הייתי שאני יכולה לקבל ועכשיו איני יכולה לקבל.
וחכמים אומרים: מקבלת היא על כרחה חוץ ממוכה שחין מפני שממקתו.
מעשה בצידון בברסי אחד שמת והיה לו אח בורסי, אמרו חכמים — יכולה שתאמר: לאחיך הייתי יכולה לקבל ולך איני יכולה לקבל.[16]

A man who has developed blemishes cannot be coerced to divorce [his wife, if she requests it].

Rabban Shimon ben Gamliel says: This was only stated with regard to minor blemishes. But with regard to major blemishes, one is coerced to divorce [his wife if she requests it].

And the following are coerced to divorce [their wives]: A person with severe skin disease, one with a bad odor emanating from his nose, one who gathers the dung of dogs, one who forges copper, and a tanner. [Divorce is coerced] whether these conditions prevailed before they were married or whether they arose after they were married.

Concerning all of these, R. Meir says: Even though she agreed [to these physical conditions before they were married], she is able to say: I thought I would be able to accept [them], and now I [see that I] am unable to accept [them].

The Sages say: She must accept [these conditions] against her will, [since she originally agreed to them,] with the exception of a one with a severe skin disease, since cohabitation erodes his skin.

An incident occurred in Sidon, whereby a certain tanner died [having left no children], and he had a brother who was a tanner [and who would ordinarily be obligated to marry his brother's widow in a levirate marriage]. The Sages said: She is able to declare: Your brother I was able to accept, but you I am unable to accept.

The Tosefta is even more explicit than the Mishnah about a woman's right to a divorce and alimony in the case of a blemished husband.

רבן שמעון בן גמליאל אומר: אם היה חיגר מאחת מרגליו וסומא באחת מעיניו מומין
גדולים הן יוציא ויתן כתובה . . .
אימתי אמרו יוציא ויתן כתובה בזמן שהוא רוצה והיא אינה רוצה. היא רוצה והוא
אינו רוצה אם היו שניהן רוצין יקיימו.[17]

Rabban Shimon ben Gamliel says:
   If he is lame in one of his legs or blind in one of his eyes, these are [considered] major blemishes and he must divorce her and give her the alimony provided for her by marriage contract . . . .
   When do [the Sages] say: He must divorce her and give her the alimony? At the time when he wishes [to remain married] and she does not, or when she wishes [to remain married] and he does not. If the two of them wish [to remain married], they stay together.

But regarding a person with a severe skin disease, even if they both wish [to remain married], they may not remain [married].

The extent to which the Sages of the Mishnah were willing to coerce a man into giving his wife a divorce and *paying* her alimony—but only on the basis of *objective* blemishes— is seen even more clearly in the following mishnah:

בראשונה היו אומרים: שלש נשים יוצאות ונוטלות כתובה: האומרת טמאה אני לך, שמים ביני לבינך, נטולה אני מן היהודים.
חזרו לומר: שלא תהא אשה נותנת עיניה באחר ומקלקלת על בעלה אלא האומרת טמאה אני לך — תביא ראיה לדבריה. שמים ביני לבינך — יעשו דרך בקשה. נטולה אני מן היהודים — יפר חלקו, ותהא משמשתו ותהא נטולה מן היהודים.[18]

Originally [the Sages] said: Three women are to be divorced [even against their husband's will] and are to receive their alimony:

(1) One who says "I am defiled for you" [i.e., the wife of a priest who claims she was raped and is therefore forbidden to live with her husband]; (2) [one who says] "Heaven is between you and me" [i.e., only the Almighty understands the difference between us, because you are impotent or sterile]; and (3) [one who says] "I have been taken away from Jewish men" [i.e., since I vowed not to have sexual relations with anyone (including my husband), I can no longer live with you].

The Sages then revised [their views] and said that a woman must not be [so easily given the opportunity] to look at another man and destroy her relationship with her husband. [Therefore], (1) she who claims "I am defiled for you" must bring proof of her words. (2) [She who claims] "Heaven is between you and me" must be appeased [by an attempted reconciliation between the couple]. (3) [She who claims] "I have been taken away from Jewish men" must have his share of the vow nullified (that is, since he has the right to nullify that aspect of the vow which pertains to himself, he must do so) and he may then have sexual relations with her [but] she will remain "taken away from Jewish men" that is, any man other than her husband—after she is divorced or widowed; this is the new meaning of her vow).

It is obvious from these sources that in the Talmudic period only an objective blemish was sufficient cause for the Rabbis to impose a divorce. Moreover, whenever the issue was the *wife's* desire for divorce, it is clearly stated as such in the Mishnah. Since our original mishnah dealing with the *moredet* does not provide the wife with an objective reason for requesting a divorce, and further, says nothing whatsoever about her desire for divorce (even though the previous mishnah deals with legitimate grounds for the wife)[19]—it seems clear that the *moredet*'s motivation is not to get a divorce but to withhold sexual relations in order to gain some desired end. In such a case, just as the Rabbis were concerned lest a husband take advantage of his wife in regard to his conjugal rights, so were they concerned lest a wife manipulate her husband with the threat of sexual deprivation. Such a woman is to be punished, or fined, by a steady reduction of her alimony sum until she agrees to fulfill her sexual obligations to him. If she does not agree, she eventually forfeits the entire alimony. Not only economics is at stake here. Since a husband and wife are forbidden to cohabit without an alimony provision in the marriage contract, a woman's steady refusal to have sexual relations with her husband—and hence the eventual depletion of the alimony provided for her in the *ketubah*—must lead to the woman's being divorced from her husband. Since the Mishnah makes it clear that the woman does not want a divorce, but is instead employing sex as a bargaining tool, this halakhah emerges not as a penalty, but as a powerful deterrent to such action.

TOSEFTA: ONE GENERATION LATER

In the transitional period between the Mishnah and the Talmud—the era of the students of R. Yehudah HaNasi (ca. 200 C.E.), the compiler of the Mishnah—the punishment accorded to the *moredet* became far more severe. Apparently, many more women were "punishing" their husbands by denying them sexual relations, and the Rabbis saw that the gradual reduction of the marriage contract by seven *dinarim* a week was not a sufficiently powerful deterrent. The Tosefta, a compilation of laws from the Tannaitic period prior to and immediately following R. Yehudah HaNasi, which at times differs from and at times clarifies and enlarges the scope of the Mishnah,[20] preserves from this period the stringent development of the law of *moredet*. The original text of the *baraita* which deals with the *moredet* is difficult to determine, since it is quoted in a number of different forms within the classic body of halakhic literature. Yet an attempt to discover the form of the original text will shed light on the development of the law of *moredet* in the time of the Tosefta and in the subsequent generations of Amoraim.

המורדת על בעלה וכו' זו משנה ראשונה.

רבותינו התקינו שיהו בית דין מתרין בה ארבע וחמש שבתות זו אחר זו פעמים בשבת.

יתר על כן אפילו כתובתה מאת מנה אבדה את הכל. אחת ארוסה ואחת שומרת יבם אפי' נדה ואפי' חולה.[21]

"One who rebels against her husband, etc."—this is the original mishnah [of Rabbi Yehudah HaNasi].

Subsequently, our Rabbis decreed that the [Jewish] court warn for four and [or] five consecutive weeks, twice each week.

If she continues [her rebelliousness] beyond this point, even if her marriage contract is worth one hundred *maneh,* she forfeits all of it.

[The law is] the same with regard to an engaged woman, one who is waiting for a levirate marriage, and even for a menstruating woman and for an ill woman.

The *baraita*'s phrase "our Rabbis" (*Rabbotenu*) probably refers to the leaders of the Sanhedrin headed by R. Yehudah Nesia, the grandson of R. Yehudah HaNasi.[22] As suggested earlier, these stringencies were probably enacted to control the increasing number of rebellious wives. Thus the Tosefta represents a second stage in the treatment of the *moredet,* wherein a wife is given up to five weeks to mend her ways. After this period of time, she forfeits her entire alimony (not merely seven *dinarim* a week), no matter how large the alimony provision may have been. So while the Tosefta provides for a "grace period" not mentioned in the Mishnah, the subsequent penalty, if enacted, is correspondingly harsher and more immediate.

There are, however, a number of textual variations in the versions of this *baraita* cited in the Jerusalem and Babylonian Talmuds. These variants reflect interesting discrepencies in the actual procedure of penalizing the *moredet*. We shall now examine the various citations.

THE BARAITA CITED BY THE JERUSALEM TALMUD

בית דין שלאחריהם מתרין בה ארבע שבתות והיא שוברת כתובתה ויוצאה.[23]

The [Jewish] court [which came] after them [legislated that the *moredet* be] warned for four weeks, [at which time] she breaks her marriage contract and leaves [with a bill of divorcement].

THE BARAITA CITED BY THE BABYLONIAN TALMUD

רבותינו חזרו ונמנו שיהו מכריזין עליה ארבע שבתות זו אחר זו ושולחין לה בית דין: הוי יודעת שאפילו כתובתיך מאה מנה הפסדת.
אחת לי ארוסה ונשואה, אפילו נדה, אפילו חולה ואפילו שומרת יבם.[24]

Our Rabbis revised [their views] and decided that they must publicly announce her [behavior] for four consecutive weeks, [during which time] the court would send her [the following message]: "Know that even if your marriage contract is [worth] one hundred *maneh,* you have lost it."

[The law is] the same if she be engaged or married, or even if she is menstruating, or ill, or awaiting a levirate marriage.

PROBABLE TEXT OF THE ORIGINAL TOSEFTA
REGARDING PRIVATE WARNING OR PUBLIC ANNOUNCEMENT

The major difference of opinion in the two passages cited above concerns the manner in which the *moredet* is to be informed of her misconduct. In both cases, the slow reduction of seven *dinarim* a week is replaced by four weeks of intense pressure. But is the woman to be privately warned (מתרין בה), as in the Tosefta and in the baraita cited by the Jerusalem Talmud, or is she to be publicly denounced

(מכריזין עליה), as prescribed by the Babylonian Talmud? Which is the correct reading, and what was the original procedure?

It is probable, based on the relative ages of the sources in which these passages appear, that the original version of the Tosefta resembled the text found in all extant versions of the Tosefta and in the baraita cited by the Jerusalem Talmud, which is also quoted by the fourteenth-century Talmudic commentator, Menahem Ha-Meiri.[25] It seems clear that in Palestine, where the Jerusalem Talmud originated, there was no public proclamation—merely a private warning to the woman to mend her ways or forfeit her alimony.[26] The text of the original baraita probably began: רבותינו התקינו שיהו מזהירין בה . . . . "Our Rabbis enacted that she be warned . . ."[27]

PROBABLE EXPLANATION OF THE BARAITA
CITED BY THE BABYLONIAN TALMUD

What was the reason for the change from the private warning cited in the Jerusalem Talmud to the public announcement referred to in the Babylonian Talmud? As we study the discussion of the Babylonian Amoraim, we find that a fourth-generation scholar, Rami bar Hama (who lived after the closing of the Jerusalem Talmud), added the following deterrent regarding the law of the rebellious wife:[28]

אין מכריזין עליה אלא בבתי כנסיות ובבתי מדרשות.

They publicly proclaim against her in the Houses of Assembly and Houses of Prayer.

In order to establish the authority of this stringency, his contemporary, Rava, attempted to find a basis for it in the original baraita.

דיקא נמי דקתני ארבע שבתות זו אחר זו.

We can also deduce this [the public denunciation of the moredet], since we learned [in the original baraita] "Sabbaths" [which idiomatically means weeks, i.e., a seven-day cycle concluding with the Sabbath, but which can literally be read as "the Sabbaths," or in the public places where Jews congregate on the Sabbath, the Houses of Assembly and Prayer].

We may assume on the basis of this Babylonian halakhah of Rami bar Hama, which was read into the original Tosefta text by Rava, that a later redactor of the Babylonian Talmud changed the original word "warned" to "publicly announced" in order to make the *baraita* consonant with what had become normative practice. (Rami bar Hama had also added that each public announcement was to be accompanied by two private warnings, perhaps because his Tosefta text read "twice each week," but more likely in order to retain the original "warning" of the Tosefta alongside his added stringency of public proclamation. Again, the redactor of the Babylonian Talmud may well have expanded his version of the baraita so as to retain the complete halakhah of Rami bar Hama within it.)[29]

It may be concluded, then, that there were three stages of penalty in the Tannaitic and Amoraic traditions of the rebellious wife: (1) The Mishnah provided for the reduction of the alimony of the *moredet* by seven *dinarim* (or *quinarii*) each week. (2) The Tosefta established that the Jewish court would warn the woman privately once a week for four weeks, after which time she forfeited her entire alimony. This was the accepted practice in the Land of Israel, at least through the middle of the third century, the period of the Jerusalem Talmud. (3) Finally, Rami bar Hama decreed that a public announcement against the *moredet* be made in the synagogues and study houses every Sabbath, for four consecutive weeks, with two private warnings, one before and one after each public announcement.

PROBABLE TEXT OF THE ORIGINAL TOSEFTA
REGARDING "GRACE PERIOD"

The next question concerning the text of the Toseftan version is about the length of time the wife is given to mend her ways. Various texts read that she is to be warned either "four weeks" or "four and five weeks." "Four weeks" is the reading found in the Erfurt MS of Tosefta, and is confirmed by the Palestinian and Babylonian Talmuds, the students of Rabbenu Yonah, and the Genizah fragments. "Four and five weeks" is the reading found in the Vienna MS of Tosefta, and is confirmed by the text of Ha-Meiri.

Saul Lieberman suggested that the legal interpretation of "four and five weeks" is dependent upon when the wife began her rebellion.[30] The Rabbis wanted to give her four full weeks to change her behavior. Hence, if she began to rebel on a Friday night, there would be only three full weeks of grace—albeit four public announcements. This interpretation is logical only if we interpret the Tosefta in terms of public announcements on the Sabbath; in that case, if the rebellion began on Friday night, there would be four public announcements on the Sabbath but only three weeks of rebelliousness. Hence the *baraita* specifies "four or five Sabbaths," so that in the case where the rebellion began on Friday night, there would be five Sabbath announcements and *four* full weeks of warning. If, however, we accept that the original text is speaking of weeks and not Sabbaths, the version "four weeks" is preferable. And since it is likely that historically, the original warnings were privately done and not dependent upon the Sabbath, the original version of the Tosefta probably read:[31]

רבותינו התקינו שיהו מתרין בה ארבע שבתות זו אחר זו אחר זו.
יתר על כן אפילו כתובתה מאה מנה אבדה את הכל.
אחת ארוסה ואתה שומרת יבם אפי׳ נדה ואפי׳ חולה.

Our Rabbis enacted that they warn her for four consecutive weeks.
    If she continues her rebelliousness beyond this point, even if her marriage contract is worth one hundred *maneh,* she forfeits all of it.
    It is the same [law] with regard to an engaged woman and one who is waiting for a levirate marriage, even for a menstruating woman and an ill woman.

FINAL PENALTY: DIVORCE

The last issue raised by the Tosefta, explicit in the text of the *baraita* cited by the Jerusalem Talmud and implicit everywhere else, concerns the consequences of the wife's rebellion after the grace period has passed and the alimony of the marriage contract has been forfeited.

והיא שוברת כתובתה ויוצאה.[32]

> And she breaks her marriage contract and leaves [with a bill of divorcement].

It is apparent from all the Tannaitic material already cited that the ultimate penalty imposed on the *moredet* is divorce, even though this is exactly what she does not want. As stated earlier, since a husband and wife are forbidden to live together without a marriage contract,[33] the moment the wife's alimony has been depleted the husband is compelled to divorce her. Nevertheless, this entire phrase may be a later emendation, as we shall see below.[34]

MIDRASH: EARLY AMORAIC DISPUTE

Genesis Rabbah is the earliest source which cites a disagreement about the definition of the *moredet*. Although this midrash is certainly late, some of its material dates to before the closing of the Jerusalem Talmud.[35] In any case, the Midrash cites a first-generation Amoriac dispute between two students of R. Yehudah HaNasi (apparently contemporaneous with "our Rabbis" [*Rabbotenu*] of the Tosefta) concerning the nature of the act which predicated a reduction of the marriage contract.

„ואת כל ונוכחת" (בראשית כ:יז)

אמר לה: כבר תוכחתה דהההוא גברא רבה גביה דתנן: המורדת על בעלה פוחתין לה
מכתובתה שבעה דינרין בשבת ולמה שבעה דינרין, כנגד שבע מלאכות שהאשה עושה
לבעלה: טוחנה, ואופה, ומבשלת ומכבסת ומיקה את בנה ומצעת לו את הממטה ועושה
בצמר — לפיכך שבעה. וכן המורד על אשתו מוסיפין לה על כתובתה שלשה דינרין
בשבת. למה שלשה? כנגד שלשה דברים שהוא מתחייב לה: שאר, כסות ועונה — לפיכך
שלשה.

אמור: שהכניסה לו עבדים ושפחות אינה מתחייבת [var: מתחייב] לו כלום?

אמור: שלא נתן לה לא שאר, לא כסות לא עונה אינה מתחייב [מתחייבת :var] לה
כלום?

אמר ר' יוחנן: צערו של איש מרובה מצערה של אשה הדא הוא דכתיב (שופטים טז:טז).
ויהי כי הציקה לו בדבריה כל הימים ותאלצהו' — שהשמיטה עצמה מתחתיו ותקצר
נפשו למות — אבל היא לא קצרה נפשה. למה? שהיתה עושה צרכה ממקום אחר."36

"And before all have you been proven right" [Gen 20:17]. He
[Abimelech] said to her: The penalty of that man is with him (for I
have gotten what I deserve), as we learned in the Mishnah: "If a wife
rebels against her husband, the alimony provided by her marriage
contract is to be reduced by seven *dinarim* each week."

And why by seven *dinarim?* Corresponding to the seven household activities a wife must do for her husband: she must grind, bake,
cook, wash, suckle her child, make [her husband's] bed, and spin
wool—therefore seven.

"And similarly, if a husband rebels against his wife, an addition
of three *dinarim* each week is to be made to the alimony provided by
her marriage contract."

And why three? Corresponding to the three obligations a husband has towards his wife: (to provide her with) food, clothing, and
sexual gratification—therefore three.

[But] suppose she enters the marriage with man-servants and
maid-servants, is she therefore not obligated to him at all? [Or] suppose that he [var: she] did not provide her with food, clothing and
sexual gratification, is he [var: he] therefore not obligated to her at
all?

R. Yohanan says: [it is because] the pain of a man is greater than
the pain of a woman [when sexual relations are denied]. That is [the
meaning of] what is written [Judg 16:16]: "And it came to pass that
she [Delilah] irritated him [Samson] with her words all the days, and
vexed him" [because] she would remove herself from beneath him
"and his soul desired to die [since the sexual privation brought
greater pain to him than her]." And there are those who say: She fulfilled her [sexual] needs with others [and therefore was not as upset
about the lack of sexual activity].

Abimelech had to compensate Abraham for the night Sarah was
separated from him as if she had been separated of her own volition.

In order to justify this interpretation, the author of this midrash cites R. Yohanan, who defines *mored* or *moredet* as a spouse who refuses to engage in marital relations. The midrash goes on to explain why the wife's reduction of alimony would be greater than the husband's addition to the alimony in the event of rebellion, by associating the respective number of *dinarim,* seven and three, with the number of obligations each spouse has to the other. Furthermore (anticipating the logical objection to the view, since if a woman brings servants to the marriage she has no household obligations), the midrash asserts that a denial of sexual relations brings greater pain to the husband than to the wife and is therefore responsible for the inequality of the penalties. At any rate, R. Yohanan, a first-generation Amora in the Land of Israel, clearly states that a *moredet* is one who rebels by refusing her husband sexual relations.

According to either interpretation, the midrash begins by defining a *moredet* as a woman who refuses to fulfill household obligations, but concludes with the view of R. Yohanan—a first-generation Amora in the Land of Israel[37]—that a *moredet* is a wife who refuses to fulfill her side of the sexual marital bond.

CHAPTER II
MOREDET IN THE JERUSALEM TALMUD

The first lenghty explication of the *moredet* of our mishnah is to be found in the Jerusalem Talmud, which affords us a view of the Amoraic discussions of Tannaitic teachings. It records the views of the Amoraim in Palestine—specifically Tiberias, Sepphoris, and Caesarea—from 200 C.E. until approximately 350 C.E. R. Yehudah HaNasi had, towards the end of his life, established his academy in Tiberias, where R. Yohanan lived. Hence, the interpretation of R. Yohanan (which follows) may be helpful in interpreting the position of R. Yehudah HaNasi and the Sages of the Mishnah in regard to the *moredet*.[1]

DEFINITION

הכא את מר שבעה והכא את מר שלשה

אמר רבי יוסי בר חנינא: היא על ידי שהיא חייבת לו שבע הוא פוחת ממנה שבעה והוא על ידי שהוא חייב לה שלשה, הוא מוסף לה שלשה. הגע עצמך שהכניסה לו עבדים, הרי אינה חייבת לו כלום? הגע עצמך שהתנה עמה לא שאר ולא כסות ולא עונה, הרי אינו חייב לה כלום?

מאי כדין? כיי דמר רבי יוחנן: צערו של איש מרובה יותר מן (!) האשה. הדא הוא דכתיב. ויהי כי הציקה לו בדבריה כל הימים ותאלצהו (שופטים טז:טז).

מהו ותאלצהו? אמר רבי יצחק בר לעזר: שהיתה שומטה עצמה מתחתיו ותקצר נפשו למות, הוא קצר נפשו למות, היא לא קצרה נפשה למות. ויש אומרים שהיתה עושה צורכיה באחרים כ"ש שתבעי?! דאמר רב נחמן בשם רבי נחמן: האבר הזה שבאדם הרעיבתו השביעתו, השביעתו הרעיבתו. השביעתו הרעיבתו[2]

"Why is it [that with regard to the wife who rebels] you say [that there is a reduction of] seven [*dinarim*], and [with regard to the husband who rebels] you say [that there is an addition of] three [*dinarim*]?

R. Yose bar Haninah says: Since she has seven [household] obligations towards him, the alimony of her marriage contract is reduced by seven, and since he has three obligations towards her, his alimony obligation is increased by three.

[The Talmud objects to this interpretation by asking] Suppose that she brings servants into the marriage, would she then not be obligated to him at all? And suppose that he makes a prior condition with her that he not [be required to] sustain, clothe, and sexually satisfy her, would he then not be obligated to her at all? What then is the reason [for the greater penalty imposed upon a rebellious wife than upon a rebellious husband]?

It is in accord with R. Yohanan [who assumes that the rebellion constitutes a denial of sexual relations]: The pain of the male is greater than that of the female.

This is [the meaning of] that which is written [Judg 16:16]: "And it came to pass that she [Delilah] irritated him [Samson] with her words all the days and vexed him." What is [the meaning of] "vexed him"? R. Yitzhak bar Lazar said: [She vexed him since, in the midst of their love-making] she would remove herself from beneath him, "and his soul desired to die"—his soul desired to die, but her soul did not desire to die [since the sexual privation brought greater pain to him than to her]. There are those who [give another explanation and] say that she fulfilled her sexual needs with others.

[If this is true, then this verse is not proof of the fact that a male experiences greater pain than the female from sexual deprivation. But the Talmud objects to this argument, for if she were sexually more active than he], certainly she would demand [sexual gratification from him, and be in even greater pain were it denied her], as Rav Nahman said in the name of Rav Nahman: "This [sexual] organ of the human being: if one starves it, one gratifies it, and if one gratifies it, one starves it [the more sexually active one is, the greater one's sexual appetite]."

It appears that the first generation of Amoraim in Palestine were divided in their opinion of the parameters of a *moredet*. R. Yose ben Haninah maintains that a *moredet* is one who rebels by refusing to fulfill her household obligations, while his teacher and colleague R.

Yohanan maintains that the woman's rebellion constitutes a denial of sexual relations. The source of their disagreement does not lie in their interpretation of the two mishnayot preceding the mishnah of *moredet* (as has been suggested), but rather on the basis of the seven and three *dinarim* referred to in our mishnah. It is certainly possible, however, that R. Yose bar Haninah would agree that a woman who refuses to fulfill her household obligations might also refuse to have sexual relations with her husband; this does not take her out of the category of *moredet*. It is unlikely that R. Yose felt a wife had no sexual obligation towards her husband, if only to submit to him. Logic would dictate that he links the seven and three *dinarim* of our mishnah with the female's seven household obligations of the previous mishnah (which are distinct from her obligation to have sexual relations) and with the male's three obligations towards his wife, as a kind of numerical tour de force.[3] The anonymous opinion, which disagrees with R. Yose ("but suppose . . .") understands R. Yose's numerical linkage both literally and exclusively, assuming that if the wife has provided servants for the household tasks, she is free of her obligations. R. Yohanan, on the other hand, limits *moredet* to a woman who denies her husband sexual relations, and this is the apparent conclusion of the Jerusalem Talmud.

I would merely add that the disagreement between R. Yohanan and R. Yose bar Haninah may very well be based upon two different conceptions of the fundamental nature of the marital relationship. Is marriage basically a financial partnership, in which case rebellion is expressed by a refusal to perform a household obligation? Or is it fundamentally an intimate relationship between two individuals? If this is the case, rebellion is best expressed by a refusal to engage in sex, the fullest expression of the marital bond. What we have before us as a debate about the meaning of the term *moredet* may indeed be a debate about the very nature of the institution of marriage.

PENALTY

The Jerusalem Talmud now begins to analyze the various possibilities of and conditions for the reduction of the alimony provided by the marriage contract. What would be the result if a wife declared her intention not to engage in sexual relations with her husband at a time when those relations were not mandatory—if, for example, he was a sailor and in accordance with Mishnaic law was obligated to have sexual relations with his wife only once in six months? What if her refusal came at a time when sexual relations were forbidden, such as during the time of her menses? Is such a woman also considered a *moredet?*

REDUCTIONS FROM ALIMONY WHEN SEXUAL RELATIONS ARE OPTIONAL OR PROHIBITED

וכרבי אליעזר עד כמה הוא פוחת? נשמעינה מן הדא: תני ר' חייא ארוסה וחולה ונדה
ושמרת יבם כותבין לה איגרת על בעלה — מה אנן קיימין? אם בשמרדה עליו והיא נדה,
התורה המרדתה עליו! אלא כן אנן קיימין שמרדה עליו עד שלא באת נדה ובאת לנדה
הרי אינה ראויה למרוד, ואת אמר כותבין! וכא פוחת!

And according to R. Eliezer [who has established in the mishnah prior to that of *moredet* the minimal obligation of sexual gratification which various husbands have towards their wives], at what point is the alimony reduced?

Let us learn it from the following:

R. Hiya taught: An engaged woman, a sick woman, a menstruating woman, and a woman awaiting her levir, [if they refuse to marry or to engage in sexual relations] each receives a "letter of rebellion" reducing the alimony contract [from the time of her rebellion]. What does this mean? For if a woman refuses to have sexual relations with her husband while she is menstrually impure, it is not she who is rebelling but rather it is the Torah which compels her to rebel [since she is forbidden from engaging in sexual relations at that time].

But we establish the principle that as long as she initiated her rebellion before she began to menstruate, we include the period of her menstrual impurity in the letter of rebellion, despite the fact that she is not then [halakhically] fit to rebel. And her alimony is reduced for the entire period.

Thus, the Jerusalem Talmud concludes that so long as the

woman initiated her rebellion at a time when sexual relations between the couple were permissible, the penalty includes even that time when sexual relations were forbidden.[4] It is interesting to note that according to this discussion, the wife's obligation to have sexual relations with her husband is predicated upon his obligation to have relations with her. If, for example, as a sailor, he is obligated to provide her with sexual gratification once every six months, she is required to have sexual relations with him only once in six months. Her obligation is not dependent upon his (subjective) appetite, but upon his (objective) obligation. The sexual relationship as it is conceived of here is mutual and two-sided.[5]

REDUCTIONS FROM ADDITIONS TO ALIMONY AND FROM GIFTS AND DOWRY

What is the extent of the reductions which may be made from the alimony provided for the wife by the marriage contract? Does the reduction apply merely to the basic contract of two hundred *zuzim* for a virgin and one hundred *zuzim* for a widow or divorcee, or may it be taken from any additional sum which the husband might have contracted for at the time of the marriage? May gifts and property which a woman brought with her at the time of her marriage be similarly reduced?

מה מיפחות מפרא פרנון דידה? נשמעינה מן הדא. ר' יוסי אומר לעולם הוא פוחת
והולך שמא תפול לה ירושה ממקום אחר ויחזור ויגבה ממנה. לא אמר אלא ירושה, דבר
שאינו מצוי. הדא אמרה אפילו לפחות מפרא פרנון דידה, פוחת!

Do we deduct from the addition to the alimony as well as from the gifts which she received as an engaged woman?[6] Let us learn from the following [statement in the mishnah]:

R. Yose says: Since she may receive an inheritance from elsewhere, the husband [has the right] to continue "collecting" (i.e., deducting [the weekly fine].

The mishnah mentions of the possibility of an inheritance (a totally unexpected source of income) as a potential source of income which may be garnisheed, implying that all else now available to her is available to her husband for collection. The only dispute (in the mishnah) is with regard to an inheritance which was unanticipated at the time of marriage. R. Yose, disagreeing with the anonymous opinion, insists that reductions be made from it, but we can certainly understand from this that any additions to the *ketubah* and any gifts brought into the marriage are also included. The Jerusalem Talmud thus excludes from the penalty only that income which was unanticipated at the time of the marriage.

DOWRY GARMENTS

We have already seen that the *moredet* loses all her anticipated revenue, goods, and property, including any additions to the alimony provided for in the marriage contracts, and the engagement gifts. But what of the garments which she brought with her into the marriage and which can certainly still be used? The Jerusalem Talmud records disagreement on this matter between two first-generation Amoraim in Palestine, Rabbi Hanina and Rabbi Yehoshua ben Levi, as to whether or not a *moredet* receives those dowry garments still in existence. R. Hanina maintains that they are hers; R. Yehoshua insists that she must forfeit them.

ר' חנינא בשם ר' ישמעאל בר ר' יסא: היוצאה משם רע אין לה בליות; מורדת יש
לה. ר' סימון בשם ר' יהושע בן לוי: דמורדת והיוצאת משם רע אין לה לא מזונות ולא
בליות.[7]

R. Hanina [said] in the name of R. Yishmael of the School of R. Yose: A woman who is divorced because of an immoral reputation does not receive the garments [she brought with her into the marriage, whose value was estimated and included within the marriage contract, and which are still in existence]; a rebellious wife does [receive these garments].

R. Simon [said] in the name of R. Yehoshua ben Levi: A rebellious wife and a woman who is divorced because of an immoral reputation receive neither food nor the garments.

REFUSAL OF LEVIRATE MARRIAGE

The Bible stipulates that if a man dies and leaves his widow childless, his brother must marry the widow, so that "the first-born that she bears shall rise up in the name of the dead brother, that his name be not blotted out of Israel."[8] This is what is called levirate marriage, or *yibbum*. If, however, the brother does not wish to marry her, the widow performs a ceremony called *halitzah*, during which she removes the shoe from the brother's foot and spits before him in the presence of the elders of the city.[9]

Although providing for this contingency, the Bible does not explicitly deal with the implications of a woman's refusal of levirate marriage. Is the widow to be considered a *moredet?* Can this woman be regarded as a *moredet,* since (per our definition of withholding intercourse) sexual gratification is not even the tactical issue involved, for she has no obligation (even implicitly) to provide this for her brother-in-law before marrying him? Rather, the emphasis of the Rabbis' approach to rebellion has been the concern for the marriage and the continuation of the institution of the family. The Jerusalem Talmud states:

ר' זעירא בשם שמואל: כותבין איגרת מרד על ארוסה ואין כותבין איגרת מרד על שומרת יבם. והתני ר' חייה: נידה וחולה, ארוסה ושומרת יבם כותבין לו איגרת מרד על כתובתה? כאן במשנה הראשונה, כאן במשנה האחרונה. אמר ר' יוסי בר בון: אפילו תימר כן במשנה אחרונה בית דין שלאחריהם מתירין בה ארבע שבתות והיא שוברת כתובתה ויוצאה.

R. Zeira says in the name of Shmuel: A letter of rebellion is written against a betrothed woman [who subsequently refuses to get married], but not against a woman subject to a levirate marriage [who refuses *yibbum*].

But R. Hiya taught [in a *baraita*]: A menstruating woman, a sick woman, a betrothed woman, and a woman subject to a levirate marriage all receive letters of rebellion [nullifying their] alimony.

One case is according to the earlier mishnah and the other is according to the later mishnah.

R. Yose bar Bun says: You may even say that it is consistent with the later mishnah. The court which came after [reviewed the previous decision regarding *moredet* and legislated that she be] warned for four weeks, [at which time] she breaks her marriage contract [with a bill of divorce].

This passage is difficult, especially the references to an earlier and later mishnah. The following mishnah from Tractate Bekhorot may clarify matters:

. . . מצות יבום קודמת למצות חליצה בראשונה שכשהיו מתכוונים לשם מצוה ועכשיו שאינם מתכוונים לשם מצוה אמרו מצות חליצה קודמת למצות יבום.[10]

Initially the commandment to perform levirate marriage was preferable to the commandment to perform *halitzah,* when they [i.e., levirs] intended [the act of *yibbum* to be] for the sake of the commandment [as opposed to the brother-in-law's own personal and familial needs]. And now that they [i.e., the levirs] do not intend it for the sake of the commandment, they [i.e., the Rabbis] say that the commandment of *halitzah* is preferable to the commandment of the levirate marriage.

This mishnah explains that there was an earlier mishnah in which *yibbum* was considered preferable to *halitzah,* and a later mishnah which held the opposite view. In the Jerusalem Talmud, therefore, where R. Hiya maintains that a letter of rebellion is written for a woman who refuses to accept a levirate marriage, he bases himself on the earlier mishnah. R. Zeira, who maintains that such a letter is not written for this woman, bases his view on the later mishnah. R. Yose bar Bun then adds:

You may even say that [R. Hiya] is consistent with the later mishnah [for, after all, his position demanding a letter of rebellion for a woman subject to a levirate marriage is part of a *baraita* which begins:] "The court which came after . . ." [which is the "later mishnah" with regard to the law of *moredet*].

In other words, despite the fact that nowadays *halitzah* is preferable to *yibbum,* if a woman refuses to agree to a levirate marriage when her brother-in-law insists upon it, she forfeits her alimony.[11] This is a further example of the stringencies adopted regarding the law of *moredet*.[12]

One final issue warrants comment. The text cites our Tosefta, but only the first phrase, "the court which came after," is truly relevant. The final phrase, "and she breaks her marriage contract and leaves [with a bill of divorce]," appears in none of the other citations of this *baraita*. It is very possible that the original text of the Jerusalem Talmud also quoted only the beginning of the *baraita*,

בית דין שלאחריהם מתרין בה ארבע שבתות וכו'.

The latter court warns her for four weeks, etc.,

and a later redactor—anxious to stress the fact that the brother of the deceased must give the widow *halitzah* (albeit without a contract providing for alimony)—added the final words, "and she breaks her contract and leaves."

EQUALITY IN DIVORCE

It is apparent from the preceding discussion that the *moredet* almost certainly does not wish to be divorced from her husband, but rather, either refuses to fulfill her household obligations or, what is more likely, refuses to engage in sexual relations with her husband. Indeed, we see that the Halakhah uses the threat of divorce (which would become necessary when the alimony has been depleted by the steady reductions) as the chief deterrent to this kind of behavior. But what would be the Rabbis' approach if a wife requested a divorce on the grounds that her husband had become so distasteful to her that she could no longer live with him? In our passage, we find a stipulation in the marriage contract providing for just such an eventuality, and, remarkably, it is worded in such a manner as to provide complete equality between husband and wife.

א"ר יוסה: אלין דכתבין אין שנא אין שנאת תניי ממון ותניין קיים.[13]

R. Yoseh said: For those who write [a stipulation in the marriage contract] that if he grow to hate her or she grow to hate him [a divorce will ensue, with the prescribed monetary gain or loss, and] it is considered a condition of monetary payment, and such conditions are valid and binding.

The importance of this tradition recorded by R. Yoseh cannot be overstated. This means that in the third century c.e. in the Land of Israel, a wife had as much right as her husband to initiate divorce, as long as this had been so stipulated in the marriage contract. This stipulation was accorded special legal standing[14] and clearly was designed to protect each partner from the difficulties inherent in a loveless marriage.

The Diaspora Community of Elephantine

The earliest precedent we can find of a Jewish community wherein a woman was legally empowered to request a divorce of her husband dates from fifth-century (b.c.e.) Egypt, where a colony of Jewish soldiers in the Persian service comprised the garrison on the island of Elephantine, near the southern border of Egypt. Three Aramaic archives have been found there, two familial and one communal. These documents all shed remarkable light on one of the earliest Diaspora communities, antedating the Dead Sea Scrolls by at least four centuries and contemporaneous with Ezra and Nehemiah. To be sure, it is difficult to determine the extent of this community's assimilation, and therefore to ascertain how closely the evidence of these documents conforms to what was then normative Halakhah. Nevertheless, these documents show that divorce could be initiated either by the husband or the wife. Marriage contracts from this community contain a clause stipulating that either spouse may rise up in the congregation, declare that he or she "hates [wishes to divorce]" the other, and make a payment of hatred [divorce] money (כסף שנאה) totaling seven and one-half shekels.[15] Presumably, this would have been all that was necessary for the Jewish courts to issue a bill of divorcement. Thus, in general principle—although not necessarily in specifics—this fifth-century B.C.E. stipulation pre-figures the clause we have examined in the Jerusalem Talmud.

PARALLELS IN OTHER TRACTATES OF THE JERUSALEM TALMUD

The next source we know of which allows equality between husband and wife in the matter of divorce was complied seven hundred years after the Elephantine archives, and is universally recognized as being the normative Halakhah in the Land of Israel. yKet 7:7 (31c) records an incident in which a woman displayed her dislike for her husband by "placing her mouth upon the mouth of another." R. Yoseh, whom we previously cited in the passage from the Jerusalem Talmud concerning the stipulation of "if he [grow to hate] her and if she [grow to hate] him," ruled that in this case the husband must grant his wife a bill of divorce along with one-half of the alimony pro-vided for by the marriage contract. The wife's relatives challenged this ruling, the marriage contract was produced, and the following stipulation was found:

„איתיון פרנא ואשכחון בגוה אין הדא פלנית תישני להדין פלוני בעלה ולא תצבי
בשותפותיה תהוי נסבא פלגות פרן"[16]

> They brought the *ketubah* and found [written] in it: "if this one [fem.] hates this one [masc.], her husband, and does not wish to [remain] married [to] him, let her take half her *ketubah*."

With this in mind, R. Yoseh's words in our Jerusalem Talmud text become clear. The *moredet* of the original mishnah was not a woman who wanted a divorce, but rather one who had refused to fulfill her marital duties—however they are defined—and as such was penalized by the reduction and possible depletion of the ali-mony provided for her in her marriage contract. But the Jerusalem Talmud understood that it might be possible for a woman to come to hate her husband and prefer to live without him (contrary to Resh Lakish's above-stated assertion of a woman's preference for mar-riage under all circumstances). In this case of true unhappiness rather than sex as the tactical medium, the Rabbis ensured, by a special stipulation in the marriage contract, that the woman would receive at least partial alimony, and—more importantly—that she could virtually initiate the divorce herself.[17] Her power was not truly *de jure*—that is, upon her stating her desire for divorce, the court would then coerce her husband until he acquiesced, and in the end it would still be he who gave the divorce to his wife—but it provided her with a *de facto* means of getting both her freedom and a livelihood. The *ketubah* lived up to its original function by both protecting the woman who could not live with her husband and (by discouraging the *moredet* from her selfish behavior) protecting the institution of marriage.

CHAPTER III
MOREDET IN THE
BABYLONIAN TALMUD

The Babylonian Talmud is made up in large part of Amoraic discussions of the Mishnah which took place in the academies of Babylonia from 200 to 500 C.E. as well as later material from the rabbinic Sabboraim. A great many traditions are recorded in the names of Palestinian Amoraim, and it is always most instructive to compare them with those preserved in the Jerusalem Talmud. The Babylonian Talmud has had a far greater influence upon the development of normative Halakhah than its Palestinian predecessor.[1] A careful study of the text in the Babylonian Talmud which comments on the mishnah of *moredet* reveals some interesting differences between the Palestinian and Babylonian approaches to the rebellious wife, and even within different Babylonian academies themselves. Most important, some of the later Amoraim of Babylonia came to redefine the entire concept of *moredet*. They considered the term "rebellious wife" to apply even to the woman who finds her husband repulsive and refuses sexual relations with him in order to force him to divorce her. But their interpretation is far from universally accepted, and the question of how to treat such a woman clearly perplexed many Babylonian Sages. It continues to be an important and delicate issue until this very day.

DEFINITION

גמרא: מורדת ממאי?

רב הונא אמר מתשמיש המטה

רבי יוסי ברבי חנינא אמר ממלאכה

תנן: וכן המורד על אשתו, בשלמא למאן דאמר מתשמיש — לחיי! אלא למאן דאמר

ממלאכה, מי משעובד לה? אין, באומר איני זן ואיני מפרנס. והאמר רב האומר איני זן ואיני מפרנס יוציא ויתן כתובה? ולאו לאמלוכי ביה בעי?!

מיתיבי: אחת לי ארוסה ונשואה ואפי׳ נדה ואפי׳ חולה ואפי׳ שומרת יבם בשלמא למ״ד מתשמיש היינו דקתני חולה, אלא למאן דאמר ממלאכה, חולה בת מלאכה היא?

אלא מתשמיש כולי עלמא לא פליגי דהוה מורדת כי פליגי ממלאכה, מר סבר ממלאכה לא הויא מורדת ומר סבר ממלאכה נמי הויא מורדת.[2]

Gemara: In what respect does she rebel?

Rav Huna replied: [In respect to] sexual relations.

R. Yose b. R. Hanina replied: [In respect to] household duties.

[In an attempt to adjudicate this dispute, the redactor of the gemara cites the end of the mishnah which in his opinion contradicts R. Yose b. R. Hanina.] We learned in the mishnah: "Similarly, a husband who rebels against his wife."

Now according to the one who holds "in respect to sexual relations," this ruling [of the mishnah] is quite logical and consistent, [since the husband is to be penalized if he denies his wife sexual relations]. But according to the one who holds "in respect to household duties," is [the husband] then obligated to her? [The passage's redactor then answers his question.] Yes, [and he becomes a rebellious husband if] he declares: "I will neither feed nor support my wife." But did not Rav state: "He who says, 'I will neither feed nor support [my wife,' must divorce her and give her the alimony provided for in the marriage contract, [and hence any addition to the *ketubah* or penalty would not be applicable?].''

[The gemara then justifies R. Yose b. R. Hanina with the argument: Is it not necessary to attempt to persuade him [before ordering him to divorce her, and specifically by adding to his alimony obligation]?

A further objection was raised [against the position of R. Yose b. Hanina]: [We learned in the *baraita*]: "The same law applies to a betrothed woman, a married woman, even to a menstrually impure woman, a sick woman, and one awaiting a levirate marriage." Now according to the one who holds [that *moredet* is defined] "in respect to sexual relations," it is quite correct to mention a sick woman [for she can usually engage in sexual relations], but according to him who said "in respect to household duties," can a sick woman do housework?

[The redactor of the *sugya* then responds and concludes,] the fact is that with regard to sexual relations everyone agrees [both R. Yose and Rav Huna] that a woman [who refuses] is termed a rebellious wife. They differ only with regard to household duties. One Master [R. Yose] is of the opinion that [her] refusal to do housework [also] makes [her] a rebellious wife, and the other Master [Rav Huna] is of the opinion that [her] refusal to do housework does not make [her] a rebellious wife.

We see that Rav Huna, a second-generation Babylonian Amora and student of Rav at Sura, and R. Yose b. R. Hanina, a second-generation Palestinian Amora, debate the same issue over which R. Yohanan and R. Yose B. R. Hanina dispute in the Jerusalem Talmud: how to define *moredet*. Rav Huna and R. Yohanan agree that a rebellious wife is one who refuses to have sexual relations with her husband; R. Yose b. R. Hanina maintains that a rebellious wife is one who refuses to perform her household obligations.

The redactor of the Babylonian Talmud, in order to remove a textual difficulty, concludes that R. Yose b. R. Hanina would agree with Rav Huna about the definition of *moredet;* but he would add that a wife who refuses to perform her household duties is *also* called *moredet.* Thus, only with regard to this last instance does Rav Huna disagree. On the basis of the Talmudic text itself, it is difficult to see the grounds upon which the redactor maintains that R. Yose b. R. Hanina includes sexual rebellion within the category of *moredet.* But once we study the original source for R. Yose b. R. Hanina's position (the Jerusalem Talmud), the conclusion of the Babylonian Talmud becomes clear. R. Yose is not so much defining *moredet* in his mention of household obligations as he is attempting to explain the logic of subtracting as much as seven *dinarim* a week when the wife rebels, though only adding three in the case of a rebellious husband. But since one of the husband's three obligations to his wife is to satisfy her sexual needs, it is logical to assume that R. Yose b. R.

Hanina may *not* be limiting a wife's rebellion to the household tasks alone. He might naturally assume that her refusal to engage in sexual relations is likewise to be considered rebellion. By putting those statements of the Palestinian Amoraim which are cited in the Babylonian Talmud into the context of the Jerusalem Talmud itself, the conclusion of our gemara is more easily understood.[3]

It is interesting to note that Rav Huna (and, indeed, the accepted majority opinion) allows for a mutual rather than a one-sided marriage contract. Rav Huna raises the possibility of a stipulation allowing that a husband need not support his wife as long as the wife is exempted from her household obligations and keeps any money she may earn.[4] This stipulation would in no way affect the alimony clause of the contract, nor the applicability of the laws of *moredet,* since all authorities are in agreement that a woman who refuses to engage in sexual relations with her husband is to be considered a *moredet* in accordance with the conclusion of the Babylonian Talmud.

FINANCIAL PENALTY

REDUCTIONS FROM ALIMONY WHEN SEXUAL RELATIONS
ARE FORBIDDEN

גופא המורדת על בעלה פוחתין לה מכתובתה שבעה דינרים בשבת ר' יהודה אומר שבעה
טרפעיקין רבותינו חזרו ונמנו שיהו מכריזין עליה ארבע שבתות זו אחר זו ושולחין לה
בית דין: הוי יודעה שאפי' כתובתיך מאה מנה, הפסדת, אחת לי ארוסה ונשואה אפי' נדה
אפי' חולה ואפי' שומרת יבם.
אמר ליה ר' חייא בר יוסף לשמואל: נדה בת תשמיש היא?
אמר ליה: אינו דומה מי שיש לו פת בסלו למי שאין לו פת בסלו.

[Let us return to] the main text:

"If a wife rebels against her husband, the alimony provided for her in the marriage contract is to be reduced by seven *dinarim* each week. R. Yehudah said: seven *quinarii.*"

Our Rabbis reviewed the issue and decided that they must publicly announce her behavior for four consecutive weeks. And the court would send to her [the following message]: "Know that even if your marriage contract is one hundred *maneh,* you have lost it."

"[The law is] the same if she be betrothed to be married, even if she be menstrually impure or ill or awaiting a levirate marriage." R. Hiya bar Yosef said to Shmuel: Is then a menstrually impure woman able to engage in sexual relations [such that if she refuse, she is to be called a *moredet*]?

He said to him: He who has bread in his basket [i.e., he who knows that he will soon be able to resume sexual relations] cannot be compared to him who does not have bread in his basket. [Therefore such a woman is called *moredet* because of the psychological pain she causes her husband, who cannot look forward to resuming sexual relations upon the cessation of her menstrual impurity.]

Prima facie, it would seem that the Jerusalem and Babylonian Talmuds agree that a woman can become a rebellious wife even during her period of menstrual impurity, when sexual relations are prohibited. However, there is a crucial difference between the texts, although each records a discussion of first-generation Amoraim. The Jerusalem Talmud unquestionably concludes that as long as a wife declared her rebellion *before* the onset of her menses, we *continue* to reduce the alimony provided for in her marriage contract, or *continue* to count the four weeks of warning, even during her menstrual period. The underlying assumption, however, is that a woman cannot become a *moredet* during the time she is menstrually impure. In contrast, the Babylonian Talmud insists that the rebellion can be initiated at this time because of the psychological pain she causes her husband. For this reason, the image of "bread in the basket" (bKet 63b) is not mentioned in the Jerusalem Talmud.[5]

AMORAIC ADJUDICATION BETWEEN MISHNAH AND TOSEFTA; ESTABLISHMENT OF NORMATIVE PRACTICE

אמר רמי בר חמא: אין מכריזין עליה אלא בבתי כנסיות ובבתי מדרשות. אמר רבא: דיקא נמי דקתני ארבע שבתות זו אחר זו ש״מ. אמר רמי בר חמא: פעמים שולחין לה מבית דין, אחת קודם הכרזה ואחת לאחר הכרזה. דרש רב נחמן בר רב חסדא: הלכה

כרבותינו. אמר רבא: האי בורכא. אמר לה רב נחמן בר בר יצחק: מאי בורכתיה? אנא
אמריתה נהליה ומשמיה דגברא רבה אמריתה נהליה ומנו? ר' יוסי בר' חנינא. ואיהו
כמאן סבר? כי הא דאתמר רבא אמר רב ששת: הלכה נמלכין בה רב הונא בר יהודה אמר
רב ששת: הלכה אין נמלכין בה.

Rami bar Hama said: One does not proclaim [the rebellious wife]
except in synagogues and houses of study.

Said Rava: A very precise reading [of the Tosefta] also [yields this
same understanding], since it has been taught: "Four consecutive
Sabbaths" [Sabbath here means weeks, as well as the seventh day when
Jews normally congregate in the synagogues and houses of study].
And this is decisive proof.

Rami bar Hama stated: [A warning] is sent twice to her, from the
Jewish court: once before the announcement and once after the
announcement.

Rav Nahman bar Rav Hisda expounded: The law is in agreement
with our Masters.

Rava stated: That is boorish.

Rav Nahman bar Rav Yitzhak said: Wherein lies its boorishness?
I said it to him, and [it was] in the name of a great man I said it to
him. And who is [the great man]? R. Yose bar R. Hanina.

Whose view, then does he [Rami] follow? He follows that which
Rava stated in the name of Rav Sheshet: "The law is that [the *moredet*]
is to be persuaded."

Rav Huna bar Yehudah stated in the name of Rav Sheshet: "The
law is that [the *moredet*] is not to be persuaded."

Just as our Talmudic discussion began with Rav Huna, a second-
generation Amoraic scholar of Sura, so does it continue with the
fourth-generation Amoraim of Sura. Rav Nahman bar Rav Hisda
apparently tried to establish what was in his opinion correct
halakhic practice, against which Rava vehemently disagrees. Our
problem is that neither the halakhic practice insisted upon by Rav
Nahman bar Rav Hisda nor the cause of Rava's disagreement is
clearly stated in the text. Rather, Rav Nahman bar Rav Hisda merely
states that the law is in agreement with "our Masters" (*Rabbotenu*).
His words may be interpreted in two ways.

The first would suggest that the *moredet* is to be treated in accordance with the view of our Masters—and not as indicated in the Mishnah. In this case he would reject the penalty of a slow reduction of the woman's alimony sum, and would uphold the view of the Tosefta that she is to be given one month of warning, after which time, if she does not change her behavior, she must forfeit the entire amount. It is in regard to this position that Rava exclaims "that is boorish," because Rava maintains that normative halakhic practice must be in accordance with the Mishnah (and not the Tosefta). Understanding that Rava is basing himself on this interpretation of Rav Nahman bar Rav Hisda helps explain both his usage of the word "boorish"—for only the Tosefta requires public announcement—as well as the support for his position in the statement of Rav Sheshet: "[the *moredet*] is to be persuaded." The Mishnah, after all, allows for a much longer period of persuasion than the four weeks of pressure determined by the Tosefta. This interpretation of the words of Rav Nahman bar Rav Hisda is the interpretation of Rashi. If it is correct, Rava, the great sage of Sura, determined the treatment of the *moredet* in accordance with the Mishnaic text, and all subsequent halakhic authorities would logically follow his example.

The chief problem with this approach is that Rava—who rejects the Tosefta—was previously cited as having cited a proof in support of Rami bar Hama from the wording "Sabbaths" in the Tosefta. It is somewhat awkward to maintain that the same man rejects the Tosefta in one place and then brings a proof from the Tosefta to support a contemporary Amora who decides in its favor.[6]

So we must turn now to the second possible interpretation of Rav Nahman bar Rav Hisda's words. It is possible that he maintains that the law is in accordance with "our Masters"—and not in accordance with Rami bar Hama. In this case, Rav Nahman would uphold the Tosefta, but disagree with the additional private warning before the public announcement which Rami bar Hama instituted. In this case, Rava's reaction "That is boorish," is in defense of Rami bar Hama, because Rava insists that normative halakhic practice must be in accordance with Rami bar Hama's view of the Tosefta.

This explains both Rava's use of the term "boorish" (a public pro-clamation without allowing the *moredet* a chance to heed earlier, private warnings may well be considered boorish) and the support for his position found in the statement of Rav Sheshet: "[the *moredet*] is to be persuaded." After all, it is by private warning that they attempted to persuade her, before making her rebellion a matter of public record! This approach has the additional merit of being con-sistent with the previous position which supported both the *baraita* as well as Rami bar Hama's interpretation.[7]

By accepting this as Rava's position, we come to the fourth state of development of the halakhot of the rebellious wife. We began with the Mishnah's gradual reduction of the alimony provided for in the marriage contract, progressed to the Rabbis' ("*Rabbotenu*") insti-tution of a month-long period of private persuasion, and then to Rami bar Hama's addition of public proclamations. What Rava does here is to combine them all. There must be a private warning both prior to and subsequent to each public announcement, and after four consecutive weeks of warning-announcement-warning, the *moredet* forfeits her entire alimony sum. This is the interpretation upheld by Rabbenu Tam, and accepted by virtually all of the major Talmudic commentators.

REDEFINITION OF MOREDET
OR SEPARATE HALAKHIC CATEGORY?

היכי דמיא מורדת? אמר אמימר דאמרה בעינא ליה ומצערנא ליה אבל אמרה מאיס עלי
לא כייפינן לה. מר זוטרא אמר כייפינן לה, הוה עובדא ואכפה מר זוטרא ונפק מיניה רבי
חנינא מסורא ולא היא התם סייעתא דשמיא הוה

What is to be understood by [the term] rebellious wife?
Amemar said: She who says "I wish [to remain married] to him, but I want to cause him pain"; if she says, however, "He is repulsive to me," she is not forced [to resume sexual relations concurrent with the steady reduction of her alimony sum].
Mar Zutra said: She is forced.
Such an incident once occurred, and Mar Zutra forced [the

woman to remain married], and R. Haninah of Sura was born [from the continued relationship].

This, however, was not [the proper course of action]. In that case it was the intervention of Providence [which brought about such a satisfactory conclusion].

We see from the text above that the Babylonian Sages of the fifth and sixth generations had reopened the question of how to define *moredet*. Their discussion, however, takes a new turn. Amemar was a student of Rava and assumed the leadership of the scholars of Nehardea, while Mar Zutra, his student and colleague, became the head of the scholars of Pumpedita in the sixth generation. They apparently agree that a *moredet* rebels by virtue of her refusal to have sexual relations with her husband; they agree, too, that she loses the entire sum of alimony provided for her by the marriage contract. What they introduce is the term "force" (כייפינן) to replace the term "persuade" (נמלכין). Apparently, they realized that causing the woman to forfeit the entire alimony sum was indeed coercion. But what about the woman who rebels against her husband, not because she wishes to cause him pain (though still wishing to remain married), but because she finds him repulsive and desires to be released from the entire marital relationship? Can she initiate divorce proceedings on the basis of this hatred, though for no objective or demonstrable reason?

It is remarkable that nowhere in the Babylonian Talmud had this issue been considered previously. The Jerusalem Talmud, as we have seen above, provided for this eventuality with a special stipulation in the marriage contract. Apparently, the Babylonian Amoraim were either unaware of or opposed to such a stipulation, and until the fifth or sixth generation had no need for it. Perhaps Resh Lakish's assumption that "a woman would rather live with grief than live alone" (bKid 41a) was widely held in Babylonia—although, interestingly enough, the Jerusalem Talmud never mentions it—and it was not until this time that the possibility of a woman *stating* her case for a divorce became a reality.

Amemar insists that a woman who claims that her husband is repulsive to her and she cannot live with him is not considered a *moredet,* and not to be judged as one. Furthermore, in no way is she to be pressured to remain with him. Yet Amemar does not specify whether or not the husband is forced to grant her a divorce, and whether or not she receives the alimony of her *ketubah,* merely saying, "she is not to be forced." Nonetheless, his words open the door for a liberal interpretation of the law, one which is concerned for the individual rights of a woman who cannot live with her husband. This interpretation would force the husband to divorce her *and* ensure that she receives her *ketubah.*[8]

Mar Zutra, on the other hand, expands the concept of *moredet* to include the woman who denies her husband sexual relations because he is repulsive to her; and he would subject such a woman to coercion either by the Mishnaic penalty of a steady reduction of the alimony sum or by the four-week warning-announcement process followed by complete forfeiture of the *ketubah,* as ordained by the Tosefta and Rami bar Hama. Mar Zutra apparently feels that the claim "he is repulsive to me" is not enough to remove her from the category of *moredet,* either because he believes that only the objective considerations stated in the Mishnah (usually physical deformities in the husband) are sufficient to make her claim valid, or because he fears that the woman may have merely "cast her eyes on another," and, in fact, is not repulsed by her husband.[9]

The Talmud takes into account the conflict between Amemar's concern to protect the woman and Mar Zutra's concern to protect the institution of marriage, and seems to decide in favor of Amemar's opinion. By attributing the birth of R. Haninah of Sura to Divine Providence and not to Mar Zutra's legal decision, it implicitly rejects the latter's action. And, indeed, the redactor cries out, "[coercion] was not [the proper course of action]."

FINAL TALMUDIC DECREE

INTRODUCTION CONCERNING DOWRY GARMENTS

כלתיה דרב זביד אימרדא הוה תפיסא חד שירא יתיב אמימר ומר זוטרא ורב אשי, ויתיב
רב גמדא גבייהו יתבי וקאמרי: מרדה, הפסידה בלאותיה קיימין. אמר להו רב גמדא:
ומשום דרב זביד גברא רבה, מחניפיתו ליה והאמר רב כהנא, מיבעיא בעי רבא, ולא
פשיט!

איכא דאמרי

יתבי וקאמרי: מרדה, לא הפסידה בלאותיה קיימין
אמר להו רב גמדא: ומשום דרב זביד גברא רבה הוא, אפכיתו ליה לדינא עילויה? והאמר
רב כהנא מיבעיא בע׳ רבא, ולא פשיט!

Rav Zevid's daughter-in-law rebelled [against her husband] and
grabbed her silk [garment, which she had brought with her into the
marriage, which was assessed and entered into the *ketubah,* and which
was still in existence]. Amemar, Mar Zutra, and Rav Ashi were sitting
[together, on a rabbinical court], and Rav Gamda sat near them.

[In the course of their deliberations] they said: She rebelled, [and]
she forfeits her worn-out garments which are still in existence.

Rav Gamda said to them: Because Rav Zevid is a great man, do
you then flatter him? After all, did not Rav Kahana say that Rava
raised this question [regarding the worn garments], but never
resolved it? [Do you then decide that it is forfeited in order to curry
favor with Rav Zevid, whose son would then be able to retrieve the
silken garment?]

Another Version

[In the course of their deliberations] they said: She rebelled, [and] she
does not forfeit her worn-out garments which are still in existence.

Rav Gamda said to them: Because Rav Zevid is a great man, do
you then turn the law against him? After all, did not Rav Kahana say
that Rava raised this question, but never resolved it?

Rav Zevid was a fifth-generation Amora, and the head of the
scholars of Pumpedita. Amemar, Mar Zutra, and Rav Ashi were
fifth-and sixth-generation Amoraim, but Rav Ashi—a disciple of
Rav Kahana—restored the preeminence of the scholars of Sura,

where he served as head. Thus the discussion of *moredet* returned to its place of origin, Sura.[10]

The present problem concerns the daughter-in-law of Rav Zevid, who apparently rebelled against her husband, declaring, "I wish to remain married to him, but I wish to cause him pain."[11] It is interesting to note that the same disagreement we see in the Jerusalem Talmud between first-generation Palestinian Amoraim concerning dowry garments still in existence, continues into the fifth and sixth generation of Babylonian Amoraim. But even these latter do not conclusively settle the issue.

DECREE OF RABBANAN SABBORAI

השתא דלא אתמר לא הכי ולא הכי, תפסה, לא מפקינן מינה, לא תפסה, לא יהבינן לה, ומשהינן לה תריסר ירחי שתא אגיטא, ובהנך תריסר ירחי שתא, לית לה מזוני מבעל.

Now that it has not been determined, either this way or that way [i.e., the law regarding the dowry garments has not been clarified], if she seized the garments, we do not take them away from her, and if she did not seize them, we do not give them to her. We also make her wait twelve months—a year—for a divorce, and during these twelve months she receives no sustenance from her husband.

This final statement in the Babylonian Talmud is anonymous, though it apparently emanates from the period following Rav Ashi (to whom the Babylonian Talmud referred as "the last of the authoritative legal authorities") and should be attributed to the Rabbanan Sabborai, those scholars whose glosses of previous material constituted the last stage of the Babylonian Talmud.[12] The halakhic decision about the status of dowry garments in the case of a rebellious wife is consistent with the rulings on similar cases of ownership when there is no conclusive evidence: "The burden of proof is upon the one who wishes to take possession," or, more commonly, possession is nine points of the law.[13]

The final words of this decree concerning the question of divorce are more problematic, for consistency would require that the Rabbanan Sabborai are dealing with a *moredet* who claims "I wish to remain married to him, but I wish to cause him pain." After all, a woman who seeks to divorce her husband by claiming "I find him repulsive" is not considered by Amemar to be a *moredet,* and we have shown that the Talmud supports his position. If indeed this refers to the woman who negotiates her sexual position for a degree of power, then we see this later generation of scholars becoming more lenient, granting the *moredet* a period of one year (and not one to seven months) before she loses the alimony provided for in the marriage contract, and even providing her with a divorce at the end of that time, albeit without sustenance from her husband. This would be the fifth stage in the history of *moredet.*

Yet this interpretation of *moredet* is difficult, for the emphasis of the decree is not the loss of the *ketubah,*[14] but rather the penalty of having to wait a full year for a bill of divorce (thus implying that they are making her wait for something she wants). So it seems that this *moredet* is not merely engaging in sexual politics.

A better interpretation is that the Rabbanan Sabborai were dealing with a woman who claimed "He is repulsive to me," and that, unlike Amemar, they believed such a woman was a *moredet.* Although she wishes a divorce, she must wait one full year—without sustenance—before she receives it. And the text does not make clear whether even then the husband is to be forced into granting her one, although it would seem that he is ("we make her wait . . . for a divorce").[15] According to this interpretation she forfeits her *ketubah,* for if she is not given her own dowry garments, she is certainly not given the alimony provided for in the marriage contract. This interpretation (and it seems to me to be the correct one) represents an intermediate position between that of Amemar and that of Mar Zutra, although weighted towards the latter: She is called *moredet,* she is pressured for a year without receiving any sustenance, she forfeits her *ketubah,* but nonetheless her husband is coerced, after all this, to free her from a marriage she finds intolerable.

The Babylonian Talmud thus raises the issue of a woman who desires to leave her husband for reasons not enumerated in the Mishnaic provision for divorce. Amemar maintains that such a woman is not a *moredet* and not deserving of punishment, and he maintains that she is to be awarded an immediate divorce as well as her entire alimony. There is a possibility that the Rabbanan Sabborai were not discussing this category of woman at all; but if they were, as the logic of the Talmudic discussion seems to dictate, their final decree repre-

sents a new stringency, for they make the woman wait a year and forfeit her sustenance before her husband can be forced to give her a bill
of divorce. She is not entitled either to her alimony or to the garments she had brought with her at the time of her marriage. Nonetheless, the very fact that the Babylonian Talmud does, in the end,
seem to ordain a coerced divorce for a woman who finds her husband
repulsive has served as the basis for subsequent legal ordinances
which have had strong reverberations even to the present day.[16]

CHAPTER IV
MOREDET IN THE GAONIC PERIOD

CHRONOLOGICAL STUDY OF RESPONSA

Until now we have found a fairly steady progression of pressure being applied against the *moredet*. This culminated in a court's proclaiming her a *moredet* and obligating her to wait one year for her divorce, with neither sustenance from her husband during that year nor the benefits of her subsequent alimony.[1] The *Geonim,* heads of the various Babylonian Academies from approximately 700 to 1000 C.E. and the authoritative interpreters of Talmudic law, initiated a much more lenient policy. The husband was immediately to grant a divorce and full alimony benefits. We shall begin by investigating the responsa of each of the individual *Geonim* on the subject of *moredet,* delineating the various opinions.

YEHUDAI GAON

Rav Yehudai Gaon, head of the Surans in 760 C.E., is cited as having sent the following responsum to Rav Aharon HaKohen:

[רב יהודאי גאון] לרבנו אהרן הכהן זצו"ל ובהלכות דמר רב יהודאי גאון ז"ל דכי בעיא איתתא לאיגרושי שלא ברצון בעלה מדחינן לה י"ב ירחי בגמרא דאף על פי. והאידנא לא קא עבדינן הכין וכד מימרדא איתתא על בעלה ותבעה לאיגרושי מחייבינן ליה לבעל ליגרשה ואי לא עביד, משמתינן ליה עד דעביד אבל כדי למיתבע שלמא בין איש לאשתו מדחינן לה שבתא ותרין.[2]

[A responsum of R. Yehudai Gaon] to Rabbenu Aharon HaKohen (may the memory of the righteous be a blessing) and found in the laws of Mar Rav Yehudai Gaon (may his memory be a blessing). When a woman desires a divorce against the will of her husband, we

put her off for twelve months in accordance with the gemara of
[Chapter] "Even Though" [bKet 63b]. But we do not act now in such
a manner. When a woman rebels against her husband and desires a
divorce, we obligate [the husband] to divorce her, and if he does not
do so we place him under the ban until he does it. But in order to
bring about peace between husband and wife we make her wait a
week or two.

In this, the earliest Gaonic responsum extant concerning *moredet,*
we perceive a fundamental change and the beginning of a far more
lenient attitude towards the woman who denies her husband sexual
relations because she finds him repulsive. It is likely that the respondent understood the Talmud (Rabbanan Sabborai) to have ordained
a *coerced* bill of divorcement after twelve months (in accordance with
the second interpretation of *moredet* in the previous chapter),
because the only exception he takes to the view of the gemara is
when the original states that "she is forced to wait twelve months."
According to the words of Rav Yehudai Gaon, the Geonim reduced
this period of time to "a week or two," after which period the husband is forced to grant her a divorce. It seems clear from the conclusion of this responsum that the Rabbis of the day had no *legal*
objections to immediate divorce, but instituted this short waiting
period only in the hope that the woman would change her mind,
thus, "bringing peace between husband and wife." But he makes no
mention of the *ketubah* or the *alimony,* and it may be assumed that at
this time the Geonim concurred with the final decree in the Talmud,
and held that a *moredet* must forfeit her alimony.

HALAKHOT GEDOLOT

The author of *Halakhot Gedolot,* generally considered to be Rav
Shimon Kiara, wrote in the ninth century:

ואי אמרה ליה גירשן והב לי כתובתאי הויא לה מורדת ומשהינן לה תריסר ירחי שתא
והדר יהבינן לה גיטא. והני תריסר ירחי לית לה מזוני מבעל. האי גמרא היא. ואי תפיסה
מידעם מכתובתה לא מהנפקינן מינה ואי לא תפישא מידי לא יהבינן לה, והאידנא בבית
דין הגדול תרתין מתיבאתא הכין קא פסקין במורדת דאע״ג דתפישא מידעם מכתובתה

קא מפקינן ליה מינה ומהדרינן ליה לבעל ויהבינן לה גיטא אלתר. והני מילי במאי דכ׳זב
לה בעל, אבל מאי דאיתיאת היא מבי נשא בין תפישא ליה ובין לא תפי״ א ליה כל
מידעם דאיתיה בעיניה דידה הוא ויהבינן לה.[3]

And if she says to him, "Divorce me and give me the value of my
marriage contract," she is a rebellious wife. And if she seizes anything
of the marriage contract [apparently, anything of that which she had
brought into the marriage], we do not take it away from her, but if
she does not seize [anything] we do not give it to her.

And we make her wait twelve months, and then we grant her a bill
of divorce. These twelve months she is without sustenance [from her
husband]. Thus the gemara [teaches].

And now, [in the Great Court] of these two academies,[4] they rule
regarding the rebellious wife that even though she seized something
from the marriage contract, we take it away from her and return it to
her husband, and we grant her a bill of divorce immediately.

But this applies [only] to that which the husband contracted with
her, but regarding that which she brought from her own home [into
the marriage], whether she seized it or not, everything which is still in
existence belongs to her and we give it to her.

The move towards granting more and more privileges to the
rebellious wife continued. She is given an immediate divorce—
apparently even in the face of her husband's objection—and she is
given all of the objects still in existence which she brought into the
marriage. This is clearly a further departure from the Talmudic ruling that she receives only that which she seizes. But at this point in
time she still loses her right to alimony, and anything else which had
originally been owned by her husband.

Natronai Gaon

Rav Natronai Gaon, the head of the scholars of Sura in the middle
of the ninth century, wrote the following responsum, the most complete explication of the Talmudic passage of *moredet* up to this point:

כך ראינו שמתניתין כך שנויה: המורדת על בעלה פוחתין לה שבעה דינרין בשבת ר׳
יהודה אומר שבעה טרפעיקין ובמורדת כך שנויה, וכך המורד על אשתו מוסיפין לה על

כתובתה שלשה דינרין בשבת ר' יהודה אומר ג' טרפעיקין . . .
ולענין הלכה מסקנא דמורדת אע"ג דפלגי ר' יהודה ורבותינו וחזרו ונמנו שיהיו מכריזין
עליה כו' ואמר רמי בר אבא פעמים שולחין לה מב"ד ודרש רב נחמן בר רב חסדא הלכה
כרבותינו ואמר רבא אמר רב ששת הלכה נמלכין בה ומסקנא כלתיה דרב זביד אימרדה,
וקאמרי' בסיפא השתא דלא אתמר לא כמר ודלא כמר דתפיסא לא מפקינן מינה ודלא
תפיסא לא יהבינן לה ומשהינן לה תריסר ירחי שתא אגיטא מיהא צריכה התראה בב"ד
קודם לכן כדקאי בפרקא ארוסה בשוטא (סוטה לה: א) והלכתא הכין הא (!)[5]
מיהא רבנן סבוראי דבתר הוראה תקינו
הלכה למעשה למישקל מינה מאי דתפסת מדילה ולמיהב ליה. ואיהו יהיב גיטא לאלתר
כדי שלא תצאנה בנות ישראל לתרבות רעה וכך עמא דבר ואין לזוז ממנה ומפקינן
ממורדת עיקר כתובה ותוספת אפ' מנה אפ' מאתים(!) אבל נדוניא שלה נוטלה את נדוניא
והא דאמר איבו א"ר ינאי תנאי כתובה ככתובה דמיא היינו דברים האמורים (נד:)
בכתובה כי היכא דאמרי' בריש אע"פ אבל נדוניא [שלה] לא שייך כל עיקר בכתובה.

We have seen that the Mishnah teaches as follows: "If a woman rebels
against her husband, seven *dinarim* are deducted each week from the
value of the alimony provided for by the marriage contract; R. Yehudah says: seven *quinarii*." This is what we have learned concerning a
rebellious wife: "And similarly if a man rebels against his wife, three
dinarim are added each week to the value of the alimony provided for
by the marriage contract; R. Yehudah says: three *quinarii*." And
regarding the halakhah, the conclusion is that a rebellious wife, even
though Rabbi Yehudah and the [later] Rabbis disagreed, they
reviewed the situation and decided that they publicly announce
against her, etc., and Rabbi bar Abba said that the Jewish court must
send [private warnings] to her twice, and Rav Nahman bar Rav Hisda
teaches that the law is according to our Rabbis [and not the Mish-
nah], and Rava says in the name of Rav Sheshet that the law is that
one must attempt to persuade her [by a private warning twice each
week in addition to the public announcement].

And the conclusion [of the Talmudic discussion is that] the
daughter-in-law of Rav Zevid rebelled, and we say at the end, since
[the law concerning her dowry garments] has not been conclusively
decided, "not in accord with one Rabbi nor the other," if she seized
any [garments] we do not take them away from her, and if she did not
seize any [garments], we do not give them to her. We make her wait
twelve months for a bill of divorce, but she must be warned in
advance by the court [of her alimony loss], as it says in the Chapter
"Betrothed Woman" in Tractate Sotah [25a]. And thus [is the law].

However, the Sabboraic Sages who came after the period of authoritative legal decision decreed normative halakhah to be that one take [from her] even that which she has seized, and give her a bill of divorce immediately, so that Jewish women should not stray towards lewdness and indecency. So do people act, and one should not depart from it. And we take from the rebellious wife the basic alimony sum, and any additions thereto [provided in the marriage contract]. But her dowry is hers [which is the money, gifts, and property which she brought into the marriage], and even if they [be worth] one or two hundred [zuzim, and thus equal to the alimony sum], she takes them. And this statement of Aivo in the name of R. Yannai, that the stipulations of the marriage contract are as binding as the marriage contract itself [bKet 44b], only applies to matters stated in the marriage contract proper, as our Sages maintain in the beginning of the Chapter "Even Though."[6] But her dowry is hers; it has no connection to the marriage contract [and is treated differently from it. We can therefore justify her forfeiture of the alimony and her right to the dowry].

Rav Natronai Gaon repeats the legal decision previously cited, deciding the Talmudic dispute in accordance with the Tosefta and Rami bar Hama. To this he adds another decree recorded earlier, identifying it with the Rabbanan Sabborai. He clearly recognized that it disagrees with the Talmudic conclusion. Thus he strengthens the Sabboraic insistence that the husband of a woman who finds him repulsive must provide her with an immediate divorce, at which time she receives everything she brought into the marriage with her.

This responsum is especially fascinating because it is the only one to give a reason for the basic change in attitude towards the *moredet* which we find in the Gaonic period. Rav Natronai Gaon explicitly states: "And he gives her a divorce immediately in order that Jewish women not stray towards lewdness and indecency." We previously explained the Talmudic debate on this issue between Amemar and Mar Zutra as being predicated upon two sometimes opposing values: protecting the sensitivities and rights of the individual woman, and safeguarding the social institution of marriage. The final statement in the Talmud seemed to tip the scales in favor of the latter.[7] The Talmudic decision forced the woman to wait one year without sustenance before she could receive a divorce, after which she would have to forfeit the entire amount of alimony provided by the marriage contract, with the exception of those dowry garments (and apparently anything else she had brought into the marriage) that she had been strong enough—or clever enough—to seize. Rav Natronai shows that in the Gaonic period another variable was taken into consideration. If the Rabbis delayed in granting her a divorce, the *moredet* might "stray towards lewdness and indecency." I believe that the meaning of this phrase is that the woman might stray to a foreign culture; evidently the social realities of the Jewish communities in Babylonia were such that the possibility of a Jewess's assimilating into Gentile society was a danger to which the halakhah had to respond.[8] At the very least, the phrase means that the *moredet* might take up with another man—Jewish or otherwise. So the Geonim determined that a woman who claimed she could no longer live with her husband was no longer forced to do so; she was granted an immediate divorce and automatically received all that she had brought into the marriage which was still in existence.

AN ANONYMOUS THIRTEENTH-CENTURY RESPONSUM

A responsum which appears anonymously as part of a collection of Gaonic responsa from the thirteenth century sheds an even greater light on the reason for the increasing leniency towards the *moredet* in the Gaonic period. The Gaon sees the danger of the woman's "coming to a bad end" (*tarbut ra'ah*); an even more explicit expression of the danger inherent in delaying the granting of a divorce to the woman who requests it.

ובתשובת הגאונים מצאתי ושאלת מאי נמלכים בה אמר רמי בר חמא פעמים שולחים
לה מב"ד הוי יודעת שאפילו כתובתך ק' מנה מפסדתן את והיינו נמלכין בה. והשתא
סוגיין והלכתא מאי דנוהגין רבנן בתרתי מתיבתא לאו הכי. אלא כי כלתיה דרב זביד
וכלתיה דרב זביד גופא אע"ג דמסקי' דתפיסה לא מפקי' מינה ומשהינן י"ב ירחי שתא
אגיטא רבנן סבוראי דהוו בתר רבנן דהוראה חזו כי משתהיין י"ב ירחי שתא דנפקן בנות

ישראל לתרבות רעה בין בזנות בין בשמד ותקון מאי דתפסה נמי מפקי' מינה וכתבי לה
גט לאלתר וטב לתרוייהו בין לבעל בין לאשה.⁹

And in the responsa of the Geonim I found: and you asked: what is
[the meaning of the Talmudic phrase] "they must attempt to persuade her"? Rami bar Hama explains: Twice they send her [a warn-
ing] from the Jewish court, [saying] "Know that even if the alimony
provided by your marriage contract is one hundred *maneh,* you shall
lose it." This is their attempt to persuade her. And nowadays the law
which the rabbis of the two schools follow is not like that, but rather
is like [the case of] the daughter-in-law of Rav Zevid. But [even] the
case of the daughter-in-law of Rav Zevid [is not the final law]:
Although we concluded there that whatever she seizes is not taken
away from her, and that we make her wait twelve months to receive a
bill of divorce, nevertheless the Sabboraim who came after the
authoritative legal decision saw that when they caused a delay of
twelve months, the daughters of Israel went out to "bad ends," either
prostitution or apostasy. Therefore, they instituted that [even the
property] she seized was taken from her, but they wrote her an immediate bill of divorce. This is good for both the husband and the wife.

Although the fear expressed in this responsum—that a woman
denied a divorce for a year might "come to a bad end"—seems
extreme, it is not difficult to imagine that a woman who was so con-
stricted by a seemingly insensitive religious leadership might well
express her outrage or satisfy her needs by turning towards more
congenial society. Moreover, a year-long period without financial
support, and an inability to finalize her legal status, might well
encourage her to enter into a relationship that provided the former
without requiring the latter.

But this responsum is not nearly as clear on the issue of a *moredet*'s monetary rights as it is about her legal status. Does the author
maintain that even that which she seizes of her own dowry is to be
taken from her (a view even more stringent than both the concluding statement of the Talmud and Rav Natronai), or does he refer
only to that which she seizes of her husband's property (as is the
opinion of Rav Natronai)? If the first interpretation is correct, the

final statement, "and this is good for both the husband and the wife," makes sense, because the decree is more stringent than the Talmud regarding both the husband (since he must grant his wife an immediate divorce) and the wife (since she does not receive even her dowry). In this case, I would place this responsum chronologically *before* that of Rav Natronai, who would then be relying on it as a basis for the change, but going beyond it in terms of the monetary payment (for he awards the woman her full dowry). However, the second interpretation of the passages makes more sense, for if the Geonim were concerned about Jewish prostitution, they would hardly leave the *moredet* divorced and absolutely penniless. If this is the correct interpretation, then we must assume that the final phrase means that it is to the husband's advantage to be free of a woman who abhors him, and to the wife's advantage to be freed from the marriage. And then this responsum would conveniently follow that of Rav Natronai Gaon.

AMRAM GAON

Rav Amram Gaon inherited the chair of the scholars of Sura from Rav Natronai Gaon, and was a leader of the Jewish community during the second half of the ninth century. In a responsum probably to be attributed to him he cites—perhaps initiates—a further advance in the lenient treatment of the *moredet*.

[הוראה לפי המשוער לרב עמרם גאון]

כל האשה (!sic) שמורדת על בעלה ואומרת אי איפשי בפל[וני] בעלי בין יבמה בין חלוצה בין אשה אחרת נוטלת כל מה שהביאה מבית אביה בין מקרקע בין מטלטלי שהם עומדים בעצמם הכל נוטלת אותם ו[נוטלת] זוזי חמשה ועשרים. שאמרו חכמים שהם מאתים זוזים מדאורייתא דמי בתולים ומפסדת כל תוספת ותצא בגט.[10]

Any woman who rebels against her husband and says "I do not wish so-and-so [to be] my husband," whether she be a levirate wife, a *halutzah,* or any other woman, is entitled to take with her anything she brought [into the marriage] from her father's house, be it real or movable property, which [is presently usable]; all of this she takes.

And [she is also entitled to receive] twenty-five *zuzim,* which the Sages said are [equivalent to] the two hundred *zuzim* Biblically ordained as the money [for] virgins. She loses any addition [which might have been made] to the [alimony sum], and leaves [her husband after receiving] a bill of divorce.

Rav Amram agrees with the decision of Rav Natronai Gaon, but adds that the *moredet* receives not only those things which she brought with her into the marriage, but also the value of her alimony. This is the third stage of the law of *moredet* in the Gaonic period, and it is by far the most lenient. We see that whereas in the period of the Babylonian Talmud decisions became increasingly more stringent, in the Gaonic period the trend was towards leniency.

HANANIAH BEN YEHUDAH GAON

Rav Hananiah ben Yehudah Gaon was the father of Rav Sherira and the head of the scholars of Pumpedita in the first half of the tenth century. His responsum contains no innovations concerning the laws of *moredet;* rather, he confirms all that we have previously discussed.

רב חנניה גאון

אם האשה היא שמרדה על בעלה ותובעת גירושין וריצוה ולא נתרצת לחתפייס על בעלה משפטה שתיטול נדוניא בלבד מה שכתוב בכתובתה שהביאה מבית אביה ומוסיף עליה לבתולה עשרים וחמשה עיקר כתובה ולאלמנה וגרושה שנים עשר וְחצי — אבל מה שכתב לה הבעל בכתובתה ממתנות עם מה שהתפיסה משלו אין נותנין לה ממנו כלום לפי שלא הקנה לה אלו אלא על מנת שתעמוד לפניו ותשמשו לא על מנת שתטלם ותצא, עכשיו שמרדה אין לה בהן כלום — וכופין את הבעל עד שיגרש — וזה משפט מורדת בישיבתנו בזמן הזה.[11]

If the woman rebelled against her husband and demanded a bill of divorce, and if they attempted to persuade her but she did not wish to be reconciled with [him], the law concerning her is that she is entitled to those things which she brought [into the marriage] from her father's house, and for a virgin they add to it twenty-five [*zuz,* which is the basic alimony sum], and for a widow or divorcee [they add] twelve and one-half [*zuz*]. . . . But anything the husband wrote into the marriage contract for her as a gift, [as well as] anything she [may have] seized from his [property], is not given to her at all, since her [husband] did not grant her possession of these save that she live with him and serve him. It was never his intention to give them to her, in order that she might take them and leave [him]. Now that she has rebelled, she is not entitled to any of these things. . . . [The court] coerces the husband until he divorces her . . . and this is the law of the *moredet* in our yeshiva at this time.[12]

By the first half of the tenth century, the Rabbis had provided that a husband be forced to grant his wife an immediate divorce, even against his will. The woman would receive a sum of money equivalent to the basic alimony sum Biblically ordained, as well as any property which she brought with her at the time of her marriage. She was not, however, entitled to receive any of her husband's property, nor any additional gifts he might have provided for her in the marriage contract.

SHERIRA GAON

The following responsum of Rav Sherira Gaon, head of the scholars of Pumpedita during the latter part of the tenth century and one of the most prolific legal authorities, attests to his broad understanding of both the Talmudic discussion and the ensuing Gaonic decrees.

רב שרירא גאון ז"ל

ושישאלתם אשה שהיא יושבת תחת בעלה ואמרה לו גרשני איני רוצה לישב עמך, חייב ליתן לה כלום מכתובתה או לא, כגון דא היא מורדת או לא? כך ראינו ששורת הדין היתה מעיקרא שאין מחייבין את הבעל לגרש את אשתו אם תבעה גירושין חוץ מאותן שאמרו רבותינו בהן שכופין אותן להוציא וכשהאשה נמנעת מן התשמיש ומן המלאכות שחייבת לעשותן לו זו היא המורדת שפוחתין לה מכתובתה כלום בכל שבת ושבת וצריכה התראה ואחר כך תקנו תקנה אחרת שיכריזו (שיהו מכריזין [ח"ג ושע"צ]) עליה ארבע שבתות זו אחר זו ושולחין לה מבית דין: הוי יודעת שאפילו כתובותיך מאת מנה הפסדת, ואמרינן עלה אמר רמי בר חמא (ראמי בר אבא [:var]) פעמים שולחין לה (שקבלם בעלה על עצמו :var) אחת קודם הכרזה ואחת לאחר הכרזה, כל אלה לענין מה

ששם (שכתב :var) לה בעלה על עצמו ואינו מצוי בעינו, או מה שבלה ואבד מנדוניתא
(שלה) ומן תכשיטיה שהן נכס' דצאן ברזל שצריך הבעל לשלם לה דמיהן משום
שאחריותן עליו היו פוחתין מאשר לה (פוחתן לה מאשה :var) על האיש שבעה שבעה
דינרין בשבת לסוף התקינו שמכריזין עליה ארבע שבתות ומפסדת (ומפסידה את :var)
כולן ואעפ"כ לא היו מחייבין את הבעל לכתוב לה גט ואם מת, נפטרו יורשיו מכתובבה
מאשר הוא כתובה עליו. אבל הנמצא בעין והוא קיים בין בין מן נדוניתה בין מן תכשיטיה,
דתפשא לא מיפקינן מינה, ודלא תפשא לא מפקינן מיניה (לא יהבנן לט"ו :var) והתקינו
שממשהין אותה בלא (כשתובעת :var) גירושין שנים עשר חדש שמא התפייס (יתפסו,
ואם לא יתפס לאחר :var).

ולאחר שנים עשר חדש כופין את הבעל וכותב לו גט

(והוא כפי הרמב"ן ובמקצת תשובה לרב שרירא ז"ל נמי ראיתו שפי' דמן דינא אין
כופין וכשאי משהינן לה תריסר ירחא אגיטא תקנתא אחרות הוה לומר דאח"כ כופין את
הבעל בגט וכו' — חידושי רמב"ן וע' שם) ואחרי (ואחרי כך :var) רבנן סבוראי
בראותא (כשראו, כשראו חכמים :var) שבנות ישראל הולכות ונתלות בגוים ליטול להן
גטין באונס מבעליהן ויש כותבין גטין באונס ומסתפק לגט מעושה שלא כדין (גט מעושה
כדין או שלא כדין :var) וקא נפיק מינה חורבא תקנו וקא נפיק מינה חורבא תקנו בימי
מר רב רבה בר מר רב הונאי ומר רב הונאי (מר רב ראבא שתקנו בימיו לתת לאלתר גט
לאשה ודלא כשמעתא דכלתיה דרב זביד ובימיו היה בסורא מר רב הונאי) נוחם עדן
למורדת ותובעת גירושין שכל נכסי צאן ברזל שהכניסה לו משלה ישלם ואפילו מה
שכלה ואבד (או אבד :var) ישלם לה תחתיו, ומה שכתב לה על עצמו מה שאינו מצוי לא
ישלם לה ומה שהוא מצוי נמי, אע"ג דתפשה (דתפשא :var) לה, מפקינן מינה ומהדרינן
ליה לבעל וכופין אותו וכותב לה גט לאלתר ויש לה מנה מאתים.[13]

And concerning your question: In the case of a woman who is living
with her husband and says to him, "Divorce me, I do not wish to live
with you," is [her husband] obligated to give her anything from the
alimony provided for by the marriage contract, and is she [consi-
dered] a rebellious wife or not?

We have seen that the original requirement of the law was that the
husband was not obligated to divorce his wife if she demanded a
divorce except in those [cases] where the Rabbis said that they can
force him to divorce [her]. And when a woman abstains from sexual
relations and refuses to perform those household duties she is obligated to do for him, she is a rebellious wife, from whose alimony a
weekly sum is deducted, and she requires a warning. Afterwards they
enacted another decree, that they make a [public] announcement
concerning her for four consecutive weeks, and they send her [a

warning] from the Jewish court: "Know that even if the alimony provided for you by your marriage contract is one hundred *maneh,* you
shall lose it." They [further add] that Rami bar Hama says, "this
[warning] must be sent to her twice: once before the [public]
announcement and once after it."

All [the discussion concerning the weekly reduction of alimony]
pertains only to those objects which the husband obligated himself to
give her but which are not now in existence, and to whatever of her
dowry has been destroyed or lost, and to those ornaments which are
nikhsei tzon barzel [property which the wife brought into the marriage
and for which the husband accepted responsibility]. From all of
these, seven *dinarim* is deducted each week. Subsequently they
decreed that they [publicly] announce [concerning] her for four
weeks, [at which time] she forfeits everything.

Nevertheless, they did not obligate the husband to give her a bill
of divorce, and if he dies, his inheritors are freed from [those obliga-
tions] of the marriage contract for which he was responsible. But
those objects which remain in existence, either from her dowry or
from ornaments [received after her marriage], belong to whoever
takes them. Those articles which she seized are not taken away from
her, and whatever she did not seize is not taken away from him.

And then they decreed that they cause her to wait without a
divorce twelve months, in case she can be reconciled. And after twelve
months the husband is forced to write her a bill of divorce.

And afterwards the Rabbanan Sabborai saw that Jewish women
were attaching themselves to the Gentiles to get divorces from their
husbands by force, and that there were those [wives] who were satisfied with a "forced" divorce which was not in accordance with Jewish
law, and from which ruin emanates. It was therefore decreed in the
days of Mar Rav Rabba and Rav Hunai, may they rest in Eden, concerning a rebellious wife who demands a divorce, that he must pay
for all the *nikhsei tzon barzel* which was property that she brought with
her into the marriage and for which he assumed responsibility; he
must even give her restitution for those articles which were destroyed
or lost. As for his own objects or property which he had included in
the marriage contract as his obligation to her in the event of his death
or divorce, [if she divorces him, their status is as follows:] those which
are not now in existence he need not give her, and whatever she seizes

of those which are in existence, must be taken from her and returned to her husband.

They force him, and he must write her a bill of divorce immediately. She also receives one hundred or two hundred [zuzim, the basic alimony sum]. In this manner do we conduct ourselves today, and have done so for three hundred years and more. So should you do, too.

It is clear that Rav Sherira Gaon interprets the final statement of the Talmud, "and we make her wait twelve months . . . ," to mean that the husband is forced to grant his wife a divorce at the end of the twelve-month period, even against his will. Rav Sherira goes on to describe the various stages of the Talmudic position towards a *moredet,* and finally delineates the position of the Geonim. His legal summary is consistent with that of Rav Hananiah ben Yehudah Gaon, although he adds that the husband is to make restitution for *nikhsei tzon barzel* which are no longer in existence but for which he assumed responsibility. He also clearly specifies the reason for all the rabbinic leniencies: fear that a woman may resort to the Gentiles, who would arrange a divorce not in accordance with Jewish law.

Rav Sherira is so detailed and specific in his responsum that it becomes possible, with the aid of another of his statements, to date the original Gaonic decree which provided the *moredet* with both an immediate divorce and her basic alimony. In his famous *Epistle* about the history of the Oral Tradition Rav Sherira writes:

ואחריו מר רב ראבא שתיקנו בימיו לתת אלתר גט לאשה דלא כשמעתא דכלתא דרב זביד וביומיו היה בסורא מר רב הונא ובתר (יה) מר רב רבה (ובתריה) רב בוסאי . . . ובתר מר רב בוסאי בפום בדיתא מר רב הונא (ובתריה) מר׳ בו מר רבי יוסף הוה גאון בשנת אלפא . . . (למנין שטרות: 689)
. . . ושמואל אביו הוא בנו של מר רב ראבא גאון שפירשנו שהיה בפום בדיתא בהדי רב הונא גאון דמחסיא בשעת תקנת הגט.[14]

And after him, Mar Rav Rabba, they decreed in his day to grant an immediate bill of divorce to the woman—not in accordance with the [case of] the daughter-in-law of Rav Zevid. And in his day Mar Rav

Huna was in Sura. And afterwards, Mar Rav Rabba, [and after him] Rav Busai. . . . And after Mar Rav Busai in Pum Bedita, Mar Rav Huna. And after him Mar bar Mar Rav Yosef, who was Gaon in the year 1000 [698 C.E.]. . . . And Shmuel his father is the son of Mar Rav Rabba Gaon, who, we explained, was in Pum Bedita together with Rav Huna Gaon of Mehasia at the time of the decree concerning divorce.

What emerges from this epistle is that the motivation of all the rabbinic decrees—even those dealing at length with the question of alimony—was to provide a woman with the possibility of receiving an immediate divorce. The Gaonic decree originated with Mar Rav Rabba in Pumpedita after the period of the Rabbanan Sabborai, and during the time Rav Huna Gaon was in Sura—the third quarter of the seventh century C.E. Thus we can attribute the final Talmudic decree to the Rabbanan Sabborai, and the first Gaonic decree to the latter part of the seventh century.

HAI GAON

Rav Hai Gaon, the son of Rav Sherira and the recognized leader of Babylonian Jewry during the first half of the eleventh century, continued to promulgate the decree cited by his father.

אבל עכשיו דתקינו רבנן בתראי לגר(ו)שה למורדת דתבעה גירושין אלתר מגרשינן לה ולית לה עליה תוספת.[15]

But now that the later Rabbis decreed that the husband [must] divorce a rebellious wife who demands a divorce, he must divorce her immediately and she does not receive any additions [to the basic alimony provided by her marriage contract].

ANOTHER ANONYMOUS RESPONSUM

An anonymous Gaon of the tenth or eleventh century continues the tradition of providing the *moredet* with an immediate divorce, but adds a complication.

אבל מורדת, כל נכסי צאן ברזל דמן דילה בין איתינון ובין ליתנון מיחייב לשלומאנון
ומאי דכתב לה הוא, וליתיה, בלא ספיק פאקע. אבל מאי דאיתיה בין בפניה ובין שלא
בפניה לא פשיט בגמארא הפסידה(!) אי לא הופסדה מן הלכתא אילא אמרי רבנן
דתפישא לא מפקינן מינה ודלא תפישא לא יהבינן לה . . . ומשהינן לה תריסר ירחי
אגיטא. ובתר דגמרא תקינו רבנן דאפילו מאי דתפישא מהנפקינן ליה מינה ויהבינן לה
גיטא לאלתר.[16]

But the rebellious wife must be given all of the *nikhsei tzon barzel* which
are hers [i.e., which she brought into the marriage and for which her
husband assumed full responsibility]; he must give them [to her]
whether or not they are still in existence. And whatever obligations he
assumed from his own property [and which he wrote into the marriage contract], and which are not presently in existence, are assured-
ly canceled.

But the Talmud has not clarified whether or not she must forfeit
the property [that she brought with] her [into the marriage], whether
or not it is in his possession. But the Rabbis have said that whatever
[of her dowry] she seizes is not to be removed from her, and whatever
she does not seize is not to be given her. . . . And they cause her to
wait twelve months for her bill of divorce.

Now after the gemara, the Rabbis decreed that even that which
she seized [of his property] is to be taken away from her, and they
grant her a bill of divorce immediately.

This anonymous respondent comments on the allocation of
alimony in regard to the *nikhsei tzon barzel,* which, he maintains, the
husband must return to his wife at the time of their divorce, since he
had assumed responsibility for them. It is therefore possible to
maintain (and this is presumed in the translation) that this Gaon
denies the *moredet* only those things she seizes of her husband's
property; he seems to agree (but does not explicitly state) that she is
entitled to her own dowry property. Moreover, it is possible to
argue that because no mention is made of her alimony, it may be
assumed that she receives it. If this interpretation is correct, then this
anonymous Gaon is in agreement with the responsa of the previous
Geonim. If, however, we link this responsum with the earlier anonymous responsum (see above, p. 52), and interpret both responsa in

light of the simple language of the texts, we might well conclude that there were two positions on this issue in Gaonic times. The alternative position, represented by the two anonymous responsa, was that the *moredet* must forfeit all her monetary rights, including any of her dowry she might have seized, but with the exception of the *nikhsei tzon barzel*. In return, her husband was made to divorce her immediately. Yet even if there were indeed two positions, it is clear that the majority of the Geonim—especially the heads of the schools—granted the *moredet* both her dowry and her basic alimony.

SHMUEL BEN ALI

Rav Shmuel ben Ali lived in the second half of the twelfth century and was, in effect, a Gaon (head of a Babylonian school) after the conclusion of the Gaonic period. His responsum is brief but explicit.

הגאונים תקנו בשתי ישיבות בדין מורדת בין אמרה מאיס עלי בין אמרה בעינא ליה
ומצערנא ליה שאפילו י״ב חדש אין משהין אותה אלא משתדלין לעשות שלום ביניהם
ואם אינה שומעת נותנין לה גט לאלתר ואין מכריזין עליה ד׳ שבתות. יפטור מכל מה
שחייב עצמו התוספות והמתנות ואפילו אם תפסה מפקינן מינה. אבל מנה ומאתים (ומה)
שהכניסה לו בין נכסי צאן ברזל בין נכסי מלוג הקיימים חייב ליתן לה. ואפילו לא תפסה
מפקינן מיניה. כך שלח רבי שמואל בן רבי עלי ראש ישיבה מבבל אל הר׳ משה
מקיאו.[17]

The Geonim decreed in both schools regarding the law of the rebellious wife. We do not make her wait twelve months, whether she says "He is repulsive to me," or whether she says "I wish to remain married to him, but wish to cause him pain." [The court] endeavors to make peace between [husband and wife], but if she refuses to be appeased they grant her an immediate divorce, and do not [publicly] proclaim against her for four weeks. [The husband] is exempted from any obligations he imposed upon himself, including any additions to the alimony, or any gifts. Even if she seizes [anything], they take it from her. But the one hundred or two hundred [*zuzum*, the basic alimony sum], as well as [whatever] she brought into [the marriage for his benefit]—whether *nikhsei tzon barzel* [for which he assumed an obligation] or *nikhsei melug* [which are still in existence and for which he receives the usufruct]—he must give her. Even if she did not seize these, they are taken away from him [and given to her]. So did Rabbi Shmuel ben Rabbi Ali, head of the yeshiva, from Babylonia, send to Rabbi Mosheh of Keyo.

This responsum proves that by the end of the twelfth century the term *moredet* applied equally to the woman who refused her husband's advances in order to cause him pain, and to the wife who refused to have sexual relations with her husband on the grounds that he was repulsive to her. Rav Shmuel ben Ali maintains that the husband was made to grant his wife an immediate divorce without the courts's proclamation against her. He apparently thought that the original Gaonic decree rescinded the four-week warning period. At the time of the divorce, the *moredet* receives whatever dowry property she had brought into the marriage, whether still in existence or not. This includes the *nikhsei tzon barzel,* property which had originally belonged to her, but for which her husband assumed full responsibility at the time of the marriage. But the *nikhsei melug,* property originally belonging to her, and always remaining in her name, but whose usufruct belong to the husband, she received only if it was still in existence.[18] (Presumably since the husband had never assumed responsibility for them, it was not incumbent upon him to replace anything lost or used up.) In accord with the previous responsa, Rav Shmuel ben Ali grants the *moredet* her basic alimony, although she forfeits any additional alimony or gifts which the husband had promised her in the event of his death or *his* desire for a divorce.

GEONIM CITED BY THE RISHONIM

ALFASI

Rabbenu Yitzhak Alfasi (1013–1103) was one of the earliest Sephardic Rishonim. Writing in Fez, North Africa, he was known by the acronym *Rif,* and composed a compendium of each tractate of the Talmud. He deleted much of the give-and-take (*shakla ve-tarya*) of the Talmudic discussion, as well as most non-halakhic material, concentrating instead on normative legal practice as he understood it. In his discussion of the rebellious wife, he cites previous Gaonic enactments.

אלפסי

והלכתא כרב הונא דאמרינן לקמן היכי דמיא מורדת אמר אמימר דאמרה בעינא ליה
ומצערנא ליה ש״מ דמתחמיש היא מורדת כרב הונא . . . דרש רב נחמן בר רב חסדא
הלכה כרבותנו ורב הונה בר יהודא אמר רב ששת הלכה נמלכין בה . . . והשתא דלא
איתמר לא כמר ולא כמר תפסה לא מפקינן מינה: לא תפסה לא יהבינן לה ומשהינן לה
תריסר ירחי שתא אגיטא ובהלין תריסר ירחי שתא לית לה מזוני׳ מבעל. הדין הוא דינא
דגמרא, אבל האידנא בבי דינא דמתיבתא הכי דיינו במורדת: כד אתיא ואמרה: לא בעינא
ליה להאי גברא; ניתיב לי גיטא יהיב לה גיטא לאלתר; ואי תפסה מידי מכתובתה מפקינן
ליה מינה ומהדרינן לבעל והני מילי במאי דכתב לה בעל מדיליה; אבל מאי דאייתיאת
מבית נשא בין תפסה ליה בין לא תפסה ליה כל מאי דאיתיה בעיניה יהבינן לה ואי ליכא
מידי דאיתיה בעיניה ואיכא מידי דאתי דאתי מחמתיה יהבינן ליה ניהלה ואי ליכא מידי
דאיתיה בעיניה ולא מאי דאתי מחמתיה אלא אתאבדו להו לגמרי, לא מפקינן מיניה
דבעל ולא כלום וה״מ בנכסי מלוג אבל בנכסי צאן ברזל כל מידי דאיתיה בעיניה שקלה
ליה ואע״ג דבלו ליה טובא, והוא דחזו למאי דהוה חזי מעיקרא כגון דחזי לאשתמושי
ביה מעין מלאכה דידיה אבל מאי דבלו ליה לגמרי ולא חזי לאשתמושי ביה כדמעיקרא
משלם לה דמיהן כדמעיקרא מדידיה וכל שכן מאי דאיגניב או מאי דאיתניס דמשלם לה
בעל מדידה דברשותיה קיימי כדתנן אם מתו מתו לו, ואם הותירו הותירו לו (יבמות סו׳).

וחזינן לגאון דמאר דיהיב לה עיקר כתובה מנה מאתים בלחוד כי הכי דלא להויין בנות
ישראל הפקר אבל מאי דכתיב לה מדיליה בין תוספת בין מתנה לא יהבינן לה מידי ודינא
דגמרא אפילו עיקר כתובה לא יהבינן לה כדאמרינן בריש פרקא: תנאי כתובה ככתובה
נפקא מינה למוכרת למוחלת ולמורדת אלמא מורדת אין לה לא עיקר ולא תוספת הדין
הוא דינא דמורדת דנהיגין רבנן במתיבתא מכמה שני עד השתא אבל ודאי הדין תקנתא
ליתא אלא היכא דאימרדת איתתא בבעלה ובעיא לאפוקי מיניה מחמת דלא בעי׳ ליה
אבל היכא דאתמרעא או היכא עלה חשש מותא ובעיא למיפק מבעלה כי היכי דלא
לירות לה ליתא ההיא תקנתא ולא עבדינן בה עובדא ובכי האי מילתא איכא למימר היכא
דמיעיקרא נחלה דאורייתא לא תקון רבנן; ואע״ג דחזינן בהאי מילתא פלוגתא ביני
רבואתא מסתברא כמ״ד לא עבדינן תקנתא בכי האי מילתא.

ולדברי הכל כל מאן דכייפינן ליה לאפוקי בין מעיקר דינא אלו שכופין אותן
להוציא ומאי דדמי להו בין מעיקר דתקנתא, אי מיתה לה איתתא מקמי דתיפוק מיניה
דבעל בגט, בעלה יריח לה דלא מיפקע ירושה דבעל אלא בגירושין גמורין וכן הלכתא.[19]

And the law is in accordance with Rav Huna, as we say later on: "What is the case of the rebellious wife? Amemar says, When she says

'I want [to remain married to] him, but I wish to cause him pain.'"
We [may] deduce from this that [abstention] from sexual relations
[makes her a] rebellious wife in accordance with Rav Huna. . . . Rav
Nahman bar Rav Hisda teaches that the law is in accordance with our
Rabbis. Rav Huna bar Yehudah says in the name of Rav Sheshet: The
law is [that we attempt] to persuade her . . . and now that the issue is
not concluded either in accordance with that Master or the other
Master, if she seizes any object, we do not take it from her, and if she
does not seize any object, we do not give it to her. And we make her
wait twelve months for a bill of divorce, and during these twelve
months she receives no sustenance for her husband. This is the Talmudic law. But nowadays, in the court of the Academy, we judge the
moredet in such a way: When she comes and says: "I do not want [to
remain married to] this man, give me a bill of divorce," [he is made
to] grant her a divorce immediately. And if she seizes any object
which is granted to her in her marriage contract, we take it from her
and return it to the husband—but this is only with regard to those
things which her husband had promised her of his own [property].
[But] she is entitled to receive whatever objects she had brought [into
the marriage] from her prior home, whether or not she seized them;
as long as they are still in existence we give [them] to her. If the
objects themselves are no longer in existence, but if there are objects
which were derived from her original [property], but everything has
been entirely used up, then we do not take anything away from the
husband. This is with regard to the *nikhsei melug*. But with regard to
nikhsei tzon barzel, whatever is in existence, she takes from him, even if
it is every much disintegrated, as long as it can still be used for its
original purpose. But the husband must compensate her from his
own property for the original value of anything which has entirely
disintegrated. And he must certainly make her compensation from
his own [property] for any goods which may have been stolen or
damaged by forces beyond his control, since they are in his domain
[and he assumed responsibility for them]. This is in accordance with
what we learned in the Mishnah: "If it dies, it dies on his account,
and if it increases in value, it increases on his account" [mYeb 7:1].

And we see that a Gaon says that he gives her the basic alimony
provided for by the marriage contract—one or two hundred *zuzim*
specifically—so that Jewish women not be left without dignity and

respect [hefker]. But whatever [the husband] wrote to her [from himself i.e., promised in her marriage contract]—either additional alimony or gifts—he need not give her at all; indeed, it is the Talmudic law that we do not even give her the basic alimony sum, as we say in the beginning of our chapter ["Even Though"; bKet 54b]: "the stipulations added to the marriage contract are as [binding] as the marriage contract itself. The significance [of this treating as equal the husband's additional monetary commitments [to the *ketubah*] and the principal of the ketubah] is realized when the wife either sells [or] forfeits [her *ketubah*] or rebels [against her husband] [in all of which cases, the ultimate disposition of the *ketubah* will apply to the supplements].

We see from here that the rebellious wife receives neither the basic alimony nor any additions. [The Gaonic decree awards her the basic alimony but no more.] This is the law of the rebellious wife which the Rabbis of the Academy enforced for several years until now. But certainly this decree applies only when the wife rebels against her husband, and wishes to be divorced because she no longer wants [to live with] him. But when she falls ill, or when she has a suspicion of her [impending] death, and [therefore] wishes to be divorced by her husband so that he not inherit her [property after her death], this decree is not operative and we do not act in accordance with it. In such a case one should say that wherever there was initially an inheritance [awarded to the husband] by Biblical law, the Rabbis did not apply their decree regarding the rebellious wife [i.e., they would not coerce him to divorce her, merely to keep him from inheriting].

And even though we see that in this case there is a dispute among the great scholars, the reasonable position is in accord with that which states, we do not enforce the [Gaonic] decree in this case.

And according to all [authorities], anyone whom we forced to divorce [his wife], either according to Talmudic law, as we learn in the mishnah, "These are those who are forced to divorce," and similar cases [gross physical afflictions], or according to the Gaonic decree, if the woman dies before she is given a bill of divorce by her husband, her husband inherits her [property] because the inheritance of the husband is not canceled without a complete divorce, and this is the law.

THE RAVIYAH

Rabbi Eliezer bar Yoel Ha-Levi, known as the *Raviyah,* was one of the great Rishonim of Ashkenaz who lived at the beginning of the thirteenth century.[20] In his responsum he cites the Gaonic tradition of granting the *moredet* the equivalent of her basic alimony sum.

ראבי״ה

ובתשובות הגאונים כתבו דלא דייני דייני בזמן הזה דינא דמורדת אלא הכי נהיג' בבית דין
הגדול בשתי ישיבות כדאמרה לא בעינא ליה יהיב לה גיטא לאלתר ולא שקלה מאי
דתפסה מכתובתה דיליה אלא מפקינן מינה לאהדוריה לבעל אבל מאי דאייתי מי נשא
— יהיב לה בעל — **ויש גאונים שאמרו** יהיב לה עיקר כתובה מנה ימאתים לא תוספת
כי היכי דלא ליהווי בנות ישראל הפקר.[21]

> In the responsa of the Geonim, they wrote that in these times we do not judge the law of a rebellious wife, but that in the Great Court [and] in the two schools, when a woman says "I do not wish [to remain married to] him," they are accustomed to grant her an immediate divorce; she cannot take what she seized from his properties [which are] enumerated in the marriage contract; they are taken away from her and returned to the husband. But that which she brings [into the marriage] from her prior home, the husband must give to her. And there are Geonim who say that he must give her the basic alimony sum, one hundred or two hundred [*zuzim*], without any additional gifts, so that Jewish women not be left without dignity and respect [*hefker*].

The Raviyah therefore substantiates what we already know to be the Gaonic decree, adding the explanation "so that Jewish women not be left without dignity and respect." This is not the reason cited by the Geonim themselves, who were concerned that Jewish women might either convert or resort to a divorce coerced by Gentiles and not in accordance with Jewish law. The word *hefker,* which the Raviyah uses, implies a condition of poverty and homelessness. It is quite possible that the situation in Ashkenaz differed from that in Babylonia. Perhaps the Moslem mosque and courts were willing to provide help for the Jewish woman, which the Christian institutions were not. So Raviyah couched his explanation in language applicable to the situation in Ashkenaz. It is also interesting to note that whereas the decrees of the Geonim emphasized coercing the husband to grant his wife a divorce, this responsum emphasizes the wife's right to monetary compensation.

HA-ITTUR

The author of the *Ittur,* Rav Yitzhak bar Abba Mari of Provence (the city of Marseilles), lived during the twelfth century (d. 1193). He wrote a commentary on Alfasi and was apparently well aware of the Gaonic decree.

ובתשובת מורדת על בעלה דינה מדתקינו רבנן סבוראי בשנת תתקס"ב למנין שטרות
וביומי מר רב(נ)א גאון מפומפדיתא (ומרבא) ומר רב הונא גאון מסורא נ"ע.[22]

In the responsum concerning a woman who rebels against her husband, the law is in accordance with the decree of the Rabbanan Sabborai in the year 965 of the Counting of Contracts [the Seleucid era, 651 C.E.], in the days of Mar Rabbana Gaon of Pumpedita (and Rava) and Mar Rav Huna Gaon of Sura, may they rest in Eden.[23]

This responsum is of value, for it serves to date the Sabboraic decree in accordance with our previous discussion, based upon the writings of Rav Sherira Gaon.

DINA De-METIVTA

DEVELOPMENT OF GAONIC DECREES

We have delineated the progressively more stringent measures which were enacted against the *moredet* during the Talmudic period. Beginning with four weekly public proclamations together with a private warning, after which time a wife who continued in her rebellion forfeited her alimony, these measures culminated in the enactment of a twelve-month waiting period for a divorce, during which time the woman received no sustenance from her husband, and after which she received no alimony. Even a wife who truly found her husband repulsive and wished to be divorced from him is subject to these stringencies. As a result of our study of various Gaonic responsa, we can list, and even date, the various counterdecrees which were enacted for the benefit of the *moredet*. Subsequent halakhic literature refers to them as *dina de-metivta,* and they are responsible for the new legal situation which emerged by the end of the tenth century.

1. Rav Yehudai Gaon, who lived in Sura during the latter half of the eighth century, provided that the husband of a woman who claims he is repulsive to her is obligated to divorce his wife after a waiting period of merely a week or two.

2. *Halakhot Gedolot* ("The Great Laws"), probably written in the ninth century, added to the husband's obligation of granting an immediate divorce the wife's right to all her remaining dowry property, whether or not she "seized" them at the time of the divorce. Rav Natronai Gaon endorsed and confirmed this practice.

3. Rav Amram Gaon, who suceeded Rav Natronai in Sura at the end of the ninth century, added that the wife was also entitled to receive a basic alimony sum of either one hundred or two hundred *zuzim.*

4. Rav Sherira Gaon, head of the scholars of Pumpedita in the late tenth century, confirmed all the previous decrees. He clarified the wife's right not only to whatever remained of her dowry (her property which she had brought with her at the time of her marriage), but also to any *nikhsei tzon barzel* (property which she had brought into the marriage but for which her husband had assumed full responsibility) that was no longer intact. Hence, there appear to be four progressive decrees, each adding some benefits for the *moredet,* and each agreed upon by the two major schools in Babylon: Sura and Pumpedita.

THE ORIGINAL DECREE: GAONIC OR SABBORAIC?

Rav Sherira attributed all of the Gaonic decrees, except the one providing for an essential alimony sum, to the period of Mar Rav Rabbah bar Mar Hunai in Pumpedita, and Mar Rav Huna in Sura,[24] which would be during the third quarter of the seventh century. These decrees were specifically dated in the portion of the responsum preserved by the *Ittur* at 651 C.E.,[25] or, in accordance with the analysis of Efrati, after 656 C.E.[26] Certainly the original decree providing for an immediate divorce can be attributed to this period, but an interesting debate exists as to whether this period is considered Gaonic or Sabboraic. The Sabboraim were the bearers of the Oral Tradition immediately following the Amoraim and directly preceding the Geonim. Their names are barely recorded and their accomplishments are shrouded in mystery. The Talmud teaches: "Rav Ashi and Ravina conclude [the period] of instruction [*hora'ah*]."[27] Rav Sherira, in his famous epistle on the history of the Oral Law, understands this to refer to the conclusion of the Amoraic period, which he dates to the year 500 C.E. He believes the Gaonic period began at Pumpedita in the year 589 C.E.[28] Therefore, in his view, the era of the Sabboraim lasted eighty-nine years, and this seventh-century decree regarding the *moredet* must be Gaonic. But Ravad, lists five generation of the Rabbanan Sabborai in his *Sefer HaQabbalah,*[29] and believed that they lasted 189 years, until the year 689 C.E.[30] According to this calculation, the initial decree providing for immediate divorce must be attributed to the Rabbanan Sabborai. Interestingly enough, two variant readings exist in the responsum of Rav Sherira Gaon himself. In the text of the *Responsa of the Ancient Geonim,* as well as in the text cited by Alfasi,[31] the *Ittur,*[32] and R. Yeruham, the reading is:

> and *after* the Rabbanan Sabborai, in the days of Mar Rav Rabbah and Mar Rav Huna (may they rest in Eden), when they saw that the daughters of Israel were dependent upon the Gentiles . . .

But in the text of *Gaonic Responsa Hemda Genuzah,* and in the responsum cited by R. Yeshayah d'Trani, the reading is:

> and afterwards, when the Rabbanan Sabborai saw that the daughters of Israel were becoming dependent upon the Gentiles, they decreed in the days of Mar Rav Rabbah . . .[33]

The former reading is more correct, substantiated as it is by a parallel statement in another responsum of Rav Sherira (which we cited earlier) in which he refers to the decree as post-Sabboraic.[34] In addition, it is, after all, Rav Sherira himself who begins the Gaonic period in the year 589 C.E., and who dates the original decree as 651 or 656 C.E.[35] Nonetheless, we must understand why Rav Sherira chooses to classify the Gaonic decree as post-Sabboraic; why not mention it only in reference to the Talmud?

Whether the Sabboraic period lasted approximately one hundred or two hundred years is far less important than is the nature and quality of the Sabboraic activity. It is clear from the Talmud itself that much of the material it contains was developed after the period of Rav Ashi and Ravina.[36] In the epistle of Rav Sherira Gaon the following description of the Sabboraim appears:

> And after these [Ravina and Rav Ashi], although there were no authoritative halakhic decisions, there was interpretation and logical analysis [sebarā] bordering on authoritative halakhic decision, and those Rabbis were called Rabbanan Sabborai. They interpreted everything which was left unresolved [lit. "hanging"] in the Talmud. . . . And they added several analyses to the Talmud, [both] they and the Rabbis who succeeded them, like Rav Elna and Rav Simona. Their analyses are cited among the early discussions of the Talmud, from the beginning of "a woman is acquired" until "how do we know [that] money [is a valid form of acquisition]?" [bKid 2a]. The latter Rabbanan Sabborai explained [this sugya, lit., halakhic discussion] and codified it [as part of the Talmud]. In addition to this, there are also [other such sugyot formed by the Rabbanan Sabborai].[37]

So Rav Sherira believes that the Rabbanan Sabborai edited the Amoraic material, resolved any unresolved issues, and even established their own sugyot which were then incorporated into the Babylonian Talmud, such as the first sugya of the Tractate Kiddushin. A similar description of the Sabboraic contribution appears in the Seder Tannaim and Amoraim, an early Gaonic work which provides a history of the Oral Law.[38] The concluding Talmudic statement on moredet, clearly coming after the period of Rav Ashi, would thus seem to belong to the period of the early Sabboraim, whose task was to resolve all unresolved issues.

> Now that it has not been decided [in the generation of Rav Ashi, Amemar, and Mar Zutra] either this way or that way, [the law regarding the dowry garments had not been clarified]: if she seized the garments, they are not to be taken away from her; and if she did not seize them, they are not to be given to her. We also make her wait twelve months—a full year—for a divorce, and during these twelve months she receives no sustenance from her husband.[39]

Moreover, the author of the *Ittur* recognizes that this passage is an addition of the Rabbanan Sabborai; and indeed, there are many manuscripts in which the latter part of this addition, beginning with the words "and during these twelve months," does not appear at all.

The proper reading of Rav Sherira's responsum and the correct order of the decrees concerning the rebellious wife are not easy to identify. In the Talmud itself is a sixth-century Sabboraic decree which grants the *moredet* who is seeking a divorce the right to any dowry garments she seized, and a divorce (according to Gaonic interpretation, *even against the wishes of her husband*) after a twelve-month period without support. Rav Sherira therefore informs us that it was *after* this Sabboraic decree that the Geonim provided an immediate divorce for the *moredet*. It is important to note that this decree, which in effect annulled the year-long period of coercion designed to persuade the woman to change her mind, was sanctioned by the scholars of both Sura and Pumpedita. Although in his responsum Rav Sherira included the provision of the wife's monetary rights as part of this decree—it is natural that he would wish to date it as early as possible—in his *Iggeret* he attributes to Mar Rav Rabbah and Mar Rav Huna only the decree of immediate divorce.

It was probably not until the ninth-century *Halakhot Gedolot* that the rebellious wife was granted the right to all her dowry properties, and not until Rav Amram Gaon, at the end of the ninth century, that she was awarded her basic alimony sum. By this time, however, the halakhah had made a complete turnabout and provided for the coercion of a husband whose wife found him repulsive, the right to her dowry properties, and the awarding of her basic alimony. Having untangled the history of the post-Amoraic decrees concerning the rebellious wife, we must now attempt to understand the reason for this change.

REASON FOR CHANGE IN THE HALAKHIC STATUS OF MOREDET

We have discussed the development of a more lenient Gaonic legislation, and shown that it was a radical departure from the trend towards stringency which we saw in the Talmudic period. The truth, of course, is that the Geonim were generally dealing with a different type of *moredet* than their predecessors; nonetheless, it was no small matter to rescind the final statement of the Talmud and to grant the woman who found her husband repulsive both the right to an immediate divorce as well as financial compensation. In our attempt to understand the reason for this seeming change in her legal status, we must study closely the words of the Geonim and attempt to understand them in the light of the historical realities of the time.

The first reason attributed to the change in attitude towards the rebellious wife is expressed by Rav Natronai Gaon, who explained that they grant the wife an immediate divorce "so that Jewish women not 'come to a bad end.'"[40] In an anonymous responsum of the thirteenth century, the reason is made even more explicit: "The Sabboraim who came after the Concluding Rabbis of [Talmudic] teaching saw that when they caused a delay of twelve months, Jewish women came to a bad end, meaning prostitution or conversion."[41] Rav Sherira Gaon describes: "And after the Rabbanan Sabborai, who saw that the Jewish women were attaching themselves to the Gentiles to get divorces from their husbands by force, and that there were those [women] who were satisfied with a forced divorce not in accordance with Jewish law, and from which ruin emanates, they decreed. . ."[42] In his *Epistle,* Rav Sherira also makes reference to this decree.[43]

There are also many secondary sources which discuss the Gaonic decrees and attempt to find the reason behind them. Heinrich Graetz, the noted Jewish historian, maintains that "the ruling nation and the ruling religion operated upon the family life of the Jewish people in Babylon," since "the Koran improved the lot of woman in society, granting the wife the right to demand a bill of divorcement from her husband without losing her acquisitions.[44] Jewish women whose husbands refused to grant them a divorce according to Talmudic law seem to have had recourse to the Babylonian courts to force their husbands' hands; the Sages therefore were compelled to "equalize" Jewish law and Moslem law in order to prevent women from "remarrying" while still married in the eyes of Halakhah.

Isaac HaLevi Weiss fundamentally agrees with Graetz that Moslem law was at this time more progressive than Talmudic law (at least concerning women and their status in the courts), but he sees the influence of the former on the latter as aggressive and coercive rather than subtle and indirect. "From this [case of *moredet*] we are able to judge that with all [the Jews'] supposed freedom, the Moslem courts ruled over them and forced them against their will even in matters of religion."[45] Jacob Mann argues similarly, insisting with Weiss that the Moslem courts forced their influence upon the Jewish jurisprudence in Babylon.[46]

Only H. Tykocinski disputes this position, maintaining (I believe correctly) that nowhere in the responsa of the Geonim is there any mention of this kind of legal interference by the Moslem courts. He points out that only Rav Sherira refers to any kind of Gentile influence, but that this was merely through the application of external pressure—bribery—upon the husband; this is by no means to be interpreted as Moslem interference with Jewish law.[47]

What is obvious from the above sources is that none of these historians felt it necessary to prove their assumptions regarding the greater leniency and humanity of Moslem law in the matter of a woman who desired a divorce. Even Tykocinski disagrees with his predecessors only concerning the aggressive nature of Moslem influence; he does not debate the axiom of a greater Moslem liberalism. In fact, the historians quoted above are patently incorrect:

Islamic law was far harsher than Talmudic law in the matter of a woman's right to sue for divorce.

In pre-Islamic times, a wife could be repudiated by her husband with the pronunciation of the words *anti talak* ("you are divorced"). The Koran instituted a waiting period of three *kuru* (periods of purity following the menses, according to most authorities), but after the husband pronounces the two-word formula for the third time, he can never again take back his wife. According to the teachings of the Fikh on *talak,* the husband has the right to pronounce it even without justifiable cause, although such an action is deemed reprehensible (*makruh*). According to the teaching of the Hanafis, such an unreasonable *talak* is forbidden (*haram*). However, nowhere is there any provision for a wife to declare *talak* and thereby repudiate her husband—even if she has an objective reason.[48] In the words of Goitein: "the dominant position of the husband was sealed in Islamic and Jewish law by *his* right of unilateral repudiation."[49] Yet in Talmudic (and, as we have seen, Mishnaic) law, there are instances when a wife could get the Jewish court to force her husband to divorce her.[50] In time, the notion that Jewish women had recourse to a more lenient Islamic court which interfered with or determined the rulings of the Jewish courts has no basis whatsoever in fact.

There was, however, one aspect of Islamic law which did have an influence on Jewish legislation. Islamic law provides for the woman's right to obtain a divorce from her husband when (both being non-Moslem) she adopts the Islamic faith and her husband refuses to be converted along with her.[51] This is what Rav Natronai Gaon means when he speaks of women "coming to a bad end," and this is behind the additional word of the anonymous Gaon, "conversion" (*shmad*). A Jewish wife who was unable to get a Jewish divorce had the option of converting to Islam, after which the Moslem courts would obtain the divorce for her. This is what Rav Sherira meant when he explained that Jewish women might become "dependent upon the Gentiles to get divorces from their husbands by force."

Thus, the Gaonic trend towards leniency in the treatment and status accorded the rebellious wife was a product of the external conditions within which the Jewish people functioned. The Sages of the Talmud mediated between their desire to preserve the institution of marriage and their equally commendable desire to protect the woman from the fate of a loveless relationship. During the Sabboraic period, emphasis was accorded to the former consideration. When, in the Gaonic period, the threat of conversion to Islam was introduced, the Sages shifted the balance to the latter position. This is a perfect example of the internal development of Halakhah, which takes into full account the personal as well as national exigencies of the period.

It is necessary to emphasize once more that this Gaonic development of the law was internally motivated and not externally compelled, and to explain precisely what is meant by the term "internal development." Undoubtedly, Halakhah is influenced by the external environment of the Jews in any particular generation; indeed, the Torah itself, in the section of the Pentateuch which grants legislative power to religious leaders, specifies that a petitioner must come "unto the judge who will live in *that* generation" [emphasis added].[52] But the legal adjudicator, to be certain that he is ruling or interpreting in accordance with the Jewish legal system and not merely assimilating the foreign legal practices of his host country, must find within the corpus of Jewish law a precedent for his decision. This precedent may be a Biblical principle, such as the injunction "thou shalt not bar the doors to borrowers," which is the basis of Hillel's *prusbul* (a method of circumventing the rescinding of all loans during the sabbatical year),[53] or it may be a reliance upon a previously rejected Talmudic opinion, such as the shift towards the position of Amemar which we see in our case of *moredet*. After all, the Mishnah itself teaches that the minority opinion is recorded together with the majority opinion in order to allow a later generation to decide in accordance with the former;[54] and it is precisely because of such situations that the Sages teach, "[both] these and those are the words of the living God."[55] Hence, the Geonim sought and found an Amoraic precedent for not forcing a woman to remain married to a husband she found repulsive. Moreover, the Talmudic decree of the Rabbanan Sabborai provided for a bill of divorce even against the wishes of the husband, according to Gaonic *interpretation*. This opened the way for subsequent Gaonic *legislation* when the Rabbis observed that Jewish women occasionally converted to Islam. The study of the development of the Gaonic decrees regarding the rebellious wife provides an excellent insight into the internal process of halakhic change.

PARALLEL GAONIC DECREE

It is interesting to note that during the period of the Geonim other decrees similar to those regarding the rebellious wife were instituted. For example, despite the fact that the Talmud allows a creditor to claim his debts and a widow to claim her alimony only from the real estate of the deceased, and not from any movable goods he may have left,[56] the Geonim decreed that both creditor and widow have rights to the deceased's movable goods as well. This decree is first mentioned in a responsum of Rav Mosheh ben Yaakov, a religious leader in Sura during the first half of the ninth century, and he provides reasons for its development which are in accord with our own explanation of the internal development of Jewish law.

והשתא בכתובתא אע״ג דלא רגילין למיכתב בכתובה למיגבי ממקרקעי ומטלטלי בחיי ובמותי ובשטר חוב נמי דכתבי׳ מקרקעי ומטלטלי לא כתבי׳ בחיי ובמותי תקינו רבנן למגבי׳ כתובת אשה ובעל חוב אפי׳ ממטלטלי דיתמי משום דהכא רובא דעלמא לית להון מקרקעי ועבדי רבנן בתראי תקנתא שלא תנעול דלת לפני לווין ולמסמך אשה בכתובתה.[57]

And now regarding the alimony, even though it is not usual to write in the marriage contract that "it may be claimed from my real estate and movable goods during my lifetime and after my death," and also regarding a contract of debt we write "from my real estate and my movable goods," [but] we do not write "during my lifetime and after my death," [nevertheless] the Rabbis decreed that the woman's alimony and the creditor's debt may be claimed even from the movable goods [of the inheritors] because here [in Babylonia] the majority of people do not own real estate.

The later Rabbis promulgated this decree in order that the door not be locked before borrowers, and so that women might be able to rely on the alimony provided for in their marriage contracts.

Based upon the economic change in Babylon from an agricultural society to a more industrialized, urban community, and on the principle of ensuring a reliable marriage contract and of encouraging loans,[58] the Geonim decreed that wives and creditors have a claim to the movable goods of the deceased. And they similarly decreed an oath for a debtor who defaults on his payment, and the necessity of a quorum to legalize an act of betrothal. In each instance the Sages took into account the exigencies of the times, and ruled on the basis of halakhic precedent,[59] much as they did on the issue of *moredet*.

CHAPTER V
MOREDET IN THE CAIRO GENIZAH

We have already seen that the Jerusalem Talmud provided for a stipulation in the marriage contract which ensured that a wife could receive a divorce from a husband she hated.[1] The Mishnah cites a number of marital stipulations, about which it is ordained that even if they are not included within the marriage contract they remain operative, since they are considered to be a stipulation of the court.[2] In the Cairo Genizah (which contained 300,000 documents, dating primarily from the tenth to the thirteenth century) were discovered fifty Palestinian *ketubot,* two of which contain stipulations regarding divorce similar to those we saw in the Jerusalem Talmud. These marriage contracts afford us a fascinating glimpse into how Palestinian authorities of the late Gaonic period dealt with the problem of a woman who finds her husband repulsive.[3]

TENTH-CENTURY PALESTINIAN KETUBAH *STIPULATIONS FOR A WOMAN WHO HATES HER HUSBAND*

This is the first of a number of stipulations which appear after a listing of the dowry, which in this case totaled $456\frac{1}{3}$ *dinarim*:

3. . . . . ואשוון ואתקנון ביניהון הדין מר׳ סעיד חתנה

4. והדה מליחה אנתתיה תנאי פרנא כדת משה ויהודאי דאן הדן סעיד חתנה יסני הדה
מליחה ולא יתרעי ביה ויבעי למפרוש

5. מינה יהוי משלם לה כל מה דכתיב ומפרש בהדן שטר פרנה עד גומרה ואין תסני הדה
מליחה להדן סעיד בעלה ותבעי למיפוק

79

6. מן ביתיה תהווי מאבדה ית כסף כתובתה ולא תהוי נסבא אלא מה דעלת מבית
אבהתה בלחוד ונפקא על פם בית דינה ועל דעתיהן
7. דמארינן רבאנן

And this Mr. Sa'id, the groom, and this Maliha, his wife, agreed[4] and fixed between themselves *ketubah* stipulations according to the law of Moses and the Jews:[5] that if this Sa'id, the groom, hates this Maliha and does not desire her, but wants to separate from her, he will pay her all that is written and specified in this marriage contract. And if this Maliha hates this Sa'id, her husband, and desires to go out from his house, she will lose her alimony and will take nothing except that which she brought from her father's house, that alone, and she will be divorced with the permission of the court and on the authority of our lords the Rabbis.[6]

This marriage contract provides the wife with benefits identical to those provided by decrees of the Babylonian Geonim: an immediate divorce and the right to all of her dowry properties, even if she had not seized them. Apparently, the courts would force the husband to grant his wife the divorce she sought: "She will be divorced with the permission of the court and on the authoritiy of our lords the Rabbis."

ELEVENTH-CENTURY PALESTINIAN KETUBAH STIPULATIONS FOR A WOMAN WHO HATES HER HUSBAND

The following stipulation was written into a marriage contract found in the Cairo Genizah, and which was dated the twelfth day of Kislev, the third year of the Sabbatical cycle, 4784, corresponding to Thursday, November 28, 1023 C.E.[7] The groom, Nathan, is a priest from Safed. Marriage is referred to her by the Aramaic term *shutfetah* ("partnership").

31. ואתנון ביניהון על עסק שנתא ורחמתא וחייא ומיתותא אן הדן נת]ן חתנא ישנא[
32. להדה רחל אנתתיה ולא ירצא בשותפתה שנאת מגן יהו' משלם לה כל מה דכ]חיב בהדן[
33. שטר פרנא מן שלם ואן הדה רחל כלתא תשנא להדן נתן בעלה ולא תרצי בש]ותפתיה תהוה[

34. [מאבד]ה מאוחר מהרה ותיסוב מה דאעלת ולא תהוה נפקא אלא על פי בית ד[ינא]

And they stipulated between themselves concerning hate and love
and life and death[8]—if this Nathan [the groom, hates this] Rachel, his
wife, and does not desire her partnership, [and it is] a gratuitous
hatred, he will pay her all that is [written in this] marriage contract.[9]
And if this Rachel, the bride, hates this Nathan, her husband, and
does not desire his p[artnership, she will] [los]e the delayed payment
of her *mohar,*[10] and will take whatever she brought in; and she will not
go out except with the permission of the cou[rt].

This marriage contract is unique in its expression of complete
equality of husband and wife.[11] Even the literary style presumes a
parallel structure between the bride and the groom: love and hate,
life and death. Marriage is defined as a partnership, a term with a
very different sound than the Mishnaic word "acquisition."[12] From a
halakhic perspective, this stipulation is even more lenient towards
the rebellious wife than are the Gaonic decrees. In this Palestinian
document the woman who wishes a divorce forfeits the "delayed
payment" of the *mohar* (marriage document). According to these
Genizah documents there are two parts to the husband's addition to
the wife's basic alimony: the *mukdam* (lit., "that which is earlier"),
which he gives her at the time of the marriage, and the *me'uhar* (lit.,
"that which is later"), which the wife collects only in the event of the
husband's death or his divorcing her.[13] Hence, this stipulation
means that the *moredet* forfeits only the *me'uhar,* the delayed payment, but that she receives her basic alimony as well as the first additions to the alimony, the *mukdam*. According to the later decrees of
the Babylonian Geonim, a *moredet* received her basic alimony, but
forfeited any additions which might have been made to it.

RELATIONSHIP BETWEEN KETUBAH *STIPULATIONS
AND THE GAONIC DECREES*

Rabbenu Menahem Ha-Meiri, a brilliant interpreter of the Talmud
who was teaching in Provence at the turn of the fourteenth century
(d. 1315),[14] suggests that the Gaonic decrees were based upon the

marriage contract stipulation cited in the Jerusalem Talmud, which was operative and normative during the Gaonic period.

ורבותי העידו על רבותיהם שפירשו במה שחדשו הגאונים בדין זה שסמכו על מה
שאמרו בתלמוד המערב בסוגייא זו, הילין דכתבין אי שנאי אי שנאית תנאי ממון הוא
וקיים, כלומר שכל שהם מתנים שאם הוא שונאה יגרש, והן בכתבתה והן בתוספת כתבה,
וכן אם היא שונאתו שיזקק הוא לגרשה אם בכל הכתבה אם בקצת פחיתה, הכל קיים כפי
מה שהתנו והם כתבו על זה שחדשו הגאונים הוא מפני שהיו רגילים לכתוב בכתובותיהם
שאם תשנאהו תטול כתבתה ותצא . . . ומאחר שנתפשט המנהג קבעוהו לעשותו אף
בזמן שלא בכתב כאילו נכתב כשאר תנאי כתבה וכו'[15]

And my Teachers[16] testified concerning their teachers, who explained concerning that which the Geonim innovated in this law [of *moredet*], that [the Geonim] relied [for their decrees] upon what was written in the Jerusalem Talmud on this legal discussion: that they write [a stipulation in the marriage contract], "that if he hates her or if she hates him, it is a monetary stipulation and it takes effect"; that is to say, whatever they stipulate [becomes operative]. If he hates her and divorces her, she receives both the alimony as well as any additions to the alimony; and similarly, if she hates him, he is forced to divorce her, whether with the entire alimony or with somewhat of a reduction [from it]. Everything takes effect in accordance with their stipulation. . . . And [the teachers] wrote concerning this that the Geonim innovated [the decrees] because they were accustomed to write in their marriage contracts that if she should hate him, she would receive her alimony and go out [with a bill of divorce] . . . and after this custom had spread [the Geonim] established that it be enforced in practice, even at a time when the stipulation was not written [into the marriage contract]. [They treated the matter] as if [the stipulation] had been written, as was the case with other stipulations of the marriage contract.[17]

Hence the Meiri feels that he has discovered the source for the Babylonian decrees: namely, the marriage contract stipulation, which became normative practice in the earlier generations.[18] Recently Mordecai Friedman quoted this passage from Meiri, and asserted that he had discovered in the Genizah a proof for the Meiri's words—examples of marriage contracts of the late Gaonic period with just such stipulations.[19] Yet it is difficult to accept fully the view of either Meiri or Friedman. If at that time a coerced, immediate divorce and the various monetary benefits were provided for a woman in a special marriage contract stipulation, then why did the Geonim need to ensure the normative procedure with a decree? And why did the various heads of the Babylonian scholars not mention such a stipulation in their responsa?

I would suggest that there were two different traditions, each of which was deeply concerned about rescuing the woman from an impossible marriage. The first tradition is that of the Land of Israel, which legislated the marriage contract stipulation in the early Amoraic period, and which continued this tradition at least into the eleventh century. It must be remembered that the Jerusalem Talmud never included the case of a woman who claimed "He is repulsive to me" under the law of the rebellious wife, and therefore had no recourse but to deal with the problem by means of a stipulation. The documents in the Cairo Genizah confirm that this was the normative practice in the Land of Israel. The second tradition was that instituted by the Babylonian Geonim, who were apparently unaware of the stipulation provided for in the Jerusalem Talmud and the inclusion of such stipulations in marriage contracts in Palestine, which began with the assumption that a woman who claimed "He is repulsive to me" is considered a *moredet*. They dealt with the problem by means of decrees based upon their interpretations of the Talmud: The husband is *coerced* into giving his wife a divorce after a waiting period of twelve months. They subsequently modified this Talmudic-Sabboraic decree by providing for an immediate (coerced) divorce, and monetary compensation of at least the woman's basic alimony. Hence by the eleventh century a woman who had no "objective reason" for her desire to be divorced save the claim that her husband had become repulsive to her was guaranteed a court-imposed divorce and generous financial benefits in both Babylonia and the Land of Israel.

CHAPTER VI
MOREDET IN THE WORKS OF
THE RISHONIM AND POSKIM

We have seen how the legal status of the rebellious wife who claimed that she found her husband repulsive and the attitude towards her, had undergone a complete change by the end of the eleventh century. Indeed, by this time the law clearly favored the wife over the husband. If a man claimed that his wife was repulsive to him, he could divorce her only if he was prepared to pay her all the money he had provided for her in her marriage contract, a not insignificant amount whose purpose was to discourage divorce and to protect a wife against the whims of an impulsive husband. But if a woman claimed that her husband was repulsive to her, the court could force her husband to grant her a divorce, and she would receive both her dowry and the basic alimony sum. This was certainly no protection for a husband who had married an impulsive wife! The early commentators on the Talmud (following the Geonim from approximately 1000 C.E. and known as the Rishonim, lit., "the first ones") and those who decided Jewish law (called Poskim) continued to be concerned with the problem of the *moredet,* and once more attempted to strike a balance within the corpus of Jewish law between the not-always-complementary issues of the stability of marriage as an institution and a sensivity towards the woman's subjective feelings regarding her mate. An analysis of representative figures in the major schools of Rishonim will provide an overview of the path which they chose. I have specifically chosen those Sages who have had the greatest influence not only on the development of Halakhah in general, but also on the development of the halakhah of *moredet* in particular.

SEPHARDIC SCHOLARS

THE SAGES OF NORTH AFRICA

Immediately following the Gaonic period, the major center of Talmudic studies shifted to North Africa, where great sages flourished at the beginning of the second millennium C.E. Earliest among these commentators was Rabbenu Hananel of Kairwan, who combined in his responsa three divergent schools of learning: the Palestinian, the Babylonian, and the European. On the issue of the rebellious wife he is cited by Mordecai ben Hillel Ashkenazi[1] as follows:

היכא דמיא מורדת? כגון דאמרה בעינא ליה ומצערנה ליה אבל אם אומרת מאיס עלי,
לא כייפינן לה להוציאה בלא כתובה יש מן הגאונים דנים כן וכן פירש רבינו חננאל.[2]

What is the case of a rebellious wife? If she says "I wish [to remain married to] him, but I [wish to] cause him pain," [that is a *moredet*]. But if she says that he is repulsive to her, she is not to be forced to leave [him] without her alimony. There are those among the Geonim who judged in this way, and so interpreted Rabbenu Hananel.

It is therefore apparent that Rabbenu Hananel upheld the practice of the Geonim and coerced the husband to divorce his wife *and* pay her both her basic alimony and her dowry.

By far the most important figure of the North African school is Rabbi Yitzhak of Fez, Yitzhak Alfasi (1013–1103). In Alfasi's abridged version of the Talmud as noted in Chapter IV, only material which represents the definitive halakhic ruling is quoted. His compilation is simultaneously commentary and legal decision, and has had an enormous influence on the subsequent development of Jewish law.

We have already seen how Alfasi cited the Gaonic position of

forcing an immediate divorce and granting the wife both her dowry
and her basic alimony as being normative halakhic practice. Despite
the fact that he concludes his commentary by comparing those husbands who are forced to divorce their wives by Talmudic law with
those who are forced by rabbinic decree, it may be persuasively
argued that he is referring to the decree of the Rabbanan Sabborai
and not to that of the Geonim. Since the words of the Rabbanan
Sabborai are considered an integral part of the Talmud itself, the
view of Alfasi seems to be that *Talmudic* law provides for a coerced
divorce in the event that a woman finds her husband distasteful,
even for subjective reasons. The importance of this position cannot
be overestimated. If it was the Geonim who initially provided for a
coerced divorce, then if the Gaonic decrees are ever rejected, their
provision for a coerced divorce must be rejected as well. If, however,
it was the Rabbanan Sabborai—i.e., the Talmud itself—who provided for a coerced divorce, then even if we were to reject the Gaonic
decrees granting the wife monetary compensation, we would
nevertheless be forced to uphold the provision for a coerced
divorce. Such is the position of Alfasi.

One of Alfasi's outstanding students, Rav Yosef Ibn Migash
(1077–1141), seemingly agrees with his teacher, and notes:

והיכא דאימרדה מעיקר האישות שהוא התשמיש, אי אמרה מאיס עלי לא משהינן
לה . . .[3]

> And whenever she rebels from the essential aspect of marriage, which
> is sexual relations—if she says "He is repulsive to me," we do not
> have her remain [with him].

Apparently Rav Yosef upholds the immediate, and most probably
coerced, divorce for the woman who finds her husband repulsive.

An exception to this ruling is to be found in the writings of a
brilliant and creative sage, Rabbenu Zerahyah HaLevi. Born in
Spain but having studied in Provence (Lunel), he was the author of
the *Sefer Ha-Maor,* which was written between 1171 and 1186 and
published as strictures on Alfasi.[4] In it, he maintains that the Gaonic

decrees were promulgated because of specific historical exigencies, but that the operative halakhah of his time must be in accordance with the Talmud. Moreover, he insists that a coerced divorce was one of the Gaonic decrees, and is not provided for by the Rabbanan Sabborai.

והיכא דאמרה לא בעינא ליה היינו מאיס עלי ולא כייפי' לה ומפסדא לכתובתה כולה לאלתר, ונפקא ומדעתו של בעל. ומסתברא לי שההתקנה שתקנו בישיבה לתת גט במורדת זו לאלתר הוראת שעה היתה לפי הצורך ממה שראו בדורם, אבל בדורות הבאים בדינא דגמרא דייניגין לה.⁵

And whenever she says, "I do not want him—that is, he is repulsive to me," we do not force her, and she loses her entire alimony immediately, and goes out [with a divorce, but only] *in accordance with the will of the husband* [emphasis added].

And it seems reasonable to me that the decree which was promulgated in the academy to give an immediate divorce to this rebellious wife was an emergency decision [*hora'at sha'ah*] in accordance with the need which [the Geonim] saw in their generation.

But in the succeeding generations we make judgment based on Talmudic law.

It is clear that Rabbenu Zerahyah HaLevi believed that the coerced divorce was a Gaonic decree, and that the decrees of the Geonim were no longer operative. He was aware of the fact that they had originally been established out of fear of apostasy and prostitution, and felt that these fears were no longer legitimate concerns. With one stroke of the pen, Rabbenu Zerahyah HaLevi eliminates the provision for a coerced divorce, and reverts to the position which insists that a woman must remain even in a loveless marriage unless she can provide objective reasons for wanting to be free of it.⁶

MAIMONIDES

The Spanish tradition reached its apex with R. Mosheh ben Maimon, popularly known as the Rambam (1135–1204), whose father was a pupil of R. Yosef Ibn Migash, disciple of Alfasi. Maimonides called his halakhic compendium—organized topically instead of in the order of the Talmudic tractates, as was Alfasi's—the *Mishneh Torah,* lit., the "Repetition of the Torah." Like R. Zerahyah HaLevi, he maintained that Gaonic decrees were no longer in effect, but he insisted that the provision for a coerced divorce for a woman who felt she could no longer live with her husband was of Talmudic origin. His interpretation remains an important legacy for subsequent legal authorities, even until today.

ח. האשה שמנעה בעלה מתשמיש המטה היא הנקראת מורדת ושואלין אותה מפני מה מרדה אם אמרה מאסתיהו ואיני יכולה להבעל בו מדעתי כופין אותו להוציא לשעתו, לפי שאינה כשבויה שתבעל לשנוא לה ותצא בלא כתובה כלל ותטול בלאותיה הקיימין בין מנכסים שהכניסה לבעלה ונתחייב באחריותן בין שנכסי מלוג שלא נתחייב באחריותן ואינה נוטלת משל בעל כלום ואפילו מנעל שברגליה ומטפחת שבראשה שלקחן לה, פושטת ונותנת וכל מה שנתן לה מתנה מחזרת אותו, שלא נתן לה על מנת שתטול ותצא.

ט. ואם מרדה מתחת בעלה כדי לצערו ואמרה הריני מצערת אותו בכך מפני שעשה לי כך וכך או מפני שקללני או מפני שעשה עמי מריבה וכיוצא בדברים אלו. שולחים לה מבית דין ואומרין לה: הוי יודעת שאם את עומדת במרדך אפילו כתובתך מאה מנה, הפסדת אותה. ואחר כך מכריזין עליה בבתי כנסיות ובבתי מדרשות בכל יום ארבע שבתות זו אחר זו ואומרים פלונית מרדה על בעלה.

י. ואחר ההכרזה שולחין לה בית דין פעם שנייה ואומרים לה: אם את עומדת במרדך, הפסדת כתובתיך. אם עמדה במרדה ולא חזרה, נמלכין בה ותאבד כתובתה ולא יהיה לה כתובה כלל. ואין נותנין לה גט עד שנים עשר חדש ואין לה מזוונות כל שנים עשר חדש ואם מתה קודם הגט, בעלה יורשה.

יא. כסדר הזה עושין לה אם מרדה כדי לצערו ואפילו היתה נדה או חולה שאינו ראויה לתשמיש ואפילו היה בעלה מלח שעונתו לששה חדשים ואפילו יש לו אשה אחרת.

יב. וכן ארוסה שהגיע זמנה להנשא ומרדה כדי לצערו ולא נשאת הרי זו מורדת מתשמיש וכן יבמה שלא רצתה להתיבם כדי לצערו כסדר הזה עושין להן.

יג. המורדת הזאת כשהיא יוצאת אחר שנים עשר חדש בלא כתובה תחזיר כל דבר שהוא של בעל אבל נכסים שהכניסה לו ובלאותיה הקיימים אם תפסה, אין מוציאים מידה ואם תפשן הבעל, אין מוציאן מידו וכן כל מה שאבד מנכסיה שקבל הבעל אחריותן עליו אינו משלם לה כלום זה הוא דין מגמרא במורדת.

יד. ואמרו הגאונים שיש להם בבבל מנהגות אחרות במורדת ולא פשטו אותן המנהגות ברוב ישראל ורבים וגדולים חולקים עליהם ברוב המקומות וכדין הגמרא ראוי לתפוס ולדון.[7]

8. A woman who refuses to engage in sexual relations with her husband is called a rebellious wife. And they [the court] ask her why she

is rebelling. If she says, "I find him repulsive and I cannot willingly engage in sexual relations with him," they force him to divorce her immediately, because she is not like a captive woman who must have sexual relations with one whom she hates. And she goes out [with a divorce] but without any alimony at all. She does receive the existing dowry garments, whether they be from the property which she brought into the marriage for which her husband was responsible, or whether they be from the property which she brought into the marriage [nikhsei melug] for which he was not responsible. She does not take anything of her husband's. She must even remove the shoe from her foot or the kerchief from her head which he had given to her. And everything which he had given her as a gift she must return to him, for he did not give [them] to her so that she would take [them] and leave [him].

9. And if she rebelled against her husband in order to cause him pain, and she says: "Behold, I am causing him this [pain] because he did to me such-and-such or because he cursed me or because he argued with me, or similar things," then [the court] sends her [the following message] and says to her: "Know that if you stand by your rebellion, even if the alimony provided by our marriage contract is one hundred maneh, [ten thousand zuz], you have lost it." And afterwards they announce concerning her in the synagogues and study houses every day, for four consecutive weeks, and they say: "So-and-so has rebelled against her husband."

10. And after the proclamation, the court sends to her a second message, and says to her: "If you stand by your rebellion, you have lost the alimony provided by your marriage contract." If she stood by her rebellion and did not change her mind, they attempt to persuade her. [Eventually] she will lose the alimony provided by her marriage contract, and she will receive no alimony at all. And they do not give her a bill of divorce for twelve months, and she receives no sustenance all of the twelve months. If she dies before [receiving] the divorce, her husband inherits her [property].

11. In this matter they deal with her if she rebels in order to cause him pain. And even if she was menstrually impure, or ill, so that she was unfit for sexual relations, or even if her husband was a sailor,

whose obligation [to his wife is to have sexual relations] once every six months, and even if he has another wife [who could then supply him with sexual gratification, nevertheless, in all of the above cases she is considered a *moredet*].

12. And similarly, a betrothed woman whose time has come to be married, and she rebels in order to cause [her fiancé] pain and refuses to get married—behold, she is a *moredet* from sexual relations; and similarly, a *yevamah,* who did not wish to enter into a levirate marriage in order to pain [her brother-in-law], all these are dealt with in accordance with [the laws of *moredet*].

13. This *moredet,* when she goes out [with a divorce] after twelve months without any alimony, must return everything which is her husband's. But as for the property and existing garments which she had brought into [the marriage], whatever she seized, they [the court] do not remove from her possession. And whatever her husband seized they do not remove from his possession. And similarly, regarding the property for which her husband took responsibility but which is no longer in existence, he need not make any restitution to her. This is the law of the Talmud regarding *moredet.*

14. And the Geonim said that in Babylonia they have other customs concerning the *moredet,* but these customs did not spread to the majority of the Jewish people, and many and great people disagree with them in the majority of places. And is proper to hold by and to judge in accordance with Talmudic law [and not Gaonic decrees].

Maimonides, the great codifier and interpreter, thus rejects the Gaonic decrees because "they did not spread to a majority of Israel"—and this despite the testimony from R. Shmuel ben Ali that the Gaonic decrees were normative practice throughout Babylonia during this period.[8] What is most important about his interpretation, however, is that despite this opinion, Maimonides nevertheless insists that a woman who claims her husband is repulsive to her is entitled to an immediate and, if necessary, coerced divorce "because she is not like a captive woman who must have sexual relations with one whom she hates." His ruling is in no way bound up with any historical reasons of adultery, apostasy, or dependence upon Gentiles, but is rather a humane consideration of the sensitivities of an unhappy wife. Maimonides decides the halakhah in accordance with the statement of Amemar in the Talmud: "[a woman who finds her husband repulsive] is not to be forced [to remain married,]"[9] and interprets this to mean that the husband must be forced to grant a divorce.

Hence the incident of Rav Zevid and the subsequent Talmudic-Sabboraic mandate of a twelve-month delay in the divorce refers only to a wife who claims, "I wish [to remain married to] him, but [I wish] to cause him pain."[10] She is the woman who is truly a rebellious wife, and it is she who must be coerced by means of a public proclamation and an ultimate forfeiting of her alimony.[11] But according to Maimonides, the woman who claims "He is repulsive to me" is simply stating a fact beyond her control, has no desire to gain anything from her husband, and must therefore be given her freedom, even if it means coercing her husband to do so. This, according to him, is Talmudic law.

Thus, Maimonides, in deciding the law in accordance with Amemar (and interpreting it to refer to coerced divorce) and in canceling the Gaonic decrees, has actually equalized the position of husband and wife. If the husband finds his wife repulsive he may divorce her even against her will, but must pay her the alimony provided for by the marriage contract. If she finds him repulsive, she may obtain a divorce even against his will, but receives no alimony at all. This, according to Maimonides, is the true Talmudic law, and is to be operative in every country in every situation.[12]

ASHKENAZIC SCHOLARS

THE PRECURSORS OF RABBENU TAM

Interestingly enough, it was the Franco-German communities which were the first to promulgate decrees that seemingly were concerned with a special sensitivity to the position of the woman, especially in regard to her marital situation. Indeed, the greatest advance for the woman's position in marriage and divorce was brought about by Rabbenu Gershom of Mayence (960–1028), called the "Light of the Exile," who decreed in the early part of the eleventh century that no man may marry more than one wife, and that no woman may be divorced against her will.[13] This latter development went a long way towards creating an equality in divorce between husband and wife. Nevertheless, the price paid for this equality was high, since the need for mutual agreement severely limited the possibility of any divorce at all. Too, the husband was still the only one who could initiate divorce, while the wife had only the power of veto. (How very different were the equality of the Jerusalem Talmud's *ketubah* stipulation, the accommodation of the Babylonian Geonim, and the affirmation of Amemar's position by the Spaniard Maimonides!)

Rabbenu Eliezer ben Natan, known as the Raban, or Ravan (born 1090 in Mayence), an older contemporary of Rabbenu Tam, makes reference to the decree of Rabbenu Gershom prohibiting a man from taking more than one wife. He also discusses the problem of the rebellious wife, and ultimately accepted the position ensuring an immediate divorce for a woman who claimed her husband was repulsive to her.

ואי אמרה מאוס עלי, לא כייפינן לה לשהות עמו אלא אלא יוציא מיד ונ"ל בלא כתובה ואין בין אומרת בעינה ליה וכו' לאומרת מאיס עלאי אלא דהתם דחיינן ד' שבתות אולי תחזור בה כיון דאמרה בעינא ליה אבל הכא אבל וזו וזו בלא כתובה ומשהינן לה למורדת האומרת בעינא ליה (וכו') שנה אחת בלא גט, לקונסה שתתעגן, וה"מ בדורות הראשונים שהיה אדם נושא אשה על אשתו ולא הוה הוא מיתעגן אבל בדורותינו שאין אדם נושא אשה על אשה והיה לו להתעגן עמה לא משהינן לה ואם בשביל אחרות שיתווסרו קנסינן לזו יתיר לבעל לישא אחרת והיא תשב ותתעגן.[14]

... And if she says "He is repulsive to me," we do not force her to remain with him, but he [must] divorce her immediately, and, it seems to me, without the value of her alimony. And there is no difference between the case of the woman who says "I want [to remain married to] him" and the case of the woman who says "He is repulsive to me," except that in the former case we delay four weeks [and proclaim against her] in the hope that she will return to him, since she said "I want him;" but here [in the latter case] he [must] divorce her immediately. In both cases [she is divorced] without alimony. We also cause the *moredet* who says "I want him" to wait one year without the divorce, to penalize her by being "chained" [until she receives a divorce]. However, this was in effect only in earlier times, when a man could take another wife in addition to his own wife, so that he would not be "chained" [i.e., unable to marry].

But in our generations, when a man cannot take a wife in addition to his own wife, and he would be "chained" along with her, we do not make her wait [to receive a divorce]. And if we [wish to] penalize her, because by this [penalty] others will learn a lesson, her husband is permitted to marry another wife, but she must sit and be "chained."

The Ravan insists, therefore, that in all cases of the rebellious wife the wife is to be divorced immediately, apparently even against her husband's will. Yet his assumption is that generally, the husband will *want* to divorce her, because it is not to his advantage to remain with a woman who refuses him sexual relations. In either case, however, the woman forfeits all her alimony.

We see too that the Rashbam (Rabbenu Shmuel ben Meir, the older brother of Rabbenu Tam) is quoted in his citation of the *Geonim* to the effect that the woman who claims her husband is repulsive to her is not delayed twelve months before she receives a divorce, but that her husband is coerced to grant her one immediately. The atmosphere among the early Franco-German leaders seems to have been one which was sensitive to the needs of the woman, and which therefore upheld the Gaonic decree (although there were still those who maintained that the divorce was Talmudically based).

RABBENU TAM

Rabbenu Ya'akov Tam of Ramerupt (1100–1171) was a grandson of Rashi, and a preeminent contributor to the *Tosafot* (lit., "additions"), notes on the Talmud, and a supercommentary on Rashi. A giant in Talmudic analysis, he had a profound effect upon the methodology of Talmudic interpretation and, correspondingly, upon the direction of all future Jewish law. His position towards the rebellious wife was clearly opposed to the Gaonic decrees and to the tradition of Alfasi, as mentioned above, and he argued it persuasively in his *Tosafot* commentary on the Talmud, as well as in his responsa. Since he spoke so vehemently against the practice of coercing a husband to divorce his wife—even if she claimed she found him repulsive— subsequent legal authorities were reluctant to oppose him on so sensitive and far-reaching an issue. For if, indeed, such a coerced divorce was not halakhically bona fide, any later relationship the woman might enter into would be adulterous, and any offspring from that union would be *mamzerim* (illegitimate, and thus prohibited from marriage with native born Jews). In effect, Rabbenu Tam single-handedly changed the course of the halakhic attitude towards *moredet*. To understand any subsequent legal developments we must first analyze his views.[15]

... ומיהו מסקנא דשמעתין דמשהינן לה תריסר ירחי שתא אגיטא ולית לה מזוני **אמורדת דהכא קאי ולא אמורדת מאיס עלי**, כמו שמפרש ר״ת דהא כיון ששניהם חפצים בגירושין כמו שנפרש למה נשהה אותה מלהתגרש אלא אמורדת דהכא קאי. ומצא רבינו יהודה בכתב רב שרירא שתקנו בימיו לתת גט לאשה לאלתר דלא כשמעתין דכלתיה דרב זביד וכתב נמי רבינו יהודה דרבנן סבוראי תקנן למישקל מינה מאי דתפיסא ומייתי לה גיטא לאלתר ...[16]

... וי״מ דכופין אותו להוציא ואין נראה לר״ת, דניחוש שמא עיניה נתנה באחר כי ההיא דתנן בפרק בתרא דנדרים (דף צ:) גבי שלש נשים יוצאות ונוטלות כתובה ויש לדחות דהתם נוטלות כתובה דוקא איכא למיחש שמא עיניה נתנה באחר, אבל הכא דיוצאה בלא כתובה, לא ...

ועוד הקשה ר״ת דבריש הניזקין (גטין מט:) אמר וכ״ת כי נפקא איהי, נתקנו ליה כתובה מינה ת״ש האיש אינו מוציא אלא לרצונו ואמאי, אי כופין במאיס עלי להוציא א״כ נתקנו ליה כתובה מינה ומיהו יש לדחות דלא מציא למימר מאיס עלי אלא היכא דיש רגלים לדבר שהבעל אינו מתקבל לה ובשביל אותן נשים ...

ועוד מקשה ר״ת דבכל השמועה אינו מזכיר כפיית הבעל אלא כפיית האשה ונראה לר״ת דהכי פירושה: בעינא ליה ולא בעינא ליה ואינה רוצה להתגרש בלא כתובה ומצערנא ליה עד שיגרשנה ויתן לה כתובה אבל אמרה מאיס עלי ולא בעינא ליה לא הוא ולא כתובתו לא כייפינן לה שתחזור בה על ידי שנאמר שלא תועיל מחילה משום דהוי מחילה בטעות אגב צערה קא

אמרה הכי ומתוך כך לא יגרשנה בעלה שאינו רוצה ליתן כתובה — אלא מחילה גמורה
היא ומתוך כך יעלה בדעתו לגרשה.
מר זוטרא אמר כייפנן לה, דהויא כמחילה בטעות, והיינו כפיה דעל ידי כך תשאר תחת
בעלה שלא ברצונה כי בעלה לא יגרשנה כיון שחייב ליתן כתובתה ואין חילוק למר
זוטרא בין מורדת דבעינא ליה ומצערנא ליה בין אומרת מאיס עלי
ור״ח נמי פירש דאין כופין הבעל ליתן גט וגם בקונטרס לא פירש שיכופו הבעל ליתן
גט.[17]

However, the conclusion of the legal discussion [in the Talmud] is
that they make her wait twelve months for her bill of divorce and
[she] does not receive sustenance [during this period]. This refers to
the rebellious wife we are discussing here [who wishes to live with her
husband, but wants to cause him pain] and not to the rebellious wife
[who says] "He is repulsive to me," as Rabbenu Tam explains.

Since [in the latter case] both [the husband and the wife] wish a
divorce, as we will explain, why delay her [the second type of *moredet*'s] divorce?

Thus, it refers to the rebellious wife we are discussing here. And
Rabbenu Yehudah[18] found in the writing[s] of Rav Sherira that they
decreed in his days to grant the woman an immediate divorce, which
is not in accordance with the legal discussion concerning the
daughter-in-law of Rav Zevid.

And Rabbenu Yehudah wrote also that the Rabbanan Sabborai
established that we take from her whatever she seized and we give her
the bill of divorce immediately. . . . [But if she says "He is repulsive to
me" we do not force her. . . .] And there are those who explain that
they force him to divorce her, [but] this does not appear [reasonable]
to Rabbenu Tam, because we fear lest she has cast her eyes on
someone else, like the case we learned [in the mishnah] in the last
chapter of Nedarim [90b] concerning three women who are granted
divorces and receive their alimonies [where the mishnah expressly
states that the law changed and they must bring proof of their words,
for we fear lest they had cast their eyes on someone else]. But this
[parallel case as proof that he is not forced to divorce her] can be
pushed aside, because [in Nedarim] it is precisely *because* they take
their alimony that we fear lest they cast their eyes on someone else,
but here, where she leaves without her alimony, [we] do not [fear
this]. . . .

And Rabbenu Tam raised a further problem. In the beginning of Chapter Nezakin [bGit 49b] it is said, "And if you will say that when she leaves him [on her own initiative], we ought to establish an alimony obligation from her [to him], come and hear [the rebuttal]: A man does not divorce his wife unless he wishes to. [But this is not an adequate rebuttal. After all,] if the Sages were to force him to grant her a divorce if she claims "He is repulsive to me," then let them establish an alimony obligation from her to him. [Could we then have an instance of her divorcing him on her own initiative?]

However, this [question] can be pushed aside, for she cannot claim he is repulsive to her unless there is some objective reason that the husband is not acceptable to her. [Our Sages] did not wish to establish an alimony obligation for such a [minority of cases], since it would not be applicable to most women.

And Rabbenu Tam raised another problem, that in the entire [Talmudic] discussion there is no mention of forcing the husband, only of forcing the wife, and it appears to Rabbenu Tam that such is the [correct] interpretation: [When the woman claims] "I want him," she means she does not wish to be divorced without alimony. [She continues to say] "and I am causing him pain;" [this means,] she is causing him pain [so that] he will divorce her and give her the alimony. But when she claims "He is repulsive to me," [she means] she does not wish him or his alimony, [then] we do not force her to return to his domicile. [And the law must specifically tell us that her divorce is valid] since we might think that her forfeiture [of the alimony] is not effective, because it is a mistaken forfeiture. After all, it was as a result of her pain that she said this. Therefore the husband should not divorce her, because he does not wish to give her alimony. Rather [we do not say this and] it is a complete forfeiture, and therefore it will occur to him to divorce her [since he need not pay the alimony].

Mar Zutra says that we force her [to remain married] because it is like a mistaken forfeiture, and this is the coercion by which she remains under her husband's authority against her will, since her husband will not divorce her as long as he is obligated to pay her alimony.

There is no distinction, according to Mar Zutra, between the

rebellious wife [who says] "I want him and I am causing him pain"
and [the one] who says "He is repulsive to me."

Rabbenu Hananel also interpreted [this to mean] that they do not
force the husband to grant a divorce; and also Rashi did not explain
that they force the husband to grant a divorce.

. . . ומה שכתב רבי' שמואל (רשב"ם) שתקנו הגאונים דלא משהינן תריסר ירחי שתא
אגיטא אלא כופין אותו, חלילה לרבינו להרבות ממזרים בישראל דקי"ל רבינא ורב אשי
סוף הוראה, ונהי דהגאונים יכולים לתקן כתובת אשה על המטלטלין או על פי הלכה או
על פי דעתם דהיינו ממונא, אבל להתיר גט פסול אין כח בידינו מימות רב אשי ועד ימות
המשיח. וזה גט פסול, שאנו שנינו בתלמוד שאין כופין עד תריסר ירחי שתא והם
הקדימו טרם כפיית דין (פשיטא שהגט) פסול, אפילו יאמר רוצה אני, דהא אמר רב
נחמן בשילהי גיטין (גטין פח:) גט המעושה בישראל, כדין כשר, שלא כדין פסול ופוסל.
וזה בתוך י"ב חודש שלא כדין, אפילו לפי פירוש רבינו שלמה במורדת. ומה שכתב
רבינו שמואל שכתב בהלכות גדולות הרב ר' יצחק אלפסי "ומשהינן לה תריסר ירחי
שתא אגיטא ובהדין תריסר ירחי שתא לית לה מזוני מבעל הדין הוא דינא דגמרא" — נ"ל זה
פתרונו: הדין הוא דינא דגמרא דמורדת דעל ידי פחיתה וכרוז. ומה שכתב ר' יצחק אבל
האידנא בבי דינא דמתיבתא הכי דייני במורדת בדאתאי ואמרה לא בעינא להאי גברא
ליתב לי גיטא, יהיב לה גיטא לאלתר. וגם זה פתרונו במורדת בלא פחיתה, אבל מוחלה
ורוצה מגרש לה בלא כתובה, ולא חש לפרש רצון הבעל דפשיטא ליה. והמפרש בענין
אחר משהינן ליה טועה גמור ומרבה ממזרות. שכן אני מורה ובא

גופא דשמעתתא המורדת על בעלה פוחתין לה מכתובתה וכו' ורבותינו נמנו וגמרו
שמכריזין עליה ד' שבתות ופעמים שולחין לה מבית דין ומפסידין כל כתובתה כאחת.
ופלוגתא דנמלכין בה אחר כל זה, דאיכא דאית ליה אין נמלכין.

ובתר הכי מפרש אמימר היכי דמי מורדת דאמרה בעינא ליה ומצערנא ליה, בעינא
ליה אם לא ירצה לגרשני וליתן כתובתי בעינא ליה כדי לצערו, ולעגנו עד כלות כתובה
ע"י פחיתה (שפירשנו ותוספת) בז' דינרין בשבת לפי משנתינו, ולפי רבותינו כדאית
להו, וזימנין דהוי כלין לפי משנתנו בעשר שנים או יותר, וכל מה דאגידא ביה לא יהבין
ליה אחריתא והיא מתכוונת לצערו ולעגנו, אולי יגרשנה ויתן כתובה. והיינו פי' דמורדת
דמתניתין, ואפי' הוא רוצה לגרש ליתן לה כתובה עד שתפחות אבל אמרה מאיס
עלי לא בעינא ליה, לא הוא ולא כתובתי, כן פי' רבינו זקני זצ"ל, והכל אני מוחלת, לא
כפינן ליה כדין מורדת להשהותה כדין משנתנו עד שתפחות או לרבותינו עד ד'
שבתות וכרוז והמלכה וי"ב ירחי שתא דלקמן, דהא לא הוה מורדת גמורה כיון שרוצה
לצאת בלא כלום אם הבעל רוצה לגרש.

מר זוטרא אמר כפינן לה, כלומר גם זו הוה מורדת גמורה, שא"כ לא הנחת בת
לאברהם אבינו יושבת חתת בעלה, דמצער לה עד דאמרה הכי כלומר מאוס עלי כדי
לפטור מכתובתה. ולית הילכתא כמר זוטרא, דלא הוה מורדת, והכי סלקא שמעתא.

ובתר הכי מסיק דין מורדת דכלתיה דרב זביד אימרד ולא במאיס עלי אלא בשאמרה
בעינא ליה וכו' והכי [פירושא] אימרדא ואמרה בעינא ומצערנא ליה ומפרש דין בלאות,
ובתר הך מימרא מפרש דמשהינן למורדות תריסר ירחי שתא אגיטא לאחר כרוז ד'
שבתות והמלכה למאן דבע' המלכה, אבל למאוס עלי ליכא שהייה כיון שמוחלת וכגון
שהבעל רוצה לגרש.

ועל זה ידון כל הדווים, איך יטעה חכם לומר שכופין הבעל לגרש באמירת מאיס עלי,
הלא בשמים ביני לבינך ובנטולה אני מן היהודים חזרו לומר שמא עיניה נתנה באחר,
ועוד אמרינן שלא יהא כל אחת ואחת הולכה ותולה עצמה ביד גוי ומפקעת עצמה מיד
בעלה בחנם (גטין פח:) תתלה בעכו"ם אם מורדת [ועוד] דא"כ מצינו חוטא נשכר. ובלא
שום פירכא בעולם כפייה לבעל לא אשכחן בכולה שמעתא.

וראיה גדולה שפי' ר"ח בהדיא, ואם אמר הבעל אתן לה גט משהינן ליה וכו' וכל
מביני שמועה יבינו מתוך הלכה, ישמעו ויאמרו אמת, ואפי' מה שכתב בה"ג דייהבינן
גיטא לאלתר הכל צריך לפרש לדעת הבעל, וכך אני מורה ובא, ומעשה היה מהחתן ר'
יחיאל לפניך ודבתי לפניך.

ואם שנינו מנהג עוקר הלכה, חלילה גבי איסורא וחנק ומזרות,

ואשר כתבו רבותינו שבפריש: והננו מסכימים על ידיכם לכל אשר תעשון להכריח
את האיש בכל צידי הכרחות שתוכלו להכריחו ולכופו עד שיאמר רוצה אני, גם זה לא
ישר בעיני, ואולי משגגה הוא בידי שהרי זה לא מצינו שכופין אותו להוציא כדפסק לעיל
ר"ח, וכיון שאומר כן בשילהי גטין גט המעושה **בישראל כדין כשר, שלא כדין פסול
ופוסל,** ולא ידענא רווחא דמלתא אי פסולא דאורייתא כגון ע"י גויים אפי' אמר רוצה
אני לא מהני כלל, אי מדרבנן. ואם אומר האומר לא נכפין בשוטי אבל בגזרות וחרמות
נכפינן, זאת לא זאת דאמרינן בדרבנן לא מזקקינן ליה אבל משמתינן ליה ופריך האי
נקטי בכובסיה דלישבקי לגלימיה הוא, ותו אמרינן במערבא מימנו אנגדא דבר בי רב ולא
מימני אשמתא, ורב יוסף אמר דטבא ליה עבדו ליה ותברא חברי בתי רמי, שמתא שם
מיתה ושממה (מ"ק דף יז:). הרי לך דחמיר מנגדא ואין כפייה גדולה מזו, וכן גבי כלבא
דאכל וכו' שמתיה וכו' איתלי נורא בגנובתיה וכו' טוב ללקות מלהתנדות.

ועל ידי היה היה מעשה על אחד שקדש בת [Chappes—not far from Troyes]
ר' שמואל מקפש גזרו על המקדש לגרש ועשיתי שהתירו לו וחשחירווהו בממון ובדברים
עד שגירש. והמעשים ידועים וכתובים למען לא יאמרו עלי חולק על רבותיו שהרי כך
אני מורה ובא, שלום שלום

And that which Rabbenu Shmuel [Rashbam] wrote—that the Geonim decreed that we do not delay twelve months for a divorce but
rather, they force him—far be it from our teacher to increase the
number of *mamzerim* in Israel. We hold the halakhic principle that
Ravina and Rav Ashi are the last authoritative halakhic decisors, and
even were the Geonim able to decree that a woman could collect her
alimony from movable property, whether it be on the basis of Tal-

mudic law or their own reasoned judgment, that is only as far as monetary value is concerned. But as for permitting an invalid bill of divorce, we have not had the power to do so from the days of Rav Ashi [nor will we] until the days of the Messiah. And this is an invalid bill of divorce. After all, we learned in the Talmud that [the Sages] did not force [a divorce] until twelve months, and they [the Geonim] advanced the forcing of the divorce before [the time which] the law [allows].

It is obvious that the divorce is invalid, even if he says "I wish it" [after having been forced], for Rav Nahman states at the end of Tractate Gittin [86b], "A divorce which is forced by a Jewish [court] in accordance with the law is valid, but a divorce which is not in accordance with Jewish law is invalid, [and she may] not marry anyone else. If she does so, her children from that union are illegitimate. But nonetheless, this invalidates [her from marrying a *kohen*, even if her husband should die]. And this [divorce] within the twelve-month period is not in accordance with Jewish law, and [this is the situation] even according to the interpretation of Rabbenu Shlomo [Rashi] concerning the rebellious wife. And that which Rabbenu Shmuel wrote, quoting HaRav Yitzhak Alfasi, who wrote in [his] great code that we cause her to wait twelve months for a divorce, and during these twelve months she receives no food from her husband, and that this is the Talmudic law—it appears to me that this is the interpretation. This is the Talmudic law concerning the rebellious wife, [that it should be] through a reduction [of the alimony provided for in the marriage contract] and a public proclamation. And that which Rav Yitzhak wrote: "But now in the court of the *Metivta* [Academy] in such a manner do they adjudicate concerning a rebellious wife who comes and says: 'I do not wish [to be married to] this man, let him give me a bill of divorce' and she is given a divorce immediately." This is the interpretation concerning a rebellious wife without a reduction of the alimony, who [voluntarily] forfeits [her alimony] and merely wishes a divorce. [Alfasi] did not [think it necessary] to explain that the husband's consent [is necessary for a divorce], for this is obvious to him. Anyone who interprets [it] in another way is considered to be in complete error and increases [the number] of illegitimate children; and so do I always rule.

[To revert to the original] teaching: [As to] one a rebellious wife, the alimony provided for in her marriage contract is to be reduced, etc. Our Rabbis voted and decided that they proclaim against her for four weeks, and occasionally the court deprives her of all her alimony all at once. And the [question of whether we make an additional effort to] persuade her after all this is a matter of dispute.

After this, Amemar explains [the essential elements] of the [case of] a *moredet*—that she says: "I want him, but I wish to cause him pain," [meaning] "I want him if he does not wish to divorce me and give me my alimony, I want him—in order to cause him pain and keep him tied [to me] until my alimony gives out by means of [its weekly] reduction"—[that is,] by seven *dinarim* per week, according to our mishnah [mKet 5:7], and according to our Rabbis, each according to his view. At times, the alimony will not give out for ten years or more, according to our mishnah; whatever is tied to [the requirements of her alimony] cannot be given to another, and she intends to cause him pain and tie him to her, perhaps he will divorce her and give her her alimony. This is the explanation of the [law of] a *moredet* of our mishnah, even if he wishes to divorce [her] he must give her her alimony [as much as remains after] reduction.

But if she says: "He is repulsive to me, I do not want him, not him and not my alimony"—so explained our Master, my grandfather [i.e., Rashi], may the remembrance of the righteous be a blessing— "I forfeit all," we do not force him to delay her [divorce] according to the law of our mishnah until [the alimony is totally] reduced, or according to our Rabbis, for four weeks, proclamation and persuasion, and twelve months [as explained] further on, since she is not an absolute *moredet*, since she is willing to be divorced without any [financial benefit], as long as the husband is willing to divorce [her].

Mar Zutra says [that] we force her, that is to say, this case too is one of a complete *moredet*, for if [it is not] so, you will not have left our father Abraham a daughter living with her husband, for he can [then] cause her pain until she says as follows: "He is repulsive to me!" in order to rid himself [of the obligation of paying] her alimony. The law does not follow Mar Zutra, for she is not [considered] a *moredet*, and that is how the law was decided.

After this, [the *sugya*'s redactor] decided the law of *moredet* [in the case of] the daughter-in-law of R. Zevid [who] rebelled, but not [by saying] "He is repulsive to me," but by saying "I want him [but I want to cause him pain]," etc. This is [its explanation]: She rebelled and said: "I want him, but I wish to cause him pain," and [the redactor] explains the law regarding the dowry garments. After that [comes] the statement that we delay the [divorce of a] *moredet* for twelve months of a year after the proclamation of four weeks and the persuasion (according to the one who requires [a final attempt at] persuasion), but [in the case of one who says:] "He is repulsive to me" there is no delay, since she is willing to forfeit [her rights], and when the husband agrees to the divorce.

And regarding [this ruling], all those suffering [the Exile] suffer [further pain]! How could a scholar make [such a] mistake as to say that we force a husband to divorce [his wife] when she says "He is repulsive to me!" Did they not state that she had perhaps cast her eyes on another [even in such extreme cases as when she states] "The Heavens are between me and you" or "I am taken from the Jews!" And did they not further state that "each one should go and become dependent on a Gentile and take herself out of her husband's authority for nothing" [bGit 88b]!—she will become dependent on a Gentile, and [furthermore,] if so, we will have a case in which a sinner is rewarded for his sin! And we do not find in any [part of the laws of divorce] that the husband is forced to give a divorce without any [logical] difficulty at all [in the law's formulation]!

A great proof [for the correctness of my view] is [the fact] that R. Hananel explained [the matter] explicitly [in a similar manner]: If the husband said: "I will give her a divorce," we delay, etc. And all those who understand Halakhah will understand from [this] halakhah and will admit the truth [of my words]. And even that which the author of *Halakhot Gedolot* wrote, that we give a divorce immediately, all must be explained [as occurring] according to the will of the husband [and not as coerced]; and this is how I continually rule. There was the case [which came] before you of the groom R. Yehiel, and I reasoned [thus] before you.

And if we have learned [the rule] that custom may overcome a law, God forbid that [this should apply in a case which involves] a ritual prohibition, [the penalty of] strangulation, [the penalty for adultery], and the [birth of] illegitimate offspring.

And regarding that which our Rabbis of Paris wrote: We hereby agree to whatever you will do to force [this] man—with whatever means of coercion lie at your disposal—until he says "I wish [to grant this divorce]"—this too is not proper in my eyes (perhaps it is an error on my part), for we do not find that we force him to divorce [his wife], as R. Hananel decided [as quoted] above, and since he states at the end of [his commentary] to Gittin: "[As to the case of an] Israelite's coerced divorce, [if it is arranged] according to law, it is valid; if not according to law, it is invalid and [prevents the woman's future offspring by another husband from marrying native-born Jews]." [Now,] we do not know the exact nature of this invalidity, whether its source is in Scripture, as when the coercion is by Gentiles, and even when he says "I wish it," his statement has no effect, or of rabbinic authority. If someone would wish to say that we do not force him by means of whips but by decrees and excommunication, here too we do not force him [to obey] rabbinic ordinances, but we do excommunicate him! [Is that not similar to the case mentioned in bSheb 41a, where the Talmud comments on the extreme nature of the penalty of excommunication:] We hold him by his privates until he releases hold of his [fellow's] garment! And further, they said [as is stated in bM.Q. 17a that] in the West [i.e., in Amoraic Palestine] they convened a court for levying stripes but not for excommunication [i.e., the latter penalty was considered too severe], and R. Yosef stated that they did to him what was good for him [see bM.Q. 17a–b], [and the Talmud further states in bM.Q. 17b that excommunication] brings down great families, and [interprets on 17a the Aramaic *shamta* as *sham mitah ushemamah*] "there is death and desolation." You see from this that excommunication is more severe than stripes, and there is no coercion greater than that! And so too from [the story there] of a dog that would eat [the Rabbis' shoes. The Rabbis could not discover the culprit and placed a ban of] excommunication on him, etc., and a fire began in its tail [and burnt it to death]. [In short,] it is better to give stripes than to excommunicate.

A case was once decided by me regarding someone who had betrothed the daughter of R. Samuel in Chappes. The one who had betrothed her was ordered to divorce her, and I arranged it by having them give him money and goods [to get him to agree]. These matters are well known and recorded, [and I state them] in order that people not say that he disagrees with his masters, since I continually so rule. I should be obeyed [in this].

אין אדם עומד על דברי תורה אלא אם כן נכשל בהן [גטין מג]. כי כמה פעמים יצתה
מלפנינו הוראה בטעות על ההיא דאמרינן בפרק אף על פי אבל אי אמרה מאיס עלי לא
כייפנן לה, והיינו מפרשים על כל הנשים האומרות לבעליהן מאיס עלי. והיה קשה לי
היא דאמרינן השמים ביני וביניך יעשו דרך בקשה דלמא נתנה עיניה באחר איכ' [נדרים
צ]. ועוד היא דאמרינן שלא תהא כל אחת ואחת תולה עצמה בגוי ומפקעת עצמה מיד
בעלה כל שכן שעל ידי (מאי) מאיס עלי לא תפקיע לעולם [גטין פח:]. ועוד קשאי לי
דהא כולה שמעתא במורדות מיירא. אך צריך לפרש כולה שמעתא אמורדת. והכי פי'
המורדת על בעלה פוחתין לה שבעה טרפעיקין ובגמ' מפרש מורדת מתשמיש. והדר
קבעי' היכי דמי מורדת? כגון דאמרה בעינא ליה ומצערנא ליה פי' בעינא ליה אם לא
יגרשני ויתן לי כתובתי ומצערנא ליה עד כלות כתובתי ותוספת דידיה בשבעה דינרין
לשבת, דזמנין הוי בחמש שנים או בעשר שנים, וכמה דאגידא גביה לא יהבי ליה אחריתי
והיא מתכוונת לעגנו ולצערו, אולי יגרשנה ויתן לה כתובתה והיינו מורדת דפוחתין לה
מעט מעט ואינו יכול לגרשה אפילו אם הוא רוצה לגרשה אם אינו נותן לה כתובתה עד
שתפחות כל כתובה בשבעה טרפעיקן. אבל אי אמרה מאיס עלי, לא כפינן לה. כלומר, אי
אמרה לא בעינא ליה — לא הוא ולא כתובתו — אלא הכל אני מוחלת לו, לא הויא
כמחילה בטעות ולא כייפינן לה לשהות' אולי תחזור בה. אם בעל רוצה לגרשה בלא
כתובה יכול לגרשה ואין עליו כתובה, דמחלה ליה, ומחילה גמורה היא. מר זוטרא אמר
כייפי' לה כלומר כופין אותה להשהותה ואולי תחזור בה כדין בעינא ליה ומצערנא ליה
דחדא היא ותרוייהו מורדות הויין, דכיון דמחמת מרד מוחלת לא הויא מחילה גמורה,
ואם בעל רוצה לגרשה נותן לה כתובה. ולא היא אלא כדאמרינן לקמן דמאיס עלי לא
הויא מורדת. אבל מורדת דמשהינן תריסר ירחי שתא אגיטה אחר הכרזה אולי תחזור
ואם לא חזרה מגרשה בלא כתובה אם ירצה. והוא דפסיק הכא כלתיה דרב זביד אימרד,
משום דאמרד דכלה דרב זביד הוא מרד דמאיס עלי כדמוכח מהפסידה בלאותיה, דאלו
במרד דבעינא ליה ומצערנא ליה לא אמרינן הפסידה בלאותיה דהא אית לה כתובתה.
ועוד דפוחתת שבעה דינרין תנן, הפסד בלאות לא תנן. אבל אם לא ירצה הבעל לגרש את
אשתו לא כך ולא כך אין לנו לכופו אלא יעגנה לעולם כדמוכח מתני' שאם תפול לה
ירושה ממקום אחר פוחת עליה. וכל שמועה זו מיירא בשאין הבעל רוצה לגרשה בלא
כתובה ו[קיי"ל] שאם היתה מוחלתו ע"י מיאוס מפני שסבורה שבעל מעכב מפני
שכתובתה עליה מרובה, אפילו הכי כופין אותה, שלא תהא מחילתה מחילה אפילו הוא
רוצה לגרשה עד מלאת לו שנה תמימה, שלא יהו בנות ישראל הפקר. אבל לאחר י"ב
חודש, אם ירצה לגרש יגרש, פטור מן הכתובה. וכן פר"ח אם הבעל נותן גט משהינן ליה
תריסר ירחי שתא להימלך בה וכן עיקר. ולשון כפינן לה [הטעה] רבותינו להעמיד
השמועה בכל הנשים אפי' אינן מורדת, מה שלא היה ומה שלא נברא, אבל כל דבר שאין
רצונה מיקר' כפייה שמכריזין עליה ומפסידין כתובתה ומעגנין אותה. ותו לא מידי.[19]

A person does not appreciate the truth of the words of Torah until he
rules wrongly [stumbles] in them [bGit 43a; see Rashi]. For many
times a mistaken ruling went out from before us regarding that which

we say in Chapter "Even Though" [bKet 63b], "But if she said, 'He is disgusting to me'—we do not force her [to remain with him]." We used to explain [this] regarding all women who said to their husbands, "You are repulsive to me." And that which we say [bNed 90b] [became] problematic to me. "[If she says] 'The Heavens are between me and you'—let [the court] act by making a request [and not by forcing a divorce], lest she has cast her eyes upon another." And furthermore, that which we say [bGit 88b], "so that no woman will take herself from the domain of her husband"—all the more so that by means of [the claim of] "he is repulsive to me"—she should not ever be able to remove herself. And it is furthermore problematic to me that the entire section [in bKet 63b–64a] is brought regarding a rebellious woman [i.e., one who wishes to cause her husband pain, and the section mentions nothing of a forced divorce].

Thus it is necessary to explain the entire section regarding a rebellious woman. And this is the explanation: [the court] deducts seven *quinarii* from [the alimony] of the woman who rebels against her husband, and the Talmud explains: [this means] one who rebels against sexual relations.

And [the Talmud] then asks: What is the specific case of a rebellious woman? [And answers:] for instance, if she said: "I desire him, and I am causing him pain," the explanation being: "I want him [only] if he will not divorce me and give me my alimony; [otherwise] I will cause him pain until my alimony runs out." And the reason for [the deduction of] seven *dinarim* per week is that sometimes [this situation] could last for five or ten years; and so long as she is bound to him, he will not be given [i.e., will not be able to marry] another. She intends to isolate him and cause him pain [so that] perhaps he will divorce her and give to her her alimony. And therefore the rebellious wife [is the one] regarding whom they deduct from her [alimony] little by little. He cannot divorce her even if he wishes to divorce her, without alimony, until the alimony has been reduced by seven *quinarii* [each week until nothing is left. For a woman who was a virgin when she married, the period of time involved would be at least fifty-seven weeks, in the hope that she might change her mind during this period.]

But if she said "He is repulsive to me"—we do not force her [to remain married]. That is to say: if she said, "I do not desire him, neither him nor his alimony; rather, I forfeit everything to him," this is not considered a forfeiture in error, and we do not force her to remain [in the marriage in the hope that] she will change her mind. If the husband wishes to divorce her without alimony he may divorce her, and he has no alimony obligation, for she has forfeited [it] to him; it is a complete forfeiture.

Mar Zutra says: we force her; that is, we require her to remain, and perhaps she will change her mind, as with the case of "I desire him and I am causing him pain," for it is one case, and they are both considered rebellious [wives]; for since she forfeits on account of rebellion, it is not a complete forfeit, and if the husband wishes to divorce her, he gives her alimony. However, this is not [the law]; rather, as we explained before, [the woman who says] "He is repulsive to me" is not a rebellious wife.

But we make a rebellious wife wait twelve months for a divorce after the proclamation—perhaps she will change her mind. If she did not change her mind, he divorces her without alimony if he wishes. And that is the decision here [bKet 63b–64a] regarding the daughter-in-law of Rav Zevid who rebelled, because the rebellion of the daughter-in-law of Rav Zevid was a rebellion of "He is repulsive to me," as is clear from the fact that she lost her used property. For if it were the rebellion of "I desire him and am causing him pain," we would not have said that she loses her used garments, for she [receives] her alimony. And, moreover, we learn in the Mishnah [bKet 63a] "seven *dinarim* are deducted"; we do not learn: "a loss of used property."

But if the husband does not wish to divorce his wife, not in this manner, and not in this manner [i.e., neither with nor without alimony], we [the court] should not force him; but let him isolate her [i.e., leave her in a status where she may not marry] forever, as it is clear from the Mishnah: that if an inheritance should fall into her possession from some other place, it is continually decreased [the implication is that she has remained with her husband for a long time after her initial rebellion, and the fine has been and is being continuously applied]. And this entire section [bKet 63b–64a] applies to a case where the husband does not wish to divorce her without alimony; and we hold that if she had forfeited [the alimony] to him in the case of her finding him repulsive, because she thought that her husband was preventing [the divorce] because the alimony he would owe her would be great—even so, we force her [to remain with him] so that her forfeiture will not be valid even if he wishes to divorce her, until an entire year passes. In this way, Jewish women will not be without dignity and respect [hefker]. But after twelve months, if he wishes to divorce [her], he may divorce [her], and he is exempt from [paying] alimony.

And thus Rabbenu Hananel explained: if a husband gives a divorce, we require him to wait twelve months [in order] to consult with her; thus is the basic [law].

And the expression "we force her" caused our Rabbis [Talmudic commentators, specifically the Geonim] to err, [and] to understand the section as referring to all women, even one who does not rebel [but says, "He is repulsive to me"], which never existed and never was created [i.e., such an understanding is impossible]. Rather, anything against her will is called "forcing," [including the court] proclaiming against her, causing her to lose her alimony, and isolating her; but [we do] nothing in addition to this [we do not force her to stay with her husband].

The two most important contentions of Rabbenu Tam—issues which are of importance in the further development of the law of the rebellious wife—are that (1) the Talmud itself never legislated a coerced divorce, and (2) the Geonim did not have the right to institute such a practice. Rabbenu Tam, therefore, vigorously opposed any actions on the part of the Jewish court to coerce the husband to grant his wife a divorce, for he saw that the consequence of this practice would be the proliferation of illegitimate children in Israel.

Now, the position of Amemar in the Talmud is that, if a woman claims her husband is repulsive to her, she must not be forced to remain married to him.[20] Maimonides interpreted this statement to mean that in such an instance the husband must be forced to grant a divorce, for "a wife is not a captive who must sexually submit to someone she despises."[21] Mar Zutra, on the other hand, concerned lest the woman had merely "cast her eyes on another," and fearing for the stability of the institution of marriage, insisted that the woman be forced to remain with her husband. Thus, Maimonides decided the law in accordance with Amemar, and rejected the position of Mar Zutra. Rabbenu Tam has a different—and entirely original—interpretation of this issue. The usual case of the rebellious wife, the woman who claims "I wish [to remain married] to him, but I wish to cause him pain," he interprets to mean: "I wish to remain married to him rather than forfeit my alimony, but I will cause him pain until he agrees to divorce me with alimony because indeed I do not wish to remain married to him." But he sees the second case of the rebellious wife, the woman who claims her husband is repulsive to her, as an instance where the woman hates her husband so much that she is willing to forfeit her alimony as long as she can be freed from the marriage. Amemar maintained that if a husband granted his wife a divorce without alimony, and *on his own volition,* that divorce is valid. Mar Zutra, according to the interpretation of Rabbenu Tam, disputed this position, claiming that since the woman in fact does want her alimony, and forfeits it merely in order to become free of her husband's authority, it is as though she had received the divorce under duress, and it is therefore invalid. According to this interpretation, Amemar never *legislated* enforced divorce in the Talmud, but rather, has ruled by the facts of the case without any supplementary interpretation of the wife's behavior.

We have also seen how the Geonim interpreted the final statement of the Talmud, attributed to the Rabbanan Sabborai, that a wife must wait twelve months and then she receives a divorce: this too they saw as referring to a woman who claimed her husband was repulsive to her. Rav Sherira restated it thus: "After twelve months the husband is forced to write her a bill of divorce."[22] Thus the Geonim *interpreted* the Talmud to have provided for an obligatory divorce even against the husband's will (albeit after twelve months), and *legislated* that this divorce be immediate, as well as providing for various financial settlements. Yet, in the *Sefer HaYashar* Rabbenu Tam insists that the Talmud never discussed coerced divorce and that the Geonim had no right to make such a decree.[23] (Rabbenu Zerahyah HaLevi had declared that such a coerced divorce was legitimate only during the generation of the original decree, but never questioned the authority of the Geonim to make such a decree.)[24] According to

Rabbenu Tam, in the issue of a divorce for the rebellious wife, there was no authority to legislate other solutions beyond the Amoraic period of Ravina and Rav Ashi.[25] The door which had been opened by the Jerusalem Talmud granting the wife the right to initiate divorce (through a stipulation in the marriage contract), by the Babylonian Talmud (by the statement of Amemar and the decree of the Rabbanan Sabborai), and by the Geonim (in a way which even provided for the satisfaction of financial claims) was tightly shut by Rabbenu Tam's novel interpretation of the Talmudic passages. He thus single-handedly reversed the direction of the halakhah, rejecting the position of the Geonim, and interpreting the Talmud in a fashion radically different than that of the Spanish authorities, Alfasi and Maimonides.

And yet there is an important question to be asked: did Rabbenu Tam simply interpret the Talmudic text as he understood it, and in accordance with the traditions of Rabbenu Hananel and Rashi as he understood them,[26] or were there any extralegal, social and historical circumstances which influenced his position? Contemporary scholars disagree regarding the extent to which extralegal considerations ever influence Halakhah. Rabbenu Tam was certainly one of the more outstanding personalities among the Franco-German Sages, and he often championed minority interpretations which soon, because of his commanding authority, became normative halakhic practice.[27] Sholem Albeck explains Rabbenu Tam's halakhic philosophy in the following manner:

> When Rabbenu Tam reconciles contradictions between the traditional halakhah and the practices of his generation, he never utilizes the argument that the conditions have changed since the days of the Talmud. He rather chooses to resolve the problem by presenting new interpretations to the statements of the Talmud, and so he manages to integrate into the practices of his day the Talmudic halakhah in accord with the (necessary) laws of his day.[28]

E. E. Urbach is in fundamental agreement with this position.[29] In this case, it would seem that the status of women was in decline at that point. Another indication comes from a dispute of Rabbenu Tam with Rabbenu Meshullam.[30] When the latter allowed women who lived in a dangerous area to purify themselves in a ritual bath on the eighth day after the cessation of their menses (and not only on the night after the seventh, in accordance with the accepted halakhic tradition), Rabbenu Tam thundered, "And even if the position were a true one (and it is false!), you ought not to have been lenient for woman and simpletons.[31]

Yet the issue of which Sages and traditions were most sympathetic to the position of women is not as clearcut as it first appears. It was Rabbenu Gershom of Mayence who made the most important advances for women by prohibiting a man from taking more than one wife, and by insisting upon the woman's voluntary acceptance of a divorce decree in order for that divorce to be valid. Moreover, Rabbenu Tam himself permitted women to recite a blessing for those time-bound positive commandments from which they are generally exempt.[32] Indeed, his own wife was apparently a very important personage, and halakhic questions were addressed to her after her husband's death.[33]

It is for reasons such as these that H. Ben-Sasson takes issue with Albeck and Urbach, and insists that "Rabbenu Tam must be seen first and foremost as a warrior on behalf of his opinion for the way of faithfulness, from which there is to be no departure."[34] He was a vigorous supporter of the customs of Ashkenaz, basing his decisions upon the Talmudic interpretations he believed to be correct; and what he considered truth was far more important than economics or sociology.

It seems clear to me that the answer to the dispute between Albeck and Ben-Sasson lies somewhere between their two positions. Although Rabbenu Tam was unquestionably a defender of the Ashkenazic tradition and a champion of the truth as he understood it, the current of the times often plays an unconscious role, and the needs of the people must be a conscious consideration in the mind of the religious legal authority. Such an attitude was considered Biblically ordained; the Jews are commanded to approach the "judge of those days,"[35] and traditionally ordained, by the principle: "The law is in accordance with the latest authority."[36] Of course, legal precedent, as discussed above, must remain the basis of any future legal determinations, but current interpretations of precedents will often be dictated by the exigencies of the times and the prevailing spirit of the land. Hence the dialectic between past and present, precedent and currency, which is the primary force behind the creative halakhic process.

It is important to remember that unlike the Gaonic and Spanish authorities, who lived in Moslem countries, Rabbenu Tam lived in Christian France, where the prohibition against divorce was a major principle in Catholicism. Indeed, in the Christian Testament it is asserted that the religion of Jesus is the extension of the Mosaic Code (Pentateuch), since the latter permits divorce, and the former, understanding it merely as a concession, forbade it, maintaining that whomsoever God had joined together man cannot put asunder.[37]

Hence the intellectual and religious climate in Rabbenu Tam's Franco-Germany militated against divorce. At a time when the prevailing culture insisted upon the permanence of the marital bond, it would hardly have behooved the religious minority to appear lax in the matter. When viewed in this light, even the case of Rabbenu Gershom's insistence upon the woman's acceptance of a bill of divorce in order for the divorce to be valid is seen not only as sensitivity to a woman's needs, but also as a practical way to curtail the number of divorces.[38] When we add to this discussion the sociological background of the Jews of early Franco-Germany—small, homogeneous, cohesive communities, generally based upon familial ties, and widely separated from each other[39]—a picture emerges which helps us to understand the position of Rabbenu Tam regarding the rebellious wife. In such a situation of limited marital prospects and natural compatibility between husband and wife, the pressure which arises from a woman's finding her husband repulsive and wishing to seek an alternative union would be less common. Simultaneously, the ideological current of the majority culture would encourage limiting divorce as severely as possible, and certainly would induce hesitation about legislating means by which the husband might be coerced into granting one against his will. Add to this the halakhic abhorrence of adultery and the traditional importance granted to the family as the vehicle for the transmission of Tradition, and it becomes clear why Rabbenu Tam interpreted the Talmudic passages (which after all are not *explicit* about forcing a divorce) as he did. Taking into account the contemporary situation, Rabbenu Tam in his interpretation of Talmudic precedent shifted the halakhic balance in favor of marital stability. The practical result of his opinion was that from his time on, Jewish courts were to be prohibited from coercing a husband to divorce his wife on the basis of her claiming, "He is repulsive to me."

RECONCILIATION OF SEFARAD AND ASHKENAZ

NAHMANIDES

Rabbenu Moshe ben Nahman (1197–1270), the Ramban, lived in Spain in the century following Rabbenu Tam, and studied under two great teachers, Rabbenu Yehudah bar Yakar and Rabbenu Natan b. R. Meir. The former was a student of R. Yitzhak b. Avraham the Frenchman, a noted Ashkenazic scholar,[40] and passed on to Nahmanides many of the traditions of Rabbenu Tam;[41] whereas Rabbenu Natan was a scholar from Provence.[42] Thus of all men, Nahmanides was best suited to synthesize the divergent traditions of Sefarad, Ashkenaz, and Provence. He was one of the great defenders of Alfasi against the Provencal Rabbenu Zerahyah. He wrote *Wars of the Lord* as such a defense.

אמר הכותב ותימה הוא, שהרי לשון דברי רבינו הגדול מכּן ונכון ופשוט שהוא ז"ל
פירש דין המורדת שאמרה בעינא ליה ומצערנא ליה ודין המורדת שאמרה מאיס עלי
דלא כייפינן לה ומפסדא לכתובתה כולה לאלתר ואמר דהדין הוא דינא דגמרא בכל
מורדת, בין במורדת דבעיא ליה ומצערא ליה ובין מורדת מחמת מיאוס אבל האידנא בבי
דינא דמתיבתא דייני בבאומרת מאיס עלי דיני אחרינא, דכייפי ליה לבעל, ולא מפסדא כל
נכסיה, ומה שאמר בעה"מ ז"ל שתקנת הישיבה הוראת שעה היתה הלא רבנו הגדול ז"ל
יודע תקנת הגאונים יותר מכלנו ומדבריו ניכר שלדורות תקנו אבל אין דבריו של בעל

המאור ז"ל בכאן אלא פיתוי שהוא רוצה לחלוק עליהם, ולומר דבדינא דגמרא דייינין
ואמרה בלשון נקיה, אבל הם באמת לדורות תקנו. ונהגו בה עד ימיו של רבינו ז"ל בחמש
מאות שנה שלא הזה תקנה זו מבניהם, כמו שידוע אצלם בהשובות שלהם. ג"כ תמצא זה
מפורש בהלכות הראשונות לרב שמעון קיירא ובכל חבורי הגאונים הראשונים, גם
בדברי האחרונים ז"ל, והם ידעו היאך תקנו אבל מי שרוצה להחמיר שלא לכוף בגט כדין
הגמ' לא הפסיד ותבא עליו ברכה.[43]

The writer says: It is a wonder, for behold, the language of our Great
Rabbi [Alfasi] is properly directed, correct, and simple. For he, may
his memory be a blessing, explains the law of the rebellious wife in
the case where she says, "I wish [to remain married to] him and I
wish to cause him pain," [as well as] the law of the rebellious wife in
the case where she says "He is repulsive to me." [In neither case] do
we force her [to remain married], but she loses her entire alimony
immediately.

[Alfasi] says that this is the law of the Talmud in the case of every
rebellious wife, either a rebellious wife who wishes to remain married
to [her husband] and to cause him pain, or a rebellious wife who
finds her husband repulsive. But now in the courts of the *Metivta*
when she says "He is repulsive to me," they judge according to
another ruling, and they force the husband [to grant a divorce], and
she does not lose all of her property. And that which the author of
the *Sefer Ha-Maor,* may his memory be a blessing, claims, that the
decree of the Yeshiva was an emergency ruling for the house [i.e., for
a limited time], does not our Great Rabbi, may his memory be a
blessing, know the Gaonic decrees better than all of us? And from his
words, it is obvious that they decreed for [all] generations. But these
words of the author of the *Sefer Ha-Maor,* may his memory be a blessing, are only misleading [lit. "seductive," and are not to be taken
literally], because he wishes to argue with [the Geonim] and to say
that we judge in accordance with the law of the Talmud, although he
says it euphemistically. But in truth they decreed for [all] generations.
This decree did not move from their midst for five hundred years,
and they practiced it into the days of our Rabbi, may his memory be a
blessing, as is known from their responsa.

You will find this explicit in the "First Laws" of Rab Shimon
Kaira and in all the writings of the early Geonim, and also in the
words of the later authorities, may their memories be a blessing; and
[the later authorities] knew how [the Geonim] decreed.

But he who wishes to be stringent and not to force [the husband to grant] a divorce in accordance with the law of the Talmud does not lose, [i.e., has not done anything wrong, and in fact we say] may a blessing come upon him.

It is interesting to note that although Nahmanides writes this in defense of Alfasi he makes two statements which have far-reaching implications. First, he believes that the Gaonic decree introduced the coerced bill of divorcement, whereas we have seen that the Geonim themselves believed this was already legislated in the Talmud. So although Nahmanides himself accepts the validity of the Gaonic decrees, he lends credence to the view of those who reject them in denying the possibility of a coerced divorce. (In this matter we have the advantage of being able to study the original decrees of the Geonim, something apparently impossible for Nahmanides.)

Secondly, he concludes by saying that despite the permissibility of accepting *dina de-metivta,* anyone who wishes to be stringent and not permit a coerced divorce "will not lose, and may a blessing come upon him." Unfortunately, the woman who is then forced to live with a man she hates stands to lose a great deal. Apparently, once Rabbenu Tam took the position he did, each of the later Rishonim—even those, like Nahmanides, who did not live directly in his sphere of influence—became increasingly more reluctant to enter into a controversy with such enormous and irrevocable ramifications. For if Rabbenu Tam was correct, and a coerced divorce was not a divorce at all, those who permitted such a divorce were condemning any future children of the "divorced" wife to illegitimacy.

Ibn Adret

Rabbenu Shelomo ben Avraham Ibn Adret, the Rashba, lived in Barcelona, Spain (1235–1310), and was a student of Nahmanides as well as of Rabbenu Yonah of Gerona.[44] The relevant case is particularly fascinating, for in it we see how that which was "beyond the requirement of the law" for the teacher becomes the normative law for the student.

[תעקב] שאלתם בראובן שנשא בת שמעון ושהתה עמו ג' חדשים ורצתה ללכת לבית
אביה הדר בעיר אחרת לבקרו בשביל שהיה חולה והלכה שם והמתין לה בעלה כשני
חדשים ולא שבה, והלך ראובן אליה כסבור שהיא בשלום עמו ופייסה לשוב אליו ולא
נתפייסה. ולקצת ימים בא לביתו ובא לו שני שומרים לבקש ממנו לגרשה כי כן רצונה
ורצון חמיו ולא אבה ראובן שמוע בקולם ושאלו את פי האשה רבים ונכבדים למה לא
היתה הולכת עם בעלה ואמרה כי היה זקן כי היא בת עשרים והוא בן מ' ומאיס עלה.
וששאלתם אם הדין נותן לכוף לאיש לגרשה כדברי אמימר דאמר אבל אמרה מאיס עלי
לא כייפינן לה או נאמר שמא עיניה נתנה באחר כי ההיא דהלין אהלויי כי יש רגלים
לדבר שהוא יפה תואר ויפה מראה . . . מכל מום יכולה אשה מאיס עלי או לא . . .

תשובה

במה שהסתפקתם במה שאמרה היא מאיס עלי אם ניחוש שעיניה נתנה באחר מפני
שהוא חזק ותקיף בחור כארזים ואיש כזה אין בו שום דבר לתלות בו שיהיה מאוס עליה.
ויראה מדבריכם כי לולי זה שהיה הדין פשוט בעיניכם שכופין אותו מדאמימר אין הדין
נראה כן בעינינו. ולא כך קבלנו מרבותינו, לפי שאין האיש מוציא אלא ברצונו זולתי
אותם הרשומים בפרק המדיר (דף ע') שכופין אותו להוציא, והראיה מדאמרינן בריש
פרק דהניזקין (דף מט) כי נמי היכי דכי מפיק לה איהו תקיני לה [רבנן] כתובה מיניה, כי
מפקא איהי תקינו ליה [רבנן] כתובה מינה ופרקינן האשה יוצאה לרצונה ושלא לרצונה.
והאיש אינו מוציא אלא לרצונו, איפש' דמשהו לה בגט, ואם איתא כל אשה יוצאה
לרצונה ותתן טעם לדבריה משום דמאיס עליה ואם נפשכם לומר שאינה יכולה לומר
מאיס עלי אלא במה שאיפשר שיש לו דבר שהוא מאוס, אבל לא על איש יפה תאר וחזק
כמו שאמרתם ועליו הוא מה שאמרו שאינו מוציא אלא לרצונו, אין לזה, שאין החן
והמיאוס תלויין אלא ברצון הלב וכמה אנשים מכוערים מוצאין חן בעיני בעליהן ובעיני
נשיהם ויפים וטובים וסברי טעם בעיניהם, אלא אין הכל אלא ברצון הבעל ותדע לך
מדלא מני הא דאמרת מימאיס עלי גבי אותן שכופין אותם להוציא. והא דאמימר לא
קאמר אלא דלא כייפינן לה כלומר לא כייפינן אותה לביישה ולהכריזה עליה בבתי כנסיות ובבתי מדרשות
באומרת בעינא ליה ומצערנא ליה, ולא לפחות לה כתובתה בכל שבת ושבת **מפני שאנו**
אינו חושבין אותה כאנוסה. ומשהינן לה בלא כפייה זו תריסר ירחי שתא, **אם חזרה בה**
תוך זמן זה לא הפסידה מכתובתה כלום. וזהו שאמר אמימר דלא כייפינן לה קאמר, אבל
כייפינן ליה לא אמר, ומקשי שכתב רב אלפסי ז"ל שתקנו הגאונים ז"ל, לא פשטה אותה
תקנה בארצותינו כלל. גם ר"ת ז"ל צווח עליה וכן הורו כל רבותינו, וגם מה שכתב
הרמב"ם ז"ל באומרת מאיס עלי שכופין אותו להוציא תהא כשפחה שתבעל לשנוי לה
גם זה פלא בעינינו מהראיות שכתבנו ולא הודו לו כל סיעתו . . . [45].

You asked concerning Reuven, who married the daughter of Shimon.
She stayed with him three months and then wished to go to her
father's house—who lived in another city— to visit, since he was sick.
She went there, and her husband waited for her approximately two

months, and [still] she did not return. Reuven went to her, for he
believed that she was at peace with him, and he urged her to return to
him, but she could not be appeased. He went home after a few days,
and two guards [presumably sent by her father] came to him and
requested that he divorce her, for such was her desire and the desire
of his father-in-law. Reuven did not wish to accept their words, and
many respected men asked the woman why she did not return to her
husband. She said that he was old—she was twenty and he was
forty—and that he was repulsive to her. And you asked if the law provides for the husband to be forced to divorce her in accordance with
the words of Amemar, who says, "But if she says 'He is repulsive to
me' they do not force her." Or do we say [that] perhaps she has cast
her eyes upon another, as in this instance where there is objective
evidence [that he is not repulsive], for he is of goodly form and
appearance. Can a woman declare "He is repulsive to me" regarding
a man such as this, who is free of any blemish, or not? . . .

Response: Concerning that about which you were in doubt, [the case]
when she says "He is repulsive to me," do we suspect that she has cast
her eyes upon another, since [her husband] is strong and powerful, a
young man like a cedar tree, and in whom there is nothing upon
which to base the claim that he is repulsive to her? It seems from
your words that had it not been for this, the matter would have been
obvious to you; they would force him based upon [the words of]
Amemar. The law does not appear to be so to us, and we did not
receive [the tradition] thus from our teachers. For a husband does not
divorce [his wife] except when he is willing [and if he has been forced
to divorce her it is an invalid divorce], except for those [cases] listed in
Chapter Ha-Madir [bKet 70a], in which they force him to divorce
[her]. And in the beginning of Chapter Ha-Nizakin [bGit 49b], [it is
asked] in the same way that [the Rabbis] established alimony from
him to her when he divorces her, so they ought to have established
alimony from her to him when she divorces [him]. The Talmud
answers that [although] the woman [is divorced both] willingly and
unwillingly, a man divorces [only] willingly, [and as such her "divorcing" him was never accompanied by the wife's alimony to her
"departing" husband]. The prime action of the divorce is exclusively
the husband's and he, in spite of "coercion," can procrastinate the

giving of the *get,* thereby weakening her divorce suit. If [the law] existed [in accordance with your understanding], a woman could [receive a divorce] whenever she wished, [if] she could provide a reason for her claim that he was repulsive to her. And if you want to say that she is not able to claim "He is repulsive to me" unless he has something which is [indeed] repulsive, but regarding a handsome and strong man such as you described, [the Talmud] said that [this man] only divorces [his wife] willingly—this is not [the case], *for good favor* [charm] *and distaste are dependent upon the will of the heart* [emphasis added]. Many ugly people find favor in the eyes of spouses who are beautiful and good, and they enjoy a good relationship; everything depends upon the will of the husband. And know that [the Rabbis] did not include [a woman] who says "He is distasteful to me" among with those who are forced [by the court] to divorce [cf. bKet 70a]. And when Amemar said, "we do not force her," he meant to say [we do not] embarrass her, and [do not] proclaim against her in the synagogue and study houses when she says "I wish [to remain married to] him but I wish to cause him pain." We do not deduct from her alimony every week, *because we do not consider her to be as one who is sexually violated against her will* [emphasis added]. And we delay her [divorce] without this coercion [the proclamations and fine] twelve months. If she changes her mind within that time she loses nothing of her alimony. This is why Amemar says "we do not force her," but does not say "we force him." And they raise a problem with what Rabbi Alfasi, may his memory be a blessing, wrote, [regarding] that which the Geonim, may their memory be for a blessing, decreed, [the problem being that] their decree did not spread in our countries at all. And Rabbenu Tam also cried out against it, and so taught all our Teachers. And also that which Maimonides, may his memory be a blessing, wrote, regarding a woman who says "He is repulsive to me," they force him [to divorce her] so that she not be as a captive woman abducted by one who is hateful to her, this too is a marvel in our eyes, because of the proofs we have written [disproving this], and all of his followers disagreed with him.

Elsewhere the Rashba writes:

הא דאמרינן נמלכין בה פי׳ אומרין לה: הוי יודעת שאם תעמדי במרדך לצער אותו אפילו
כתובתיך מאה מנה הפסדת ואי בע׳ מפיק לך ואם אמרה כתובה אני רוצה ואם אי אפשר

לגבותה ממנו איני רוצה להיות צרורה עמו מכריזים עלה ד׳ שבתות ובתר הכי נפקא בלא
כתובה. ואם אמרה איני רוצה לצאת ממנו ובע״י דתפחות כתובה ז׳ דינרין, שומעין לה
וכן פירש הראב״ד ז״ל אבל הר״י הלוי ז״ל כתב פירוש נמלכין בה — פוחתין ז׳ ז׳
דינרין בכל בשבת ושבת עד שבגמור כל כתובתה ופסק הלכתא הכי אבל לדעת הרי״ף
ז״ל נראה שהוא נוטה לפירוש ראשון, שמפני כך כתב דברי רבותי ודברי רמי בר אבא
שני פעמים שולחין לה דאתי׳ אליבא דרבותי אע״פ שלא כתב ר״ח כן . . . אבל אמרה
מאיס עלי, איני רוצה לעמוד עמו לעולם, לא כייפינן לה אלא אבדה כתובתה לאלתר,
ומשהינן לה תריסר ירחי שתא . . . וכולי ה״ל דמורדת ברצון הבעל, ואי לא אין כופין
אותו להוציא. . . . אלמא לעולם אין כופין אלא או לפסולות או לבעלי מומין ותו גרסינן
בירושלמי בפרק אלמנה ניזונת אמר שמואל: אין מעשין אלא לפסולות כגון אלמנה לכהן
גדול . . . אלא ודאי הך מימרא טעות היא, וכל מי ששומע למי שמורה כך ועושה
מעשה בדבר טועה גמור הוי, ומרבה ממזרים בישראל ומתיר אשת איש וקשין לעולם
מאנשי דור המבול אלא מנדר׳ ברצון הבעל היא יוצאה ומאי לא כייפינן לה? להשהותה
בפחיתת כתובה, אלא יוצאה לאלתר ומפסידה כתובתה ברצון הבעל ומדברי הגאונים ז״ל
אין צריך להביא ראיה ראיה שכלם אמרו שאין כופין אותו להוציא מדין התלמוד כמ״ש רש״י
ז״ל בהלכותיו. ולכ״ע כל מי שכופין אותו להוציא בין מעיקר דינא כגון אלו שכופין
אותו להוציא ובין מעיקר תקנתא וכו׳ דהיינו מורדת דאמרי מאיס עלי והגאונים הוא
שתקנו לכופו, ולא מדין הגמרא ובמקצת תשובות רב שרירא ז״ל נמי ראיתי שפרש דמן
דינא אין כופין וכשאמרנו לה תריסר ירחי אגיטא תקנתא אחריתי הות לומר
דאח״כ כופין את הבעל בגט ואין לדברים הללו עיקר כלל ודבר ברור הוא שאין כאן
תקנה חדשה לכוף מעולם לא עלתה על דעת חכמי התלמוד כפיר׳ זו לעולם ח״ו לא
הייתי חולק על תקנת הגאונים כי מי אנוכי לחלוק ולשנות במה שנהגו בו גאוני ישיבות
מרבותי ולא עוד שאני קורא תגר על שאומרים שאינו ראוי לילך אחר תקנתם אלא בדין
התלמוד אלא ראוי היו לשמוע להם ולעשות כתקנתם והמחמיר בכגון זה לא הפסיד אבל
לענין דין התלמוד אמרת שאין כופין והדבר גדול ומפורסם ועכשיו ראוי לחוש בדבר
הרבה שלא לנהוג בתקנה זו כלל עכ״פ שכבר בטלה מפני פריצות הדור ואי קשיא לך אמאי
דאמרינן דכל היכי דאמר רבנן יוציא ויתן כתובה, כופין משמע א״ל כופין אותו לאו
דווקא, אלא עד שכופין אותו ליתן כתובה וכמו שכופין אותו ליתן גט יכפה לזון ואני
צריך לכתבה עוד במקומה בארוכה . . . והוי יודע דהא דהא דאמרינן משהינן לה תריסר ירחי
שתא אגיטא לא נאמרו הדברים אלא ביוצא כגון אמרה מאיס עלי, אבל מי
שפחתה לה ז׳ דינרין בשבת אין משהין אותה לאחר שכלתה כתובתה תריסר ירחי שתא
ולא עוד אלא אפילו חזרה בה ואמרה רוצה אני לשמש עמו כל שעה שירצה, הפסידה מה
שפחתה לה כבר . . .⁴⁶

Regarding that which we say, [namely] that they [attempt to] persuade
her, the interpretation is that they say to her: "Know that if you
remain in your rebellion to cause him pain, even if your marriage
contract is one hundred *maneh* you [will] lose [it], and if he wishes, he
may divorce you." If she says, "I want [the] alimony, [but even] if it is

impossible to collect it from him I do not wish to be chained to him," they proclaim against her for four weeks, and at the end of that time she leaves [is divorced] without alimony. And such is the interpretation of the Ravad [Rabbi Avraham ben David], may his memory be a blessing. But the Ri HaLevi [Yoel ben Yitzhak HaLevi, ca. 1115-1200], may his memory be a blessing, wrote: The interpretation of "they [attempt to] persuade her" is that they deduct seven *dinarim* each week until they exhaust the entire alimony—and this is the definitive halakhic judgment. But the view of the Rif [Rabbi Yitzhak Alfasi], may his memory be a blessing, seems to lean towards the first view, and for this reason he recorded the words of our Rabbis [the *baraita*] and the words of Rami bar Abba, [to the effect] that they send [the agents of the court] to her twice, which follows the position of our Rabbis, even though Rabbenu Hananel does not write so. . . . But if she said, "He is repulsive to me, I do not wish to remain with him at all," we do not force her [to remain married], but she loses her alimony immediately, and we make her wait twelve months. . . .

And in all of these cases of the rebellious wife, [the divorce] is with the consent of the husband, and if [he does] not [consent], they do not force him to divorce her. . . .

Thus we see they never force [the husband to divorce] his wife except [in the case of] women who are invalid [e.g., a divorcee to a priest] or men who are afflicted with gross physical blemishes [as listed in mKet 7:10]. And the Jerusalem Talmud, Chapter Almanah Nizonet, further states [that] Shmuel said: "They do not force [a divorce] unless they are invalid, [to each other] like a widow to a High Priest." . . .

But certainly that statement [that they force] is a mistake, and anyone who listens to one who rules thusly and follows such a ruling in actual practice is in complete error, and increases the number of illegitimate children [*mamzerim*] in Israel, and permits a married woman [to marry another man], and this is harsher [more destructive] to the world than the men of the generation of the Flood. But . . . [only] with the consent of her husband is she divorced.

And what [does it mean] that they do not force her? [They do not force] her to remain by deducting from [the] alimony, but she receives an immediate divorce and forfeits the alimony with the consent of her husband. And one should not bring a proof from the words of the Geonim, may their memory be a blessing, because they all said that they do not force him to [divorce] her according to Talmudic law [but rather according to the specific decree of the Geonim], as Rashi, may his memory be for a blessing, wrote in his laws.

And according to all opinions, everyone who forces [a man] to divorce [his wife] does so either according to Talmudic law, such as "These [are the cases in which] they force him to grant her a divorce" [i.e., gross physical affliction], or from the Gaonic decree, that is, [in the case of] a rebellious wife who says "He is repulsive to me."

And it was the Geonim who decreed that they force [him], and not the Talmudic law, and in some responsa of Rav Sherira, may his memory be a blessing, I saw that he explained that according to Talmudic law they do not force [a husband to divorce his wife]. And when [the Talmud] says that they make her wait twelve months for a divorce, [one could say] that this is another [Talmudic] decree [which mandates] that afterwards they force the husband to divorce [her]. But this argument has no basis, and it is clear that [in the Talmud] there is no new decree to force [a divorce]. And an interpretation like this never occurred to the Sages of the Talmud, ever.

Heaven forbid I should dispute a decree of the Geonim, for who am I to dispute or to change that which the Geonim of the Schools—my masters—were accustomed to do? And further, I rail against those who say that it is not fitting to follow their decrees but [rather to follow] the law of the Talmud.

But it is fitting to listen to them and to do in accordance with their decree, and one who is stringent in this fashion will not lose.

But concerning the ultimate decision, the Talmud says that they do not force [the husband to divorce her], and the matter is great and well-known. It is now fitting to be very cautious about this issue, and not to act in accordance with this decree at all, for it has already been nullified because of the generation.

And if you have a problem regarding that which we say, that wherever the Rabbis say "Let him divorce her and give her the alimony," this implies coercion, I will say to you that [the word] "coercion" is not to be taken literally; [rather, strong measures are taken] up to [physically] forcing him to give her the alimony. In the same way [without the use of physical force] that they force him to give a bill of divorce, he is forced to support [her].

And I must write more at greater length in its place. . . . And know that that which we say, that we make her wait twelve months for the divorce, was only said when she is divorced immediately, for instance, [when] she said "He is repulsive to me."

But whenever they deduct seven *dinarim* a week there is no delay of twelve months after the alimony provided by the marriage contract has been used up. And moreover, even if she changed her mind and said, "I wish to have sexual relations with him whenever he wishes," she loses what has already been deducted from her. . . .

The Rashba takes a strong stand, forbidding the coercion of the husband to grant a divorce, and insists that the Talmud never mentioned coercion of the husband. He explains the words of Amemar, "She is not to be forced" (which we have so far taken to mean that she is not forced to remain married to him), to mean that a woman who claims her husband is repulsive to her is not forced to suffer the humiliation of a four-week period of public proclamation and subsequent forfeiture of alimony, nor the slow deduction of seven *dinarim* weekly from that sum. Rather, she is to be divorced immediately—if her husband so desires. Ibn Adret emphasizes that Amemar uses the words "She is not forced" rather than the words "He is forced." He interprets the final statement of the Talmud (Rabbanan Sabborai) to mean that in the case of a woman who claims "He is repulsive to me" there is a twelve-month waiting period for the bill of divorce, without proclamations or alimony reduction. At the end of that time the husband is not coerced to grant her a divorce, although it is probable that he would, since he would not have to pay her the alimony.

Ibn Adret cites the Gaonic decrees, although he notes the position of Rav Sherira that the Talmudic law did not provide for an enforced divorce, and insists that despite the fact that he (Ibn Adret) accepts the authority of Gaonic legislation, in this particular instance the decrees are rescinded and nullified. In his *Hiddushim* (novellae) to the Talmud he cites the immorality of his generation as the reason for this nullification. If the Gaonic decrees were to remain in effect, too many women would claim that they found their husbands repulsive, when, in fact, they had merely cast their eyes upon another man. Ibn Adret felt it necessary to protect the institution of marriage. It is interesting to note that in his responsum he proposes another, psychological, basis for his ruling: that *love is a matter of will,* as attested to by the fact that many objectively ugly people are loved by their mates. Thus a woman can—and must—*will herself* to love her husband, even in a case where he is twenty years her senior. Hence, the only possible grounds for coercing a divorce are when the husband possesses any of the objective, physical blemishes outlined by the Mishnah.[47]

ASHERI

Rabbenu Asher ben Yehiel, known as the Rosh (1250–1327), is the most authentic bridge between the traditions of Ashkenaz and Sefarad. He initially achieved eminence in Germany, but persecution and pillage forced him to flee to Toledo, Spain, where he became rabbi, teacher, and judge. In his Talmudic commentary (generally printed after each Talmudic tractate) he usually cites Alfasi and Rabbenu Tam verbatim, and proceeds to mediate between them.

Similarly, in the case of the rebellious wife, he begins with Rabbenu Tam, deciding in favor of the *baraita* (*Rabbotenu*) and his interpretation of Rava—that a woman is warned privately before as well as after each public proclamation. He interprets the classic case of *moredet* to be "I wish to remain married to him but to cause him pain," but if a woman claims "He is repulsive to me," then the divorce can occur immediately *with the husband's consent,* and without payment of alimony. The twelve-month waiting period was initially established by the latter Amoraim for this second case, but would now apply to the first case as well. Asheri quotes the decree of the Geonim as cited by Alfasi, but insists that the husband is not coerced into giving a divorce. It is possible to deduce from his words that the Geonim decreed an immediate divorce (lest a woman come to a bad end) without explicitly adding that they also meant that the husband was to be coerced. Asheri underscores his opposition to forced divorces by warning that they would increase the number of illegitimate children, and decides in accordance with the mandated twelve-month waiting period.

ורש"י פירש בענין אחר ופירוש ר"ת עיקר . . . אבל אמרה מאיס עלי לא הוא ולא
כתובתו בעינא, ודאי לא תחזר בה ולא כייפינן לה בשהייה, אלא אם ירצה יגרשנה בלא
כתובה מיד ורשב"ם ז"ל פי' אבל אמרה מאיס עלי לא כייפינן לה שתשהה ותמתין עד
כלות כתובתה ז' דינרין בשבת אלא יגרשנה מיד בעל כרחו וכן כתב הרמב"ם ז"ל . . .
ואין נראה לר"ת . . . כלתיה דרב זביד אימרידא פירוש דאמרה מאיס עלי מדמיתי עלה
שהפסידה בלאותיה דמשמע לאלתר דאילו במרד דבעינא ליה ומצערנא ליה לא שייך בה
למימר הפסידה בלאותיה מיד דהא אית לה כתובה כל זמן שלא כלתה והכריזו עליה . . .
ומשהינן לה תריסר ירחי שתא ולית לה מזוני מבעל תקנה זו נעשית בימי האמוראים
האחרונים כאשר ראו כי גבהו בנות ישראל ודעתם זחה עליהם וכאשר היה להם כעס עם
בעליהן היו אומרות לא בעינא ליה והבעל מגרשה מיד כיון שפטרתו מכתובה, ושוב היו
נשים מהחרטות, תקנו שתשהה שנה ואם יגרשנה בתוך השנה שלא תהא מחילתה מחילה
ויצטרך ליתן לה כתובה אולי יתפייסו בתוך השנה וכיון שתקנו כך לאומרת מאיס עלי
שהיתה ראויה להתגרש מיד בלא כפייה, כל שכן למורדת . . . הדין הוא דינא דגמ'
במורדת אבל האידנא דייני דייני דבי דינא דמתיבתא, כדאתיא ואמרה לא בעינא ליה להאי
גברא ניתיב לי גיטא, יהבינן לה גיטא לאלתר ואי תפסה מידי מכתובתה מפקינן מינה
ויהבינן ליה לבעל ונכסי מלוג אם ישנן בעין או דבר אחר הבא מכחן כגון שמכרו בתים
וקנו בדמים שדות שקלה להו אבל כלו אבל כלו לגמרי לא מיחייב בעל לשלומי אבל נכסי צאן
ברזל כל שישנו בעין מהן אפילו כלו הרבה שקלה להו ואפילו נפחתו מדמיהן הרבה, אינו
משלם הפחת, ובלבד שיהו ראוין להשתמש בהן מעין מלאכתן ראשונה, אבל אינן ראוין
להשתמש מעין מלאכתן הראשונה חייב לשלם כל דמיהן כל שכן אם נגנבו או נאנסו
משום דברשותיה קיימי כדהנן אם מתו מתו לו אם הותירו הותירו לו. וחזינן לגאון דאמר
דיהיב ליה עיקר כתובה מנה או מאתים לחוד כי היכי דלא להויין בנות ישראל הפקר אבל
מאי דכתב לה מדיליה בין תוספת בין מתנה לא יהבינן לה מידי. הדין הוא דינא דמורדת
דנהיגי בה רבנן דמתיבתא כמה שנין עד השתא ואפשר לפי שראו הקלקול בבנות ישראל
וכי משהו להו תריסר ירחי שתא תלות עצמן בעובדי כוכבים ויוצאות לתרבות רעה
בטלו שהייה ונתנו רשות לבעל לגרשה מיד בלא שהייה אבל לא שיכפוהו לגרשה, דאף
במונע ממנה תשמיש או מזונות אין כופין אותו להוציא כדאיתא בירושלמי אין מעשין
אלא לפסולות כ"ש כשהיא מונעת לעצמה שלא תקנו להרבות ממזרין בישראל, מוטב
שבנות ישראל הרעות יתגרשו ולא שיוסיפו רעה על רעתן . . . ואע"ג דחזינן להאי
מילתא פלוגתא דרבוותא, מסתברא כמ"ד לא עבדינן תקנתא בהאי מילתא . . . וכן
הלכתא וכן היה דין רבינו מאיר ז"ל בדינא זמתיבתא . . . הלכך לא היה דן דין מאיס עלי
אם לא שתתן אמתלא לדבריה למה אינו מקובל עליה או שהיה מכלה כל מההון.[48]

And Rashi interprets [it] in another way, but the interpretation of
Rabbenu Tam is fundamental [and should be followed]. . . .

But [if] she said "He is repulsive to me, and I want neither him nor his alimony," she will certainly not change her mind, and they will not coerce her by making her wait, but if he wishes, he may immediately divorce her without alimony.

And the Rashbam (may his memory be a blessing) interpreted: But [if] she said "He is repulsive to me," we do not make her wait until her alimony has been depleted [at the rate of] seven *dinarim* a week, [rather] he must divorce her immediately, [even] against his will, and so wrote Maimonides (may his memory be for a blessing). . . . This does not appear [reasonable] to Rabbenu Tam. . . . The daughter-in-law of Rav Zevid rebelled, the interpretation being that she said "He is repulsive to me," since they brought into [this case] the loss of her used garments, which implies [an] immediate [loss]. Had the rebellion been one of "I want [to remain married to] him, but I want to cause him pain," it would not have been appropriate to say that she immediately lost her used garments, for she has her alimony [and therefore receives compensation for dowry property which has been used up], as long as it is not used up [from the deduction]. And they publicly proclaim regarding her, and we make her wait twelve months, and she receives no support from her husband.

This decree was made in the days of the latter Amoraim when they saw that Jewish women had become haughty and arrogant, and [that] when they became angry with their husbands they would say, "I don't want him," and the husband would divorce her immediately, since she exempted him from [payment of] alimony. Then the women would regret [it]. They [therefore] decreed that she remain [with him] one year, and if she is divorced during the year, her forfeiting [of the alimony] is no forfeiture, and he must give her the alimony, for perhaps they would be reconciled during the year. And since they decreed thus for the [woman] who says "He is repulsive to me," who was fit to be divorced immediately without coercion, all the more so for the rebellious wife [who says "I want to remain married to him but wish to cause him pain"]. . . .

This is the Talmudic law concerning the rebellious wife, but now they judge in the Court of the *Metivta* [Academy]. When she comes and says, "I do not want that man, give me a divorce," we grant her a divorce immediately. If she grabs anything from her alimony, we take it from her and give it to her husband.

And, regarding *nikhsei melug,* if it is in existence or [if] anything which came from it [is in existence], for example, if they sold [some] homes [which were her *nikhsei melug*] and purchased fields with the money, she receives them, but if they have completely been used up, her husband is not obligated to pay [her for them]. But regarding *nikhsei tzon barzel,* she receives everything which remains intact from them, even if it has been greatly diminished, and even if their value has greatly depreciated. He does not make up the depreciation, if they are fit to be used for their original purpose. But if they are not fit to be used for their original purpose, he must pay their entire value, and this is certainly so if they were stolen or destroyed by circumstances beyond his control, since they are in his possession [and he assumed responsibility for them], as we learned in the Mishnah [Yeb. 7:1]: "If they die, they die on his account, if they increase in value, they increase on his account." And we saw a Gaon who said that [the husband] must give her the basic alimony sum—one hundred or two hundred [*zuz*] alone—so that Jewish women not be left without dignity or respect [*hefker*]; but whatever he wrote for her [in her marriage contract] from his own property, whether an addition [alimony sum], or a gift, we do not give her anything [of it]. This is the law of the rebellious wife which the Rabbis of the *Metivta* [Academy] have practiced for several years until now. And it is possible [that] since they saw the depravity of Jewish women, and that [when] they would make them wait twelve months, they would make themselves dependent upon the Gentiles and come to a bad end, they [therefore] nullified the waiting period, and gave permission to the husband to divorce her immediately. But they did not force him to divorce her, because even if he withholds sexual relations or food from her, they do not force him to divorce her, as it [says] in the Jerusalem Talmud: "They only force [divorce] with women who are invalid for him." All the more so [we do not force him] when she herself is the withholder.

[This is] because they did not decree [in order] to increase the number of illegitimate children [*mamzerim*] in Israel; it is better that the evil daughters of Israel should be divorced, and not add evil upon their evil. . . .

And even though we have seen a dispute among the great scholars on this issue, it is reasonable [to follow] the position which states that we do not effect a decree in this matter [i.e., we do not force divorce under Gaonic decree]. . . . And thus is the law, and thus Rabbenu

Meir [of Rothenburg, ca. 1215–1293] (may his memory be a blessing)
used to judge regarding the law of the *Metivta* [Academy]. . . .

Therefore he did not judge the case of [a woman who says] "He is
repulsive to me," if she did not give a reasonable basis [*amatla*] for her
words—why he was not acceptable to her—or that he squandered all
[their] financial resources.

A much clearer insight into the motivations of Asheri, and one
which brings us back to our original understanding of the Talmud,
can be obtained from his responsa.

תשובה על ענין אשה הכתובה לעיל החכם ר׳ יעקב אלפאסי ש״צ תשובתו על ענין
מורדת אין אדם צריך לימלך בו בהכרחת נתינת גט ראיתי לרבותנו חכמי אשכנז וצרפת
מתרחקין עד הקצה האחרון מכל מיני הכרחות כפיית האיש לגרש בעסק מרידת האשה
כי נראה להם דברי רבינו ר״ת ז״ל וראיותיו עיקרים וראוי לסמוך עליהם ואף אם היו
הדברים מוכרעים, צריך אדם להרחיק מספק אשת איש ומלהרבות ממזרים בישראל ואם
ראו בדורות שהיו אחר חכמי הגמרא בימי הגאונים ז״ל בישיבות של בבל שהיה צורך
שעה בימיהם להסיע על דברי תורה ולעשות גדר וסייג ותקנו שיגרש האיש את אשתו
בעל כרחו כשהיא אומרת לא בעינא ליה לגבראי כדי שלא תתלה עצמה בכותי ותצאנה
בנות ישראל לתרבות רעה וסמכו על זה כל המקדש אדעתא דרבנן מקדש והסכימה דעתם
להפקיע הקידושין כשתמרוד האשה על בעלה אותה תקנה לא פשטה על כל הארצות ואף
אם יש מקומות שנהגו לכוף זה לא נהגו מנהג זה באותן מקומות על פי תקנת הגאונים ז״ל
כגון שבשעה שתקנו הגאונים את התקנה שלחוה לאותן המקומות וקבלה אותה עליהם
ואם היה הדבר ידוע על פי הקבלה דור אחר דור היאך קבלו תקנה זו עליהם בצווי
הגאונים כי תקנה קבועה כזו לא היתה עומדת לישכח מפי דורות הבאים דוגמא לדבר:
חכם אחד היה בארצנו והיה שמו רבינו גרשום תיקן תקנות טובות בענין גירושין והיה
בימי הגאונים ז״ל ותקנותיו וגזרותיו קבועות ותקועות כאלו נתנו מסיני כי בשביל שקבלום
עליהם ומסרום לדור דור אלא אני רואה שבאלו הארצות רוב הגיונם בספר ר״ף ז״ל
שראו כפייה זו כתובה בהלכות ונהגו ביש מקומות לדון כך ועוד אני אומר שהגאונים
שתקנו תקנה זו תקנוה לפי הדור ההוא שהיה נראה להם לפי צורך השעה בשביל בנות
ישראל והאידנא נראה להפך בנות ישראל בדור הזה שחצניות הן אם תוכל האשה
להפקיע את עצמה מתחת בעלה באמרה לא בעינא ליה לא הנחת בת לאברהם אבינו
יושבת תחת בעלה ויתנו עיניהן באחר וימרדו בבעליהן על כן טוב להרחיק הכפייה ויותר
התימה הגדול על הרמב״ם ז״ל שכתב שאם אמרה מאסתיהו ואיני יכולה להבעל לו
מדעתי כופין אותו לשעתו לגרשה לפי שאינה כשבויה שתבעל לשנוי לה ומה נתינת טעם
לכוף האיש לגרש ולהתיר אשת איש? לא תבעל לו ותוצרר אלמנות חיות כל ימיה, הלא
אינה מצווה על פריה ורביה וכי בשביל שהיא הולכת אחרי שרירות לבה ונתנה עיניה

באחר וחפצה בו יותר מבעל נעוריה נשלים תאותה ונכוף האיש שהוא אוהב אשת נעוריו
שיגרשנה חלילה וחס לשום דיין לדון כן ורבי מאיר ז״ל בעסקי מורדת בענין הממון היה
דן בדינא דמתיבתא שיתנו לאשה כל מה שהכניסה אבל לא היה כופה לגרשה וקודם
שיחזירו לה מה שהכניסה לו היה מצוה להחרים אם שום אדם השיאה עצה זו כדי
להוציא מיד בעלה מה שהכניסה לו וכשהיה נראה לו שהיה ערמה בדבר לא היה מצוה
להחזיר אפי׳ מה שהכניסה לו ולא היה דן כלל דין דמאיס עלי אם לא שתתן אמתלא
לדבריה למה אינו מקובל עליה או שרוואין בו שהוא מכלה הממון, אז היה מצוה להחזיר
לה מה שהכניסה לו ומדבריו לענין הממון כ״ש לענין כפיית הגירושין דיש לחוש לערמה
ולנתינת עיניה באחר ואשר[י] יבחר וירחיק הגירושין. הרי כתבתי לך בענין כפיית גט
מורדת אמנם בנדון זה ספר לי אחיה אמתלאות שנותנת למרידתה ואתה דיין בדבר הזה,
תחקור על הדבר אם יש ממש בדבריה. ואם דעתו לעגנה ראוי הוא שתסמוך על מנהגכם
בעת הזאת לכופו ליתן גט לזמן ועוד כי זאת כבר נתגרשה אלא שנולד ספק בתנאי ואם
היה בא להחזירה היתה צריכה להתקדש ויפה דנת שיתן לה מה שהכניסה . . .⁴⁹.

Responsum concerning a woman which was mentioned above [by]
the Sage R. Yaakov Alfasi (may his memory be a blessing), his responsum concerning a rebellious wife. No one must seek advice regarding
the coercing [of the husband to] give a divorce, because I have seen
that our Rabbis, the Sages of Germany and France, keep as far away
as possible from any type of coercion of a man to give a divorce in the
matter of a rebellious wife, because the words of our Rabbi Rabbenu
Tam appear [reasonable] to them, and his proofs are basic [to a
proper understanding of the matter] and it is proper to rely on them.
And even if the matters were convincing [i.e., if there was strong
reason to force a divorce], a person must keep far away from the possibility [that, since Rabbenu Tam rules that forced divorces are invalid, a woman divorced under such a procedure would still be] a
married woman and of increasing the number of illegitimate children in Israel. And if they saw in the generations which were after the
Sages of the Talmud, in the days of the Geonim (may their memory
be a blessing) in the Schools of Babylonia, that there was a temporary
need in their day to go beyond the words of the Torah and to build a
fence and a barrier, they decreed that the husband should divorce his
wife [even] against his will, when she says: "I do not wish [to remain
married to] this man." This was enacted in order that she not be
made dependent upon the Gentiles and that Jewish women [not]
come to a bad end. For they relied on this dictum: "Everyone who
marries, marries in accordance with the will of the Rabbis" [bKet 3a],

and they agreed to annul the marriage when a woman rebels against her husband. This decree did not spread to all countries, and even in those places where they are accustomed to force [divorces] according to Gaonic decree, they did not practice this custom in those places. For instance, at the time that the Geonim established their decree they sent it to those places and they accepted it upon themselves. If this [had been the case], the matter would have been known by tradition, generation after generation, that they [had] accepted upon themselves the decree of the Geonim as an established decree, and as such it would not have been forgotten by the later generations.

An example of the matter: a Sage was in our lands whose name was Rabbenu Gershom [960–1028]; he made good decrees concerning divorce and lived in the days of the Geonim (may their memory be a blessing), and his decrees and enactments are established and entrenched as if they had been given at Sinai, since [the Jews of Northern France and Germany] accepted them upon themselves and handed them down from generation to generation. But I see that in these countries the majority of their study is in the book of Alfasi (may his memory be a blessing). And since they saw this coercion written in the laws [of Alfasi], they were accustomed in some places to judge thusly [and to force divorces]. And furthermore I say that the Geonim who made this decree made it for that generation [only], for it seemed to them that it was necessary at the time because of Jewish women [who would otherwise rely on Gentiles for divorce but who nonetheless would not divorce their husbands lightly]. And now the matter seems to be reversed: Jewish women in this generation are vain. If a woman will be able to remove herself from under her husband['s rule] by saying "I don't want him," not a [single] daughter of Abraham our Father will remain with her husband. They [the women] will cast their eyes upon others and will rebel against their husbands. Therefore it is good to place coercion at a far distance. And it is very astonishing that Maimonides (may his memory be a blessing) wrote that if she said "I find him repulsive and I am unable willingly to have sexual relations with him" they force him to divorce her at that time, for she is not [to be made] like a captive woman who must have sexual relations with one who is hateful to her. But what kind of reason has he given for coercing the man to divorce [his wife] and to permit a married woman [to someone else]?

[Rather,] let her not have sexual relations with [her husband] and let her remain chained all of her days, for after all, *she* is not commanded to be fruitful and multiply! Because she followed the dictates of her heart, [and] cast her eyes upon another and desired him more than the husband of her youth, do we then fulfill her lust and force the man who loves the wife of his youth to divorce her? Heaven forbid that any judge should judge thusly!

And R. Meir [of Rothenburg] (may his memory be a blessing) judged regarding the financial matters of the rebellious wife according to the law of the *Metivta,* that they would give the woman all that which she had brought in [to the marriage], but he would not force [her husband] to divorce her. And before they would return to her that which she had brought in to him [in marriage], he would command that [they] place [her] under the ban and require her to swear that no individual had given her this advice [to claim that she found him repulsive] in order to take from her husband that which she had brought in to him. And if it appeared to him that there was deception in the matter, he would not command them to return even that which she had brought in to him [through marriage], and he would not judge [any cases of] "He is repulsive to me" unless she gave a reasonable basis for her words as to why he was unacceptable to her, or if they saw that he squandered money. Then he [R. Meir] would command that [the husband] return to her whatever she had brought in to him. And from his [R. Meir's] words concerning money [to the effect that we require her to give a reason], it is all the more so concerning the forcing of a divorce. We must be suspicious of deception and of [the possibility] that she [had merely] cast her eyes upon another. And [happy] is he who will choose [wisely] and keep far from divorce. Behold, thus I have written you concerning the matter of forcing a divorce of a rebellious wife. However, in this case, her brother told me that she gave reasonable bases for her rebellion. And you as judge in this matter [must] investigate the issue [to decide] if there is substance to her words. If [her husband's] intent is to "chain" her, it is proper that you rely on your custom at this time to force him to give an immediate divorce. And furthermore, if this woman's divorce has been processed, but there are questions as to the conditions [of the divorce], and if [her husband] wants to take her back, he must remarry her. And you judged well that he must give her those things which she had brought in . . .

Asheri builds a most effective case for the position of Rabbenu Tam, basing himself upon the necessity of stable marriages and his own fear that coercion of the husband might result in a rash of women leaving their husbands for no real reason. He sees the Gaonic decrees as having been legitimately based upon the right of the Sages to "cancel a betrothal,"[50] but since the Gaonic legislation was not universally accepted (unlike the decrees of Rabbenu Gershom), it is no longer to be considered operative. Moreover, perhaps the Geonim had legislated for their own time, when they were faced with the problem of women resorting to Gentile courts and apostasy in order to be freed from unhappy marriages; but "our women" are brazen (shaḥtzaniot), argues Asheri, and the Gaonic decrees are hardly applicable to them. And yet it is possible to claim that the Gaonic decrees were in fact designed for brazen women, since these were the ones who would most probably turn to the Gentiles if unable to get their way in Jewish courts. Asheri reveals his lack of sensitivity for the plight of a woman who must remain with a man she detests when he rails against Maimonides' view that "a woman cannot be held captive." Why not simply permit her to refrain from sexual relations with her husband, he writes, since the injunction to be fruitful and multiply does not apply to women!

So in effect, all those great synthesizers who were best able to reconcile the positions of the Sages of Sefarad and Ashkenaz—Nahmanides, Ibn Adret, and Asheri—judged the law of the rebellious wife in a manner consistent with the position of Rabbenu Tam and rejected the position of Alfasi and Maimonides.

THE SHULHAN ARUKH

Persecution often causes a great scholar to leave one community for another. After the expulsion of the Jews from Spain and Portugal (Sephardic Jewry) towards the end of the fifteenth century, many formerly homogeneous Diaspora Communities in other countries became polyglot amalgamations of Jews from diverse backgrounds. Since the "custom of one's country" had become confused, a general code of Sephardic practice had to be formulated, one which

would be accepted by the majority of Jews from various countries.
Rav Yosef Karo (1488–1575), scholar and mystic of Safed, set himself
to this task. He had previously written a commentary, *Beit Yosef,* to
an earlier code, the *Arba'ah Turim* ("Four Pillars"), composed by
Rabbenu Yaakov ben Asher (1270–1340), the son of Asheri, and now
he set forth his conclusions in concise form in the classic *Shulhan
Arukh* ("Set Table"). His three pillars of authority are Alfasi, Maimonides, and Asheri; he generally accepts the position held by any
two of the three. When, in 1564, Rav Mosheh Isserles (1525 or
1530–1572) of Cracow, Poland (called the Rema), added his glosses
to Rav Yosef Karo's work, reflecting Ashkenazic (French-German-
Polish) practice, the *Shulhan Arukh* with its *Mappah* ("tablecloth")
became the accepted guide to normative halakhic practice for all of
world Jewry.[51]

אבן העזר עז, ב

ב. האשה שמנעה בעלה מתשמיש, היא הנקראת מורדת, ושואלין אותה מפני מה מרדה
אם אמרה מאסתיהו ואיני יכולה להבעל לו מדעתי.

(ודוקא שמבקשת גט בלא כתובה אבל אם אומרת יתן לי גט וכתובתי חיישינן שמא
נתנה עיניה באחר ויש לה דין מורדת דבעינא ומצערנא ליה ב״י בשם תשובות הר״ן וכן
פירש רש״י בגמרא. — רמ״א)

אם רצה הבעל לגרשה, אין לה כתובה כלל ותטול בלאותיה הקיימין בין מנכסים
שהכניסה לבעלה ונתחייב באחריותן בין נכסי מלוג שלא נתחייב באחריותן ואינה נוטלת
משל בעלה כלום ואפי׳ מנעל שברגליה ומטפחת שבראשה שלקחם לה פושטת ונותנת
וכל מה שנתן לה מתנה מחזרת אותו.

ואם מרדה מתחת בעלה כדי לצערו ואמר הריני מצער אותו בכך מפני שעשה לי כך וכך
מפני שקללני או מפני שעשה עמי מריבה וכיוצא בדברים אלו שולחין לה מבית דין
ואומרים לה: הוי יודעת שאם את עומדת במרדך אפילו כתובתיך ק׳ מנה הפסדת אותם.
ואח״כ מכריזין עליה בבתי כנסיות ובתי מדרשות, בכל יום ד׳ שבתות זו אחר זו.
ואומרים פלונית מרדה על בעלה ואחר ההכרזה שולחין לה ב״ד פעם שנית אם את
עומדת במרדך הפסדת כתובתיך אם עמדה במרדה נמלכין בה ותאבד כתובתה
ולא יהיה לה כתובה כלל ואין נותנין לה גט עד י״ב חדש ואין לה מזונות כל י״ב חדש.
וי״א דבזמן הזה שאין נושאין ב׳ נשים לא משהינן לה י״ב חדש אם רוצה לגרשה ואם
אינה רוצה . . . (רמ״א)

וי״א דכל זה באינה נותנת אמתלא וטעם לדבריה למה אומרת מאיס עלי, אבל בנותנת
אמתלא לדבריה כגון שאומרת שאינו הולך בדרך ישרה ומכלה ממונו וכיוצא בזה, אז
דיינינן לה כדינא שתקנו הגאונים (טור בשם מהר״ם מרוטנבורג) ונקרא דינא דמתיבתא

שבעל צריך להחזיר לה כל מה שהכניסה לו בנדונייתא דהיינו צאן ברזל אם הם בעין
וראויין למלאכתם הראשונה נוטלת הכל כמו שהוא ואם אינם ראוים למלאכת הראשונה
וכ"ש אם נגנבו או נאבדו צריך הבעל לשלם הכל ונכסי מלוג שלה אם הם בעין או דבר
הבא מכחה נוטלתן אבל אם כלו לגמרי, אין הבעל צריך לשלם (דינא דמתיבתא טור בשם
הרי"ף) אבל כל מה שנתן לה או כתב לה אינה נוטלת כלום ואפי' תפסה צריכה להחזיר
(מרדכי פי' אע"פ) ואין כופין אותו לגרש ולא אותה להיות אצלו (גם זה טור בתשובת
מהר"ם) ואם עשה שלא כהוגן, שקדשה ברמאות ובתחבולות, כופין אותו לגרש (רא"ש
כלל לה) וי"א עד דמטילין חרם (טור בשם מהר"ם) אם בני אדם למדוה למרוד או
שעושה כך משום כעס וקטט או להוציא ממונו ממנו אז אפי' מה שתפסה מנכסיה נוטלין
מידה ומחזירין לבעל (מרדכי פי' אע"פ) ואין חילוק בין אם תפסה או לא אלא בטוענת
מאיס ואינה נותנת אמתלא מבוררת לדבריה אבל מ"מ נותנת אמתלא ואין בזה רמאות
והב"ד יודנו בזה לפי ראות עיניהם (מהרי"ו א' ז) ויכולין להשביע אותה על כך אם
טוענת באמת מאיס עלי וכן ראוי להורות וכל זמן שלא נתן גט אין לו כפייה ונגישה
עליה.[52]

2. A woman who denies her husband sexual relations is the one who
is called a rebellious wife. And they ask her why she rebelled. If she
said "I am repulsed by him and I cannot willingly have sexual relations with him"—(The Rema: and this is only when she seeks a
divorce without alimony; but if she says "Let him give me a divorce
and my alimony," we suspect that she may have cast her eyes on
another, and the law of a rebellious wife [who says] "I wish [to remain
married to] him and to cause him pain" pertains to her. [Beit Yosef in
the name of the responsa of the RaN, and so interprets Rashi in the
Talmud.])

If her husband wishes to divorce her, she receives no alimony at
all, but she may take her used garments still in existence, whether
from property which she brought to her husband [at the time of her
marriage] for which he assumed responsibility, or from the *nikhsei
melug* for which he did not assume responsibility, and she takes
nothing at all of her husband's.[53] She must remove even the shoe on
her foot and the kerchief on her head, and she returns to him anything he had given her as a gift. . . . If she rebelled against her husband in order to cause him pain, and she said "I am causing him
pain in this way because he did such-and-such to me, or because he
cursed me, or because he argued with me," etc., the Jewish court
sends [a message] to her and they say to her: "Know that if you continue in your rebellion, even [if] your alimony is one hundred *maneh*,

you will lose it." And afterwards they proclaim against her in the synagogue and study houses each day for four consecutive weeks . . . and they say: "So-and-so rebelled against her husband." After the proclamation, the Jewish court sends to her a second time [with the message]: "If you continue in your rebellion, you shall lose your alimony." And if she continued in her rebellion and did not change her mind, they attempt to persuade her. She then loses her alimony, and she receives no alimony at all, and they do not give her a divorce for twelve months, and she does not receive sustenance [from her husband] all twelve months. (. . . And there are those who say that in these times when one cannot marry two wives, we do not make her wait twelve months if [she wants a divorce and her husband] wants to divorce her [Rema].)

(. . . And there are those who say that all of this applies [only] when she gives no reasonable basis for her claim that he is repulsive to her, but if she gives a reasonable basis for her claim—for example, if she says that he does not follow a proper path [of conduct], or that he squanders money, etc.—then we judge her according to the law which the Geonim decreed [Tur, in the name of the Maharam of Rothenburg].)

And [the judgment that] the husband must return to her whatever she brought into him as a dowry is called the Judgment of the Academy [dina de-metivta]. That is, she takes as is the entire [nikhsei] tzon barzel if they are in existence and fit [to be used] for their original purpose, and if they are not fit [to be used] for their original purpose—and all the more so if they had been stolen or lost—the husband must pay their entire value, and she takes her nikhsei melug, if they are in existence, and any [property] which was derived from them, but if they have been completely used up, her husband need not pay [her their value]. (dina de-metivta of the Tur in the name of the Rif). But she takes nothing of anything her husband had given her or promised her, and even that which she seized she must return (Mordecai, Chapter "Even Though"). And they do not force him to divorce her, nor [her] to remain with him (also this is in the Tur, in a responsum of Maharam [of Rothenburg]).

And if he acted improperly by having betrothed her through trickery and deceit, they force him to divorce [her]. (Rosh, Rule 35.)

And there are those who say [that they force him] to the extent that they put [him] under the ban [of excommunication] (Tur in the name of the Maharam [of Rothenburg]). If people taught her to be rebellious or if she did thusly because of anger, argument, or in order to extract money from him, then they take from her and return to her husband even that which she seized from her (dowry) property. (*Mordecai,* Chapter "Even Though.")

There is no distinction [made] whether she seized [the property] or not, except in the case when she claims that he is repulsive [to her] and does not bring a reasonable and clear basis for her words; [in such a case only that which she seized belongs to her,] but whenever she gives a reasoned basis and there is no trickery [involved], the court will judge [the case] in accordance with what appears [reasonable] to them. (MaHaRip Ohr Zarua). And it is possible to make her take an oath to that effect [that there has been no trickery involved]. If she claims in truth, "He is repulsive to me." And so it is fitting to rule. And as long as he has not given [her] a divorce, we do not force him or apply pressure regarding her.

The *Shulhan Arukh* concludes that if a woman comes before the Jewish court and claims that her husband is repulsive to her and she wishes a divorce—but brings no reasonable basis for the claim—her husband may not be forced to divorce her. If she does bring "proof" for her claim she may take her dowry property still in existence, and if the judges feel that her claim is reasonable and legitimate they award her her complete dowry, even if she had not seized it originally. And if she insists that she can no longer live with him, and can prove that she was originally tricked into marrying him, he may be forced to give her a divorce.

Hence, it is clear that the authorities succeeding Rabbenu Tam retreated significantly from the initial position set forth by Amemar, developed by the Geonim, and confirmed by the Rashbam and Maimonides, which gave the Jewish court the authority to coerce a husband into divorcing a wife who found him repulsive. Apparently once Rabbenu Tam raised a serious objection to such an imposed divorce—and within the climate of societies wherein romantic love was a rarity and marital stability an axiom of life—few of the latter authorities would oppose his position. This is the accepted halakhic norm until this very day.

CHAPTER VII
CONCLUSION

BRIEF HISTORY TO THE PRESENT DAY

Thus far we have traced the halakhic history of the *moredet* in an attempt to understand the development of Jewish law and the forces behind its evolution, dealing particularly with the issue of a woman who tries to free herself from a marriage she finds intolerable. Despite the Biblical statement that the husband must initiate the divorce, we have seen that the Babylonian Talmud in the frame of broad powers provides for coercion by the Jewish court until the husband agrees to grant a divorce to a wife who finds him distasteful. The Jerusalem Talmud allows for a special stipulation to be written into the marriage contract in order to ensure the wife this protection. The Geonim went further, and insisted that she even receive the entire sum of the alimony provided for in her marriage contract.[1]

The early Sages of North Africa, Spain, and France, although differing in regard to her monetary compensation, upheld the right of a woman to initiate an action towards a court-imposed divorce if she so desired. In the twelfth century of the common era, the tide was dramatically turned by Rabbenu Tam, who by his interpretation influenced the overwhelming majority of subsequent halakhic decisors to deny the possibility of coercing the husband to grant his wife a divorce "merely" because she subjectively found him intolerable. With only rare exceptions, this has been the accepted halakhic opinion to the present day.

It is easy to understand why the legal position of Rabbenu Tam was accepted without significant controversy by many subsequent generations. The small, cohesive Jewish communities, generally bound together by familial ties, isolated from the surrounding Gentile society by external anti-Semitism and internal religious strength,[2] existed primarily against a backdrop of a culture that insisted upon the permanence of the marital bond and the stability of family life. Such a society would hardly rally serious opposition to a halakhah which effectively denied the woman the right to initiate divorce proceedings.

In contemporary times, however, the situation has changed radically. Our freedom of social intercourse between Jewish and Gentile society, and the consequent assimilation and intermarriage, have reached staggering proportions. A vindictive husband, or one who is unconcerned with the requirements of Jewish law, can not only deny his wife a religious divorce if he so chooses, but can also—once he has obtained a secular divorce—remarry before a justice of the peace. Thereby he forces his halakhically concerned wife to languish as an *agunah* (lit., "chained," i.e., to a husband with whom she could not formerly live) and now, due to his reluctance to arrange for a *get,* is in an inextricable situation. In most instances he can even arrange a kind of religious ceremony for his second marriage (since most Reform rabbis do not require a halakhically validated divorce), while his first wife can only depend upon an impotent Jewish court which—even if it chose to coerce the husband to divorce her—is powerless in these days to impose its law upon a recalcitrant husband who refuses to accept its authority. As a result, many Jewish women are being forced either to live out their years as *agunot,* unable to remarry within the framework of Jewish law, or to pay staggering sums of money to a husband using his halakhic power of divorce as blackmail. All too often these women choose to marry and have children with their second husbands without having secured a Jewish divorce from their first, thereby committing adultery and giving birth to children considered halakhically illegitimate. Indeed, the very situation which caused the Geonim to enact their legislation on behalf of the wife seeking a divorce—"Jewish women were becoming dependent upon the Gentiles . . . . and were satisfied with a . . . divorce not in accordance with Jewish law, from which ruin emanates"—certainly applies today. We have previously seen how the halakhic system is designed to respond to such agoniz-ing human dilemmas. What can the halakhic system do today, especially when the combination of an American legal system, a secular climate, and the relative ease with which an individual can move great distances from his original community, makes it virtual-ly impossible for a religious court to impose its will upon an intran-sigent husband? Let us summarize the various attempts which have been made in recent times to alleviate this intolerable situation.

In the early part of this century, when civil divorce was making incursions into the broad religious spectrum in France, a council of rabbis was convened to introduce a system of conditional marriage. It was their suggestion that at the time of the marriage, the bride and groom stipulate that if their marriage was terminated through civil divorce, their Jewish marriage would then be nullified retro-actively, obviating the necessity for the husband to grant a religious divorce. The halakhic precedent for such a stipulation was a decision of Rabbi Israel of Brunn (1400–1480), who concluded that a man whose brother is an apostate may stipulate at the time of his mar-riage that if he should die childless, his marriage will be nullified retroactively, thereby protecting his wife from being forever "tied" to a brother-in-law who will most likely refuse to release her via *halitzah* from levirate marriage. So we see that the concept of condi-tional marriage has a valid halakhic basis.

Rabbi Yitzhak Elhanan Spektor of Kovno, Rabbi Yehudah Lubestski of Paris,[3] and virtually all of the European luminaries of that time objected to the proposal that the council put forth. Their major argument against it was that the sexual relationship between husband and wife expresses a complete and total commitment, and it automatically rescinds any stipulation agreed upon at the time of the marriage. In the face of such serious opposition, the proposal was rejected. The rabbinic authorities similarly rejected any possibi-lity of the Jewish court's being allowed to nullify a religious mar-riage retroactively, despite the Talmudic argument that "Everyone who marries, does so by consent of the rabbinic authorities; the rab-binic authorities have the right to retroactively nullify a marriage."[4] They saw this right as being dependent upon a *unified* Jewish court, and limited to the period universally accepted as the sealing of the Talmud (ca. 500 C.E.).[5]

In 1967 Rabbi Eliezer Berkovits similarly attempted to resolve this problem by means of a conditional marriage.[6] His proposal differs from the proposal of the French council in that the stipulation involves the Jewish court as well as the secular one: The husband stipulates at the time of his marriage that if he does not acquiesce to the rabbinic court's demand to grant his wife a religious divorce, the marriage will be nullified retroactively. However, the same rabbinic opposition which befell the French plan similarly faced the Berkovits proposal.

In 1954 Professor Saul Lieberman of the Jewish Theological Seminary added a new clause to the marriage contract used by the Conservative movement. In it, the husband agreed to be bound by all decisions of the Rabbinical Assembly Beth Din in the event of a marital difficulty; he would thus be halakhically bound to grant a religious divorce if the Beth Din so ordained. In effect, Lieberman added an addendum very similar to the *ketubah* stipulation cited earlier in the Jerusalem Talmud. As far as the impotence of the rabbinic court in America is concerned, the new stipulation provides that, in the event of the husband's refusal to adhere to its ruling, "We authorize the Beth Din to impose such terms of compensation as it may see fit for failure to respond to its summons or to carry out its decisions."[7] Lieberman hoped that such a monetary stipulation could be enforced in the secular courts as well, and would therefore give renewed strength to the marriage contract and renewed power to the wife.

The Orthodox rabbinical world reacted negatively to the Lieberman proposal. They argued on halakhic grounds that any agreement to pay an indeterminate sum of money is an *asmakhta,* and that such a vague understanding is not binding in Jewish law.[8] Moreover, on legal grounds, they argued that the *ketubah,* the marriage contract, which is always read as an integral part of the Jewish marriage ceremony, is a *religious* document, and therefore the First Amendment to the Constitution of the United States precludes any power of the secular court to enforce it.[9]

Nevertheless, the New York Court of Appeals decision in *Avitzur* v. *Avitzur,* declared by a 4–3 majority, that this *ketubah* is valid and enforceable. The case involved Susan and Araz Avitzur, whose marriage in May 1966 utilized the aforementioned "Conservative" *ketubah.* They obtained a civil divorce in 1978, but although Susan summoned Araz to appear before a Beth Din and grant her a religious *get* in accordance with his initial agreement, he refused to do so.

Araz argued that the *ketubah,* as a religious document, was inadmissible as a legal contract in a civil court. The Appellate Division of the New York Supreme Court accepted Araz's contention, declaring the *ketubah* a liturgical agreement without standing in civil court (*Avitzur* v. *Avitzur,* no. 41550 [31d Dept. April 8, 1982]), only to be reversed in Susan's favor by the New York Court of Appeals.[10] That court decided that the provisions of the *ketubah* requiring the parties to enter into arbitration were merely an application of the neutral principles of contract law, entitled to the same legal status as any antenuptial agreement. Furthermore, whenever an antenuptial agreement is signed binding the parties to enter into arbitration in accordance with their accepted traditions—such as a particular Beth Din—the agreement is enforceable by the secular courts.

THE PRESENT SITUATION IN ISRAEL

As we explained above, Jewish law mandates that even in those instances where the husband can be compelled to give his wife a divorce, he must still formally present the bill of divorcement willingly. Unfortunately, therefore, there are a significant number of instances in Israel where recalcitrant husbands have chosen to spend years in jail rather than give their wives a *get.*[1] However, the Israeli Rabbinical Courts have generally been reluctant to compel a husband to give his wife a divorce merely because she claims "he is repulsive to me: without her presentation of objective reasons why she finds him so.[2] In some instances they have utilized compulsion, but only where they have some objective confirmation (*amatla*) for the wife's claim of repulsion.[3]

Thus, in general, the Israeli Rabbinical Courts have been reluctant to take advantage of the early authorities who permit compulsion when a woman claims that she finds her husband repulsive. This despite the fact that Rabbi Chaim Palaggi, a noted Talmudic authority of mid-nineteenth century Izmir, at the conclusion of his Responsa, *Ha-Hayyim Veha-Shalom*,[4] notes that if a couple is separated for eighteen months and there appears no chance of reconciliation, the Rabbinical Court must force the husband to grant his wife a *get*. Rabbi Eliezer Waldenberg, in his *Ziz Eliezer*,[5] argues that even with a slight hint or taint of confirmation, "the Court must compel the husband to grant his wife a divorce if she claims that he is distasteful to her." Rabbi Yitzhak Halevy Herzog, a former chief rabbi of Israel, likewise maintains that it is proper for the Rabbinical Court to exact compulsion "for the sake of enabling Jewish women" to be able to remarry.[6] The renowned Hazon Ish, in his commentaries on *Even Ha-Ezer*,[7] suggests in a specific instance that it is possible to rely on those authorities who allow compulsion when a woman finds her husband is repulsive. And Rabbi Ovadiah Yosef cites the decision of the former Chief Rabbi of Jerusalem, Rabbi Zvi Pesach Frank, that since in Yemen the decisions of Maimonides were authoritative, it is permissible to coerce a *get* when a woman who was originally from Yemen claims that she finds her husband repulsive.[8] Hence, אית דין ולית דיין, *it din ve-let dayyan,* the law exists, but the judges are often wanting.

A PROPOSED SOLUTION

As noted, proposed solutions in the form of a clause added to the *ketubah* have run afoul of the non-enforcibility of penalty clauses by reason of *asmakhta*. An obligation must be considered absolutely binding by the contracting parties, so that it is virtually certain that the clause will be applied at some time. Since the parties to a contract assume that the penalty will not be applied, such clauses are invalid. Moreover, there is a substantial body of opinion which holds that the threat of financial reprisals to induce the husband to issue a *get* is sufficient to make the *get* invalid as a coerced divorce.

Rabbi J. David Bleich has proposed a prenuptial agreement (see n.10 above) which is based on a concept far removed from that of penalty clauses; rather, it proceeds from the husband's freely assumed obligation to support his wife. The civil dissolution of a marriage in the eyes of the civil authorities does not affect this obligation. Rabbi Bleich suggests that a prenuptial agreement be made by which the husband obligates himself to provide more than the minimal standard of maintenance and higher than any likely alimony. This obligation would be held in abeyance by agreement of the wife during the marriage, and cancelled at its end upon issuance of a *get* or the husband's taking concrete steps to end the marriage.

Rabbi Bleich's proposed prenuptial agreement follows.*

> May good fortune sprout forth and ascend to the greatest heights even as a well-watered garden. These are the words of the covenant and the provisions which were spoken and stipulated between the two parties at the time of the nuptials on the _____ day of the month of _____ in the year _____ in the city of _____; to wit:
>
> Between _____ and his son, the groom _____, the party of the first part; and _____ and his daughter, the bride, _____, the party of the second part.
>
> Firstly, _____ wedded and married _____ by means of a wedding ring and caused her to be brought under a nuptial canopy in accordance with the law of Moses and Israel, and she accepted the wedding ring from him.
>
> _____ provided his son with dignified clothing for the Sabbath, festivals, and weekdays in a proper manner and in accordance with his status, and presented his son with marriage gifts in accordance with his status.
>
> _____ provided his daughter, the bride, with dignified clothing for the Sabbath, festivals, and weekdays, clothing, kerchiefs, marriage gifts and furnished bed, all in accordance with his status.
>
> Henceforth, the aforementioned couple will comport themselves with love and affection and will neither alienate nor conceal nor lock away, neither he from her nor she from him, any property whatever,

---

* The appendix contains a similar suggestion by the late chief rabbi of Jerusalem, Rabbi Bezalel Zolty, as embodied in a *responsum* to Rabbi Abner Weiss, who acted as chairman of the special Commission on Agunot of the Rabbinical Council of America. It was kindly provided by Rabbi Weiss and is reproduced with the permission of Rabbi Zolty's widow.

but they shall both equally exercise jurisdiction over their property.

The aforementioned groom, _____, will work, honor, support, and maintain the bride in accordance with universal custom so long as she shares his board, and at any time that she does not share his board, may it be for any reason whatsoever, the groom obligated himself that he will thereupon immediately give his wife the sum of 200 dollars to spend for food, clothing, and domicile and will give her a like sum every single day throughout the period during which she does not share his board from the time a judgment is issued by a Beth Din declaring that she is prevented from marrying in accordance with the law of Moses and Israel because of him [i.e., because of the husband's feasance or nonfeasance]. And from this day and forevermore it is the prerogative of the aforementioned bride either to share her husband's board or to receive from him the aforementioned sum to spend for food, clothing, and domicile in accordance with her desire. If, Heaven forfend, there be any dispute between them, whether with regard to payment of maintenance, whether with regard to any marital matter, or whether with regard to custody and support of their issue, they will then present their suit before an established Beth Din composed of competent judges in their city or community, and if there is no established Beth Din composed of three qualified judges, one judge designated by each party and a third judge chosen by the two judges designated by the parties, within fourteen days after the application of either of the parties. Any quarrel or controversy shall be settled in accordance with their decree, and the award of said Beth Din may be entered as a judgment in a court of competent jurisdiction.

After a settlement is reached and the wife _____ returns to her husband's home, she shall return any balance of the funds received from her husband for purposes of maintenance, clothing, and domicile which remain in her possession as well as her clothing and jewelry, to their original site.

All of the foregoing in the presence of us, the undersigned witnesses through conveyance of a *sudar* (kerchief) and in the most efficacious manner, not in the manner of an *asmakhta* and not in the manner of a mere documentary form. We have accepted conveyance in the form of a vessel halakhically fit for purposes of conveyance from each of the aforementioned parties on behalf of the other party with regard to all which is written and stated, and Everything is Valid and Confirmed.

_____ (witness)
_____ (witness)

And we also have affixed our signatures in order that our signatures may attest even as a hundred competent and trustworthy witnesses to all which is written and stated above.

_____ (Groom)
_____ (Bride)

Hence we have seen how Jewish law has endeavored to protect the rights of the woman and to provide her with the means of disengaging herself from an intolerable marriage with personal and financial dignity. The Geonim of Babylonia and the earlier authorities of Ashkenaz and Sefarad agreed, especially in a climate of assimilation and apostasy, to the necessity of enforcing a divorce when the wife claims that she finds her husband distasteful. In our own times there is certainly sufficient reason to invoke halakhic precedent and provide our women with the same legal recourse. The sad truth is that many women are remarrying and even bearing children with their second husband without having received a religious divorce because of their first husband's intransigence. The sad truth is that many other women are being doomed to loneliness and isolation because they will not rebel against rabbinic authority. The sad truth is that the entire structure of Jewish law is being charged with rigidity and insensitivity because of its seeming inability to find an acceptable solution to the plight of these women. Indeed, whenever a solution has been offered, legal objections have caused it to be set aside. And yet Amemar found a solution; the rabbis of the Jerusalem Talmud found a solution; Maimonides found a solution; the sages of our generation dare do no less. The legal precedent exists; the courageous legalists must make their voices heard and their position accepted. "May the Almighty grant courage to His nation; may the Almighty bless His people with peace."

APPENDIX

HaRav Bezalel Zolty, z.t.l., the former chief rabbi of Jerusalem, accepted the idea that a prenuptial contract can be designed to coerce the husband to give his wife a *get* at the behest of a Jewish court. Below is his *responsum*.

23 Tishri 5743

First, I must ask your[1] pardon for not responding immediately in [this] serious matter of rectifying the situation of women who are unable to remarry [because, though living apart, their husbands refuse to grant them a divorce according to Jewish law]. This issue did not slip my mind at all, but my answer has been constantly delayed by the need to decide practical halakhic questions [in specific cases, rather than theoretical] matters.

But now I have taken the time to consider the matter and record my suggestion.

As I have already mentioned to you, the simplest solution is that at the time of the marriage the husband should undertake to make provisions for [his wife]'s support, [when] there has been a civil separation or divorce, and she cannot remarry because of [his refusal to grant a divorce] (*Ketubot* 97b, *Baba Metziah* 12b). [He must pay] a sum of $2,000 a week until he grants [his wife] a divorce. However, the husband would have the right to bring the case before an authoritative rabbinic court in order to relieve himself of this obligation, in whole or in part. (This will accomplish the following: we will have forced the husband to appear before a rabbinical court to request aid, and the court will then be able to pressure or persuade him to grant a proper divorce.)

Now, this obligation applies even when [the wife] works and earns her own keep, since Rashi on BT *Ketubot* 97b writes "[as for one who has been given a divorce of doubtful validity,][2] even though a betrothed [maiden cannot claim] sustenance [from her husband-to-be], when she is prevented from marrying by him, he is nonetheless obligated to provide her with sustenance. See *Shitah Mequbetzet* [in BT *Ketubot* (142b) s.v. *ve-zeh leshon ha-Rosh*, "as to one who has been given a divorce whose validity is in doubt, Rashi has explained [that this rule applies even to] one who is [only] betrothed, etc., and some [authorities] question how it is possible to explain this as referring to a betrothed [maiden], since even when [the betrothed girl] is not divorced [i.e., the betrothal is still in effect], she has no [claim to] sustenance."

[Rosh continues:] "It seems to me that there is no difficulty, since [inasmuch as] she is in a state [in which her divorce is of doubtful validity, and] she is bound to him and cannot marry someone else, he is [therefore] obligated [to provide her] sustenance, and there is no difference [in this regard] whether [she is] betrothed or she has been married. It is equivalent to a case in which the date set for a marriage has arrived and [the couple has] not married, [where the groom-to-be must provide his betrothed with support]." The explanation of this is as follows: in a case of divorce of doubtful validity, the husband is obligated to provide [his wife's] sustenance, *not* because he is assumed liable in a case of doubt, and he is obligated to support her because of her status as a woman married [to him]. Rather, this is a new obligation to support [her] because she is bound to him, and therefore [this applies] to a betrothed woman as well, even though he had never been obligated to support her before; nevertheless, in a case of doubtful divorce he is obligated to provide her support.

This may be inferred from the Ramban's words in *Hilkhot Gerushin* 4:30: "A husband who sent his wife a divorce is obligated to provide her sustenance [along with] every [other] stipulation in her *ketubah* until the divorce document reaches her hand, etc." And in the *Magid Mishneh* on the same text (and so similarly in the *Kesef Mishneh, Hilkhot Ishut* 18) it is explained: "It is clear that even in a case where the validity of the divorce is in doubt, the husband is obligated to provide her sustenance as long as he lives, etc. We may infer from this that she does not have [the right to claim payment] of the other stipulations of her *ketubah,* since her divorce is of doubtful validity, etc. Nevertheless, from what our master writes here it seems that [the husband] is not obligated [to pay these other stipulations], for if this were not so, he should have stated [that] this [applies] even in a case where the divorce is of doubtful validity (where she does not have the right [to claim payment of the] other stipulations of the *ketubah*), and this is the preferable view. The husband cannot be obligated except with clear proof, etc." [We are entitled to ask] why the provision of sustenance is different from the payment of other stipulations of the *ketubah.* [After all,] is it not the Rambam's opinion (*Hilkhot Ishut* 12:4, 17:19 and the *Magid Mishneh ad loc.*) that sustenance is also a stipulation of the *ketubah?* Thus, it seems clear that the obligation of providing sustenance in a case where the divorce is of doubtful validity does not proceed from [the woman's status] as a wife, but is a new obligation [which issues from the fact] she is prevented from remarrying by [his failure to give her a valid divorce], and so [the Rabbis obligated him to] provide her sustenance, but [did not obligate him to pay] of other stipulations of the *ketubah.*

This may be derived from the words of the Ramban, for in *Hilkhot Ishut* 18:25 he writes: "The woman whose divorce is of doubtful validity, etc. but has nonetheless [the right to demand] sustenance during the life of her husband, until she is granted a valid divorce." [Note] that he wrote "she has" [the right to demand] sustenance, while in *Hilkhot Gerushin* 6:30 (mentioned above) he wrote "he is obligated [to provide] her sustenance." That is to say, this case of a divorce of doubtful validity [does not involve a question of the woman's status] as a wife, but *she has* [the right to demand] sustenance until she is [validly] divorced [beyond doubt], and this is a new obligation [placed on the husband] because she is bound to him.

Accordingly, it seems that he has no right to her earnings [which is ordinarily one of the husband's prerogatives], even if he does provide her sustenance, since his obligation does not arise from her status as a married woman, but is a new obligation to provide [her] sustenance because she is prevented [from remarrying] by him. Note that the Rosh (cited in the aforementioned *Shitah Mequbetzet*) writes: "It is equivalent to a case in which the date set for a marriage has arrived and they have not married, [where he must provide his betrothed with suppport]." In this regard, there is a disagreement among the Rishonim as to whether [the husband] has a right to her earnings: the *Shitah Mequbetzet* (BT *Ketubot* 107b s.v. *ve'i*) cites [an opinion] in the name of Ra'ah that in regard to a betrothed woman, [the prospective husband] has no right to her earnings until she is married to him, but nevertheless he must provide her sustenance if the date of the marriage has arrived and they have not married. However, in *Hiddushei Ritva* on BT *Ketubot* 57a, [the author] writes: "she may support herself [from his property] that is to say, she may eat [of his property] and he is obligated to provide her sustenance. That applies to her clothing and sustenance, just as though she had been married to him,[3] and he too has a right to [whatever inheritance she receives from her family] and her earnings [just as though they were married]." See *Or Same'ah* (*Hilkhot Ishut* 10:12), where doubt is expressed about this matter.

It appears that even according to the Ritva, when the date for the marriage arrives and they have not married, he is obligated to provide her sustenance, her earnings and [whatever inheritance she receives from her family] are his. That is, he writes, "just as though she had been married to him," i.e., she is bound by the laws [pertaining to] a married woman, and therefore he writes [that the husband] is obligated to pay all the stipulations of the *ketubah* and as a result he acquires the rights to her earnings and [whatever inheritance she receives from her family], acccording to the rules governing a married woman. But in the case of a woman whose divorce is of doubtful validity, regarding which the *Magid Mishneh* writes, as noted above, [that] the Rambam holds that she has no right [to claim payment of] all the stipulations of the *ketubah,* but only sustenance, her status is not that of a married woman and thus he has no right to her earnings and [whatever inheritance she receives from her family].

However, the *Shitah Mequbetzet* (BT *Bava Metzi'ah* 12b s.v. *uleinyan pesaq*) [writes]: "The Remakh writes that the [articles] found by a woman whose divorce is of doubtful validity belong to her, but even so [her husband] is obligated [to provide] her sustenance. And he is also obligated [to fulfill] all the monetary stipulations of her *ketubah*. If she dies, because of the doubt [as to whether she really was validly divorced], [the presumed husband] inherits all [her property] in his possession, [but] it is likely [*garov lomar*] that if she is taken captive he is not required to ransom her since there is the question of whether she is divorced from him, [and] the clause "I will take you back as a wife" does not apply. Likewise, he does not acquire [the usufruct of the property he manages during the life of the marriage], since he has given her a divorce [even though it is of doubtful validity]. And it may be that since her divorce is not certainly valid, she is still [considered] his wife in every respect [as pertains to monetary matters] aside from [the matter of his rights regarding [any inheritance she receives from her family]."

It is clear from his words that a woman whose divorce is of doubtful validity is [considered to have the status of] a married woman, and [her husband] is obligated [to provide] her with all the monetary stipulations of the *ketubah*; if she dies, because of the doubt he inherits all [her property] in his possession. The reason [for this] is [that] since her divorce is not certainly valid, she is still his wife in every respect [in regard to monetary matters].

[We may] also infer from the words of Raavad in his critique of the Rif on BT *Ketubot* 63a, who cites the Yerushalmi [to the effect] that he is obligated to provide her sustenance even before he gives her a *ketubah,* and he writes there, *inter alia,* "therefore [even though] he has not given her a *ketubah,* they have a legal connection, he has some claim on her, i.e., her earnings in exchange for [his obligation] to [provide] her sustenance, etc." It seems that the Raavad is consistent in his opinion, since he writes *ad Hilkhot Nahalot* 1:9, that in the case of a woman whose divorce is of doubtful validity, her husband inherits her [estate], and so too the aforementioned Ramakh, that because of the doubt he inherits all [her property] in his possession, that is, she is [considered as] his wife in regard to all [monetary] respects [of the marriage]. The Raavad writes that this too is according to the opinion of the Yerushalmi: [even though] he has not yet given her her *ketubah,* she is considered his wife in every respect in regard to monetary matters.

However, in should be noted that the Rambam writes in *Hilkhot Nahalot* 1:9 that the husband does not inherit [the estate of his] wife, whose divorce is of doubtful validity, and she has no [right to claim payment] of any stipulation of her *ketubah,* as he writes in the aforementioned *Hilkhot Gerushin* [6:]30, and the fact that he is obligated [to provide] her sustenance is a new obligation [which devolves upon him] because she is prevented from remarrying because of him. Thus, we can again say that he has no claims on her, as explained.

Now, the essential basis of the obligation of sustenance is because she is prevented from marrying because of him. [But] this applies not only to [a woman] whose divorce is of doubtful validity, but [also] to [a woman] who is his wife beyond doubt; so long as she is prevented from marrying because of him, she [has the right to claim] sustenance. See *Derush Ve-Hiddush* of R. Akiva Eger ("Ketavim," 91b), who cites the Magen Avraham [to the effect] that if she had an extramarital affair, [in the case where the husband] is not obligated to divorce her, he is obligated to provide her with food and clothing, and R. Akiva Eger comments that "in truth, I cannot understand the words of the Magen Avraham, since she is forbidden to him because of her deeds, there is no obligation of sustenance, see BTT *Yebamot.*"

Indeed, it seems that the Magen Avraham's intent is that since the husband does not want to divorce her, she is [thereby] prevented from remarrying because of him, [and] therefore this obligation constitutes a new obligation of sustenance and [does not come into effect] because of [her status] as a married woman, but because she is [thereby] prevented from remarrying because of him. Therefore, this obligation exists even when her own deeds have caused [the break-down of the marriage], since after all he has the right to divorce her. And as to the statement in BT *Yebamot* 85a in regard to forbidden marriages, [that she does not have complete rights over her] sustenance because she may resist [the husband's wish to divorce her in a case] where the husband is prepared to divorce her and she is unwilling—[this clearly refers to] sustenance which is provided because she is married. In this case, she is not prevented from remarrying by him, and thus she has no claim to sustenance, since she may resist him.

And now to the situation at hand. It would seem that when they have been separated according to civil law, and the husband refuses to grant her a divorce, if at the time of marriage he is required to pay her a designated sum for sustenance—including clothing and a place to live—this obligation is valid [according to Halakhah], since she is prevented from remarrying by him. And even when her own deeds have caused [this separation], [as when] she engaged in an extramarital affair, the Magen Avraham holds that he is obligated [to provide her] with food and clothing.

But according to the opinions of the aforementioned Rishon-im, it would seem that even when she is prevented from remarrying because of him, if he provides her with sustenance, he has a right to her earnings, [and] so the husband can demand [to collect] her earn-ings when she works and earns her own living, and he can claim that he allows her to keep her earnings in exchange [for being relieved of his obligation to provide] her sustenance.

However, it seems that the *Helqat Mehoqeq* (*Even Ha-Ezer* 102) cites [an opinion] in the name of the Bah, that the customary prac-tice in these provinces is not to deprive the woman of any involun-tary preference she receives. And since [the rights to] earnings are considered an involuntary advantage, the husband can require that [we proceed] according to the customary practice of these areas, [and] he has no claim on her earnings, which are an involuntary preference.

In addition, [the decision has been codified] in *Shulhan Arukh*

(*Even Ha-Ezer* 69:6) [that if] the woman stipulates that the husband may not claim any [of his usual] monetary rights [in regard to her property], the stipulation is valid. It is thus possible to make a stipulation, before the marriage [takes place], that in the case of a civil separation [the husband] would have no claim on anything he usually has a claim to, that is, not to her earnings, nor the usufruct of her *nikhsei melug,* nor to her estate, as explained in *Shulhan Arukh,* (*Even Ha-Ezer* 69:7)—nevertheless, he is obligated [to provide] her sustenance as is proper, for she is prevented from remarrying because of him.

Now, it seems to me that this proposal [has certain advantages over] the one you sent, since [the latter] runs counter to the opinion of the Rema (*Shulhan Arukh, Even Ha-Ezer* 134:4). On the other hand, our proposal would be according to Halakhah, as noted. I have proposed that the husband is obligated [to pay] $2,000 a week for sustenance, including food and clothing. Understandably, [the precise amount] would depend on the husband's monetary situation, in accordance with the rule that the wife's social and economic status rises with that of her husband, but does not decline [with it]. However, there is still an area of doubt regarding whether this rule of "rising but not declining" applies to the provision of sustenance to one who is prevented from remarrying by her husband, since it is a new obligation, as explained above. The rule of "rising but not declining" may apply only in a case where the obligation of sustenance arises from [the wife's] status as a married woman, but, nevertheless, the husband may be obligated to provide sustenance according to his socio-economic status, and this applies also in the case of one who is prevented from remarrying by her husband.

Moreover, according to our proposal, the husband may apply to an authorized rabbinic court in order to relieve himself entirely or in part from the amount [set] for sustenance.

I want to emphasize that our proposal is only an *obiter dictum,* as it were, and not my [final] halakhic opinion in regard to this matter. Expression of a halakhic opinion in this case is the prerogative of the Torah authorities in America who are involved with practical halakhic decision-making [for American Jews], and in particular is in the province of my esteemed colleague, the authority *par excellence* of the American continent, Maran R. Moshe Feinstein, shlita, and as he decides so shall it be.

HaRav Yaakov Bezalel Zolty
Chief Rabbi and Head of
Religious Courts, Jerusalem

It would seem to me that a proposal based on the Lieberman addendum, taking into account the legal and halakhic issues involved, and based upon Rav Zolty's *responsum,* may well point to a solution to the problem both in the Diaspora and in Israel.

1. Literally, "his." As is common in rabbinic letters, the recipient is always addressed in the third person. This has been changed to conform to general American usage.

2. Literally, "divorced and not divorced."

3. Literally, "she had entered [under] the *huppah.*"

תשובת הרב יעקב בצלאל ז'ולטי זצ"ל
מכ"ז תשרי תשמ"ז

ראשית עלי לבקש את סליחתו שלא כתבתי לו מיד בענין החמור של תקנת
עגונות, לא שכחתי את הדבר כלל, אלא מרוב טרדות להורות הלכה למעשה בשאלות
המופיעות יום יום, נדחה תשובתי זו מיום ליום.

אך כעת לקחתי לי זמן לעיין בדבר ולהעלות על הכתב את הצעתי בנדון זה.

כפי שכבר אמרתי לכת"ר שליט"א, שהדרך הפשוטה ביותר היא, שהבעל
יתחייב בשעת הנשואין, שבמקרא שיהא פירוד אזרחי ביניהם, הוא מתחייב לתת לה
מזונות מדין מעוכבת להנשא מחמתו, (כתובות צ"ז ע"ב ב"מ י"ב ע"ב) סכום מזונות
של אלפיים דולר לשבוע עד שיתן לה ג"פ. אולם הבעל יהא זכאי לפנות לבי"ד רבני
מוסמך לפטור אותו מחיוב זה בכולו, או במקצתו. (על ידי כך נרויח שהבעל יבוא
לביה"ד לבקש סעד, ואז ביה"ד יכול ללחוץ עליו או להשפיע עליו שיתן גט כדין).

והנה התחייבות זו היא כדין גם במקרה שהיא עובדת ומרויחה לפרנסתה, דהרי
רש"י בכתובות צ"ז ע"ב כתב, מגורשת ואינה מגורשת "ומן הארוסין" וכו', ואע"פ
שארוסה אין לה מזונות, אבל כשהיא מעוכבת מחמתו להנשא, הוא כן חייב לה
מזונות. ועיי' בשיטה מקובצת שם (קמ"ב ע"ב) ד"ה וז"ל הרא"ש, מגורשת ואינה
מגורשת פרש"י מן הארוסין וכו', ויש מקשים היכי מצי לפרש מן הארוסין, הא
אפילו כשאינה גרושה, ארוסה לית לה מזוני.

ונראה לי דלא קשה דכיון דהיא מגורשת ואינה מגורשת ואגידא ביה ולא מציא
לאנסובי לעלמא חייב במזונותיה, ואין חילוק בין מן הארוסין בין מן הנשואין, הוי
כמו הגיע זמן ולא נשאו, ע"כ. ובאור דבריו, דהא דמגורשת ואינה מגורשת בעלה
חייב במזונותיה, זה לא מפני שבספק הוא עומד בחזקת חיוב, והוא חייב במזונותיה
מתורת נשואה, אלא שהוא חיוב חדש של מזונות משום שהיא אגידא ביה, ולכן גם
בארוסה אע"פ שמעולם לא חייב לה מזונות, מ"מ בספק מגורשת הוא חייב
במזונותיה.

וכן נראה מדברי הרמב"ם בפ"ו מה' גרושין ה"ל, "הבעל ששלח גט לאשתו הרי
הוא חייב במזונותיה ובכל תנאי כתובה עד שיגיע הגט לידה". ובמ"מ שם, "וכן
מתבאר מכ"מ פי"ח מה' אישות נתבאר שאפילו בספק מגורשת הבעל חייב
במזונותיה בחייו וכו', ומשמע שאין לה שאר תנאי כתובה כיון שהיא ספק מגורשת

וכו', מ"מ ממ"ש כאן רבינו נראה שאינו חייב, שאם לא כן היה לו להשמיענו אפילו
בספק מגורשת (שיש לה שאר תנאי כתובה) וכן עיקר שאין לחייב את הבעל אלא
בראיה ברורה וכו'", ע"כ. ולכאורה מאי שנא מזונות משאר תנאי הכתובה, והלא
לדעת הרמב"ם בפי"ב מה' אישות ה"ד, ובפי"ז שם הי"ט ובמ"מ שם, שגם מזונות
הם תנאי כתובה, אלא מוכח שחיוב מזונות בספק מגורשת זה לא מתורת נשואה, אלא
שהוא חיוב חדש משום שהיא מעוכבת מחמתו, א"כ תקנו לה רק מזונות, ולא שאר
תנאי כתובה.

וזה מדויק בדברי הרמב"ם, שהרי בפי"ח מה' אישות הכ"ה כתב, האשה שהיה
לה ספק גרושין וכו', אבל בחיי בעלה יש לה מזונות עד שתתגרש גרושין גמורים.
הרי כתב יש "לה" מזונות, ובה' גרושין פ"ו ה"ל הנ"ל כתב "חייב" במזונותיה,
והיינו שבספק מגורשת זה לא חיוב מזונות מתורת נשואה, אלא שיש "לה" מזונות
עד שתתגרש, וזה חיוב חדש משום שאגידא ביה.

ולפי זה נראה שאין לו זכות במעשה ידיה, גם אם נותן לה מזונות, כיון שאין
חיובו מתורת נשואה, אלא שהוא חיוב מחודש של מזונות שהיא מעוכבת
מחמתו. והנה הרא"ש שהביא הש"מ הנ"ל כתב, "והוי כמו הגיע זמן ולא נשאו".
ובזה הלא יש מחלוקת הראשונים אם מעשה ידיה שלו, הש"מ כתובות ק"ז ע"ב ד"ה
ואי, הביא בשם הרא"ה דבארוסה אין מע"י שלו עד שתנשא לו, ואעפ"כ חייב
במזונותיה כשהגיע זמן ולא נשאו. אולם בחדושי הריטב"א כתובות נ"ז ע"א כתב
וז"ל, אוכלת משלו, פרוש שאוכלת וחייב במזונותיה, וה"ה בכסותה ופרנסה כאלו
נכנסה לחופה, והוא ג"כ זוכה במציאתה ומעשה ידיה ע"כ. ועיי' אור שמח פ"י מה'
אישות הי"ט שמסתפק בזה, עיי"ש.

ונראה שאפילו לדעת הריטב"א בהגיע זמן ולא נישאו שחייב במזונותיה,
מעש"י. ומציאתה שלו. היינו, כמש"כ שהיא כאלו "נכנסה לחופה" כלומר שיש לה
דין נשואה, ולכן כתב שחייב בכל תנאי כתובה וממילא הוא זוכה במעש"י ומציאתה
כדין נשואה. אבל בספק מגורשת שכתב המ"מ הנ"ל בדעת הרמב"ם שאין לה כל
תנאי כתובה, אלא רק מזונות, א"כ אין דינה כנשואה וממילא אין לו זכות במעש"י
ומציאתה.

אולם הש"מ ב"מ י"ב ע"ב ד"ה ולענין פסק וז"ל, כתב הרמ"ך מציאת אשתו
שהיא מגורשת ואינה מגורשת הרי היא שלה ואעפ"כ הוא חייב במזונותיה, וה"ה
שחייב בכל תנאי ממון של כתובה, ואם מתה יורשה מכל מה שתחת ידו מספק, וקרוב
לומר שאם נָשְׁבֵּית אינו חייב לפדותה כיון שהיא בספק מגורשת אין אני קורא בה
ואהדרינך לך לאינתו. וה"ה שאינו אוכל פירות כיון שנתן לה גט.

ואפשר לומר כיון שאינה מגורשת ודאי, עדיין אשתו היא לכל דבר, חוץ מזכות
מציאתה, ע"כ.

הרי מבואר בדבריו שספק מגורשת היא כנשואה, והוא חייב לה בכל תנאי ממון

של כתובה, ואם מתה יורשה מכל מה שתחת ידו מספק, והטעם הוא, כיון שאינה
מגורשת ודאי, עדיין היא אשתו לכל דבר.

וכן משמע מדברי הראב"ד בהשגתו על הרי"ף כתובות פרק שני דייני גזירות
(ס"ג ע"א), שהביא את דברי הירושלמי שגם לפני שנתן לה כתובה הוא חייב
במזונותיה, וכתב שם בתו"ד וז"ל, אלמא כל זמן שלא נתן לה כתובתה שייכא ביה,
ואית ליה זכייה עילויה, ומאי ניהו מעשה ידיה תחת מזונותיה וכו', עיי"ש. ונראה
דהראב"ד לטעמיה שכתב בפ"א מה' נחלות ה"ט, שבספק מגורשת בעלה יורשה,
וכ"ה בדברי הרמ"ך הנ"ל, דבספק מגורשת בעלה יורשה מכל מה שתחת ידו מספק,
והיינו כאשתו לכל דבר, והראב"ד כתב זה גם לשיטת הירושלמי דכל עוד שלא נתן
לה כתובתה, הרי היא לגבי ממונות, כאשתו לכל דבר.

אולם הרמב"ם הרי כתב בה' נחלות פ"א ה"ט, דבספק מגורשת אין הבעל
יורשה, וכן אין לה כל תנאי כתובה כמש"כ בפ"ו מה' גרושין ה"ל הנ"ל, והא דחייב
במזונותיה, זהו חיוב מחודש משום שהיא מעוכבת מחמתו, א"כ שוב אפשר לומר
שאין לו זכות במעשה ידיה, וכמש"נ.

והנה יסוד החיוב של מזונות משום שהיא מעוכבת להנשא מחמתו, זה לא נאמר
רק בספק מגורשת, אלא אפילו באשתו גמורה, כל עוד שהיא מעוכבת מחמתו להנשא
יש לה מזונות. ועיי' בדרוש וחדוש הגרע"א בחלק הכתבים (צ"א ע"ב), שהביא בשם
המג"א, דבזינתה אם אין מחוייב לגרשה, הוא חייב ליתן לה שאר וכסות. והעיר על
זה הגרע"א וז"ל, "אבל באמת אין מובנים לי דברי המג"א דכיון דאסורה לו מחמת
מעשיה ליכא חיוב מזונות, עיי' יבמות פרק יש מותרות פ"ה ע"א', ע"כ.

אכן כונת המג"א היא, דכיון שהבעל אינו רוצה לגרשה, א"כ היא מעוכבת
מחמתו, וזה חיוב מזונות מחודש של מתורת נשואה, אלא משום שהיא מעוכבת
מחמתו, א"כ חיוב זה ישנו גם כשמעשיה גרמו לה, שהרי בידו לגרשה. והא דאמרו
ביבמות פ"ה ע"א בנשואי איסור, מזוני דלמא תיעכב גביה לית לה, היינו מזונות
מתורת נשואה, שהיא לא רוצה להתגרש, והבעל מוכן לגרשה, א"כ היא לא מעוכבת
מחמתו, ולכן אין לה מזונות דלמא תעכב גביה.

מעתב בנדון דידן, לכאורה כשקיים פירוד אזרחי ביניהם, והבעל מסרב לתת לה
גט, אם התחייב בשעת הנשואין לשלם לה סכום מסויים למזונות, וזה כולל כסות
ומדור, הרי ההתחייבות היא כדין, שהרי היא מעוכבת להנשא מחמתו. וגם כשמעשיה
גרמו לה שזינתה תחתיו, הרי דעת המג"א היא שחייב בשאר וכסות.

אלא שלכאורה לשיטת הראשונים הנ"ל, שגם במעוכבת להנשא מחמתו, אם
הוא נותן לה מזונות, יש לו זכות במעשה ידיה, א"כ הבעל יכול לדרוש את מעש"י,
כשהיא עובדת ומרויחה לפרנסתה, והוא יכול לטעון שנותן לה את מעש"י עבור
המזונות.

אמנם נראה דהביא החלקת מחוקק אה"ע סי' סק"ב בשם הב"ח, שכן נוהגים

במדינות אלו שלא להוציא מיד האשה שום העדפה שעל ידי הדחק. והלא כל מעשה ידיה של אשה במזונינו, הוא העדפה ע"י הדחק, א"כ הבעל יכול להתחייב לנהוג כמנהג המדינות, שאין לו זכות במע"י שהוא העדפה ע"י הדחק.

ועוד, דנפסק בשו"ע אה"ע סי' ס"ט סעיף ו', התנית האשה שלא יזכה הבעל באחד מהדברים שהוא זוכה בהם התנאי קיים. א"כ אפשר להתנות לפני הנישואין שבמקרה של פרוד אזרחי ביניהם, אין לו כל זכות באחד מן הדברים שהוא זוכה בהם, דהיינו לא במע"י, ולא בפירות נכסי מלוג שלה, ולא בירושתה, כמבואר שם בשו"ע אה"ע סי' ס"ט סעיף ז', ומ"מ הוא חייב במזונותיה כדין, שהרי היא מעוכבת להנשא מחמתו.

והנה הצעה זו, היא לדעתי יותר טובה מהצעה שהביא כת"ר שליט"א. שהרי הצעתו היא בנגוד לדברי הרמ"א בשו"ע אה"ע סי' קל"ד סעיף ד'. אולם הצעתנו יכולה להיות הכל כדין כאמור.

ומה שהצעתי שהבעל יתחייב אלפיים דולר לשבוע למזונותיה, שזה כולל כסות ומדור. נ?ב?ך שזה תלוי במעמדו הכספי של הבעל, שהרי במזונות יש כלל שהיא עולה עמו, אלא שיש להסתפק אם בחיוב מזונות של מעוכבת להנשא מחמתו, שהוא חייב מחדש של מזונות כנ"ל, אם נאמר הכלל של היא עולה עמו, שהרי אפשר לומר שזה נאמר רק בחיוב מזונות מתורת נשואה, אבל מ"מ הבעל יכול להתחייב לה מזונות לפי מעמדו, וזה כדין גם אם חיוב המזונות הוא מדין מעוכבת להנשא מחמתו.

ועוד יותר מזה, הלא לפי הצעתנו, הבעל יוכל להגיש תביעה בבי"ד רבני המוסמך לכך, לפטור אותו לגמרי מסכום המזונות, או ממקצתו.

ברצוני לציין שהצעתנו הנ"ל, היא רק הצעה גרידא, ולא חוות דעת הלכתי בנדון זה, כי זה נתון לגדולי התורה באמריקה הנוגע להם להלכה ולמעשה, וביחוד זה נתון לדעת ידידי גאון ישראל ותפארתו מריה דאתרא של יבשת אמריקה, הגאון האדיר מרן ר' משה פיינשטיין שליט"א, וכאשר יגזור הוא כן יקום.

NOTES

CHAPTER I

1. MKet 5:7. The edition of Chanokh Albeck, *Shishah Sidrei Mishnah,* (Jerusalem and Tel Aviv, 1958), is the source for all Mishnaic texts. Variant readings will be discussed when relevant.

2. MKet 1:2.

3. Roman and Jewish currency corresponded as follows:

1 as (bronze) = 24 איסר or 192 פרוטה.
1 dupondus (silver) = 6 מעה or 12 פונדיון.
1 denarius (silver) = 1 דינר.

The Encyclopedia Americana notes that the as, in 90–88 B.C.E., was worth about $0.008 in 1932 dollars. A Roman denarius was worth about 10 as, as opposed to the Jewish currency breakdown noted above. Estimates of the value of a *perutah,* in current halakhic usage, range from about $0.10 to $1.00 (but see Daniel Sperber, *Roman Palestine 200–400: Money and Prices* [Ramat Gan, 1974], p. 29). Thus, a fine of seven *dinarim* per week would in modern terms amount to about $134 per week at the very least—a not inconsiderable sum. The quinarius was worth half a denarius (Jastrow, s.v. *tarpik*); thus R. Yehudah's fines are half the value of those set by the anonymous mishnah.

4. It is quite possible that the mishnah before us is a composite of a number of layers, the earliest of which may have read:

המורדת על בעלה פוחתין לה מכתובתה שבעה בשבת וכן המורד על אשתו מוסיפין על כתובתה שלשה בשבת.

> If a wife rebels against her husband, the [lump-sum] alimony of her marriage contract is to be reduced each week by seven. Similarly, if a husband rebels against his wife, an addition of three a week is to be made to her marriage contract.

In a later generation, two additional disputes arose based upon this early text: (the anonymous opinion of the mishnah (usually identified as R. Meir) and R. Yehudah disagreed as to which currency was to be used for the reduction enjoined by the mishnah (*dinarim* or *quinarii*). R. Meir and R. Yose disagreed as to whether the reduction is to be made from the marriage contract alone or from any additional inheritance she may receive after her rebellion. If this reconstruction is accurate, the original text is much older than the second layer added during the second century of the common era. Compare mKid 1:1, which may similarly be composed of several layers, the original of which probably read:

האשה נקנית בשלש דרכים וקונה את עצמה בשתי דרכים. נקיות בכסף בשטר ובביאה וקונה את
עצמה בגט ובמיתת הבעל.

A woman is acquired in three ways and acquires her [freedom] in two ways. She is acquired by means of money, contract, and cohabitation and acquires her [freedom] by a bill of divorcement and the death of her husband.

A later dispute as to the minimal amount of money of acquisition (or rather as to the nature of the currency of acquisition) led to the following addition:

בכסף — בית שמאי אומרים בדינר ובשוה דינר ובית הלל אומרים בפרוטה ובשוה פרוטה וכמה
היא פרוטה? אחד משמונה באיסר האיטלקי.

Money: The House of Shamai says: a *dinar* or the worth of a *dinar*. The House of Hillel says: a *perutah* or the worth of a *perutah*. And how much is a *perutah?* One-eighth of an Italian *issar*.

I would further suggest that the original text of the mishnah in Ketubot spoke in terms of seven and three because of the parallelism to the seven household duties that a wife was obligated to perform for her husband (mKet 5:5) and to the three more general obligations the husband had to perform for his wife (Exod 21:10 and commentaries) The form of currency was not mentioned because it was obviously to be the same currency used in the marriage contract. If this reasoning is correct, the position of R. Yehudah (*quinarii*) becomes less defensible. This interpretation of the various layers of the mishnah follows J. N. Epstein, *Introduction to Tannaitic Literature* (Jerusalem 1957), pp. 24 ff. Jacob Neusner, however, argues that the entire mishnah must emanate from the period of the rabbis last mentioned therein. (See, e.g., *The Rabbinic Traditions about the Pharisees,* [Leiden, 1971], vol. 3, pp. 147 ff.)

    5. MKet 5:5.

    6. Despite the fact that Maimonides defines *moredet* as one who refuses sexual relations (see below), he writes: (*Mishneh Torah* [= *MT*], *Hilkhot Ishut* 21:10) "Any wife who refuses to do any of the work activities which she is obligated is to be forced to do them, even with a whip." *The Ravad* ad loc. objects:

מעולם לא שמעתי יסור שוטים לנשים אלא שממעט לה צריכיה ומזונותיה עד שתכנע עכ"ל

I never heard of punishment by whipping for women; rather, her provisions and food are lessened until she submits.

An expanded version of the Ravad, cited in the *Hidushei Ha-Ritva* and the *Shitah Mekubbetset* to Ketubot 63a, reads as follows:

If the marriage contract [of the woman who rebels by not doing her work-activity] is not reduced, in what way [does R. Eliezer rule] that she is to be forced? If it is with words, "no servant can be [successfully] chastised with words" [Proverbs 39:19]; "if it is with a whip and sanctions, a wife is not subject to such things. Certainly the forcing is by means of the marriage contract."

ואם אין פוחתין לה מכתובתה, במה הוא כופה? אם בדברים, בדברים לא יוסר עבד; ואם בשוטים ושמתא, איתתא לאו בה הכי הוא; הא ודאי ליכא כפיה אלא בכתובתה.

Hence, the Ravad objects to the position of Rav Huna, that a rebellious wife is not to be defined as one who refuses to do her work activity, and disagrees with Maimonides.

7. Cf. the discussion of the Jerusalem Talmud below, pp. 21 f.

8. BKet 58b. Resh Lakish, first-generation Palestinian Amora, disagrees, stating explicitly that a husband can force his wife to provide him with produce; however, the overwhelming majority of halakhic decisors agree with Rav. The very fact that the Torah insists upon the husband's obligation to provide sustenance for his wife (Exod 21:10) would confirm the fact that this is the primary one, and the wife's work-activity is merely in compensation for that. In "An Equal or a Ward: How Independent Is a Married Woman," *Journal of Semitic Studies* 44 (1987): 189 f., Samuel Morell argues that the position of Resh Lekish was normative and that of Rav was innovative. I respectfully disagree.

9. MKet 5:6.

10. Rabbinic opinion derives the husband's responsibility of sexually gratifying his wife from the Biblical phrase "he shall not withhold from her sustenance, garments, and sexual gratification" (Exod. 21:10). See *Mekhilta De R. Yishmael, Mishpatim* 3, ed. Horovitz-Rabin, pp. 258–259, for a further discussion of this Biblical source. Ibn Adret, in *Hiddushei Ha-Rashba* to bNed 15b, derives the responsibility not from the Biblical command but from the marital obligation which the husband assumes, and it is this marital obligation which activates the commandment. One of the ramifications of this dispute is whether or not the wife has the right to relieve the husband of his responsibility; if it is a Biblical command, one may not enter into any condition or agreement in violation of a Biblical command; if it is a result of the marital obligation, the wife has the option to forgo this benefit. Tosafot to bKet 56a, s.v. *harei,* deals with the problem, as do Maimonides, *MT, Hilkhot Ishut* 6:10; R. Shimon b. Zemach Duran, *Responsa Tashbatz*, vol. 1, *Siman* 94; and Saul Lieberman, *Tosefta Ki-feshutah, Kiddushin* 3:7, n. 29. See Nahum Rakover "Marital Relations: The Husband Coercing the Wife," *Jewish Law and Current Legal Problems* 55 (May 1984): 4–7.

11. BNed 15b.

12. See, for example, *MT, Hilkhot Nedarim* 12:9. If a wife says to her husband, "I forbid you to derive pleasure from sexual relations with me," he need not rescind

the vow. This may be compared to one forbidding the owner of fruits from deriving pleasure from his own fruit.

13. Ibn Adret cited above, as well as all of note 7. R. Avraham Min Hahar, in his interpretation of bNed 15b, suggests that this mutual obligation stems from the verse "when a man take a woman to wife . . ." (Deut 22:13), interpreted by the Amoraim (bKid 2a) to mean קנין, or "mutual obligation-consent."

14. BKid 4b.

15. See R. Mosheh b. R. Yosef mi-Trani, *Kiryat Sefer, Hilkhot Ishut,* chap. 14, who derives from the fact that the Bible places the responsibility for sexual gratification upon the male for the female that sex is "her privilege and not his privilege" (דזכותה היא ולא זכותו). Cf. R. Shlomo Luria, *Yam Shel Shlomo* (to bB. K.: 3:21) that a husband certainly cannot force his wife with brutality, and *Responsa Maharit* 1:5, that a woman's responsibility to have sexual relations with her husband is parallel to his responsibility towards her, as outlined in mKet 5:6.

The clearest statement that a husband cannot force his wife to have sexual relations is made by Rami bar Hama in the name of Rav Assi in bErub 100b, though the topic there is his demand for sexual intercourse not in the usual manner. For a complete discussion of this issue, see Rakover, op. cit., pp. 12–23.

16. MKet 7:10. Cf. Neusner, op. cit., pp. 82–83.

17. TKet 7:10–11. See Lieberman, *Tosefta Ki-feshuta, Ketubot,* p. 35, n. 45. He cites a responsum of Rabbenu Gershom to the effect that the coercion only refers to the bill of divorcement and not to the payment of the alimony. However, Lieberman cites many authorities who maintain the correctness of the reading of our text of Tosefta, "he is coerced to divorce her and grant her the alimony." See also *Tosafot,* bKet 77a: "They coerce him to grant her a divorce," in which the Ri insists, "he gives her the alimony," based on the Tosefta.

18. MNed 11:12. Cf. Neusner, op. cit., vol. 3 (Nedarim, Nazir), p. 102.

19. MKet 5:5 provides for coerced divorce in the instance of a husband who takes a vow forbidding his wife to perform any work-activity, and 5:6 assumes the wife's legitimate claim of divorce if her husband does not fulfill her legitimate sexual needs. TKet 5:6 explicitly states:

המדיר את אשתו מתשמיש המטה בית שמאי אומרים שתי שבתות כלידת נקיבה בית הלל אומרים
שבת אחת כלידת זכר וכימי נדתה
יתר על כן, יוציא ויתן כתובה.

One who vows that he will not take sexual pleasure from his wife: The House of Shamai says: [He may do so] for two weeks, as in the birth of a female child [when the wife is ritually impure and sexual relations are forbidden for two weeks]. The House of Hillel says: [He may do so] for one week, as in the birth of a male child and during the woman's menstrual period [when the wife is virtually impure and sexual relations are Biblically forbidden for one week]. [If he took an oath for a] longer [period] than this, he must divorce her and give her the alimony.

20. See Epstein, op. cit., pp. 241 ff. Individual sections are called *halakhot* or *baraitot*.

21. TKet 5:7. All texts based on Lieberman, *Tosefta Nashim,* (New York, 5726 [1966]). See Lieberman *Tosefta Ki-feshutah,* p. 266:

And so the published text, but there the words "Jewish court" [בית דין] are missing, and so, too, in any textual version, and even in the Vienna MS, there are dots above the words (apparently as a sign of erasure). And in the Erfurt MS:

"Our Rabbi enacted that they warn her [שמתרין בה] four weeks one after the other (consecutively), *once* each week," etc. In the fragments from the Genizah the page is torn here, but there remains "four weeks."

The students of Rabbenu Yonah (*Shitah Mekubbetset* 53b) wrote: "But my teacher the Master says that *twice* refers to each public announcement which make eight public announcements . . ."

22. All of the Sages of the period in which R. Yehudah Nesiah was the head of the Sanhedrin were called "*Rabbotenu.*" See bNid 66a, yNid, 3:4 (50c), bGit 76a, and bAb 36a.

And cf. bAb 38b. R. Yehudah HaNasi and his court permitted Gentile oil; and from the incident recorded in ibid. 37a it is clear that R. Yehudah Nesiah is meant.

C.f. Heiman, *Toldot Tannaim Va-Amoraim* (Jerusalem, 5724), pp. 606–611. Also compare Epstein, op. cit., p. 234, but see too p. 22, where he suggests the possibility that in this instance "our Rabbis" may be earlier. In any case, they further our mishnah.

23. YKet 5:10 (30b).

24. BKet 63b.

25. "But in the *baraita* I saw: 'they warn her four and five weeks.'" However, the students of Rabbenu Yonah, who are cited in the *Shitah Mekubbetset* on Ket 63b, read: "they publicly proclaim" (מכריזין) as do Tosafot bKet 63b, but these citations are probably based upon the *baraita* quoted in the Babylonian Talmud. R. Meir attempts casuistically to ·harmonize the two versions: "perhaps public announcement is called a warning," but even he does not appear to take this linguistic sleight of hand seriously.

26. Leiberman, *Tosefta Ki-feshutah, Ketubot* p. 267–268.

27. Ibid., p. 267.

28. BKet 63b.

29. Lieberman, loc. cit., cites both possibilities, since the word "twice" is found in our Tosefta text, the Vienna MS, and is confirmed by the Babylonian Talmud and the students of Rabbenu Yonah; and the word "once" is found in the Erfurt MS

and is confirmed by Tosafot. I would opt for the latter, since neither the Jerusalem Talmud nor the Babylonian Talmud cites the word "twice" in its quotation of the *baraita,* and Rav does not attempt to "prove" this second contention of Rami bar Hama from any Toseftan text.

30. Ibid., p. 267.

31. I believe the reading was "they," and was to be interpreted as "Jewish court," for this would connote an official but private warning. Some later readings included "Jewish court," where others saw it to mean a public proclamation in the Synagogue.

32. The same phrase is to be found in mSot 1:5:

אם אמרה טמאה אני — שוברה כתובתה ויוצאת

If [after the wife suspected of adultery is frightened by the judge of the Great Court in Jerusalem and] she said: "I am defiled," she "breaks" her marriage contract and goes out [with a bill of divorcement].

See the Amoraic discussion ad loc. The term *shoveret* ("breaks") may come from *shuvar* ("receipt"); she writes a receipt for her alimony when there had originally only been a verbal agreement. In the instance of a written marriage contract, the document would be torn and destroyed. The point of this Mishnaic statement is that she is divorced without benefit of the alimony.

33. See mKet 4:7. Even if there is no written *ketubah,* as a stipulation of the court (תנאי בית דין) the husband owes her the minimal amount (200 *zuzim* for a virgin; 100 for a widow or divorcee) if he dies or gives her a divorce, since the alimony obligation of the marriage contract is the condition *sine qua non* of every marriage. See bKet 56b, where the Talmud cites the position of R. Meir that a husband cannot live with a woman who does not have a *ketubah.* So, also, Maimonides rules in MT, *Hilkhot Ishut* 10:10:

לפי שאסור לו לאדם לשהות עם אשתו אפילו שעה אחת בלא כתובה.

Because it is forbidden for a man to remain with his wife even for one hour unless she has a *ketubah.*

34. See p. 29.

35. Cf. Tel Aviv, *Midrash Genesis Rabbah.* Y. T. L. Zunz, *Ha-Derashot Be-Yisrael Ve-Hishtalutan Ha-Historit,* ed. Vilna, 52:16, cf. rev. by Ch. Albeck (Jerusalem, 1974), pp. 77–78.

36. Theodor-Albeck, *Midrash Bereshit Rabba,* Jerusalem 1968, 552–553 (52:14–16); cf. p. 553, n. 1, "there are those who say [ויש אומרים]" in our text, on the basis of the Jerusalem Talmud. It is necessary to include this addition, because it is evident that R. Yohanan can only prove his position that the pain of sexual denial is greater for the husband than the wife from the fact that Samson wanted to die and not Delilah. If the reason for Delilah's greater patience was because she obtained

sexual gratification elsewhere, the verse can no longer serve as a proof-text for R. Yohanan. The one who interprets it in that fashion would define a *moredet* as one who rebels by not performing her household duties.

37. E. Z. Melamed, *An Introduction to the Talmudic Literature (Pirkei Mevo Le-Safrut Ha-Talmud)*, (Jerusalem, 1973), pp. 503–504.

CHAPTER II

1. See Albeck, *Genesis Rabbah,* vol. 3, who cites the possibility that the *Midrash Rabbah* was taken from the Jerusalem Talmud and is therefore later than the following passage.

2. YKet 5:9 (30b). The following sections all deal with this *sugya.*

3. Cf. David Weiss-Halivni, *Sources and Traditions, Mekorot U-Mesorot* (Tel Aviv, 1968), pp. 207–208, who disagrees with this interpretation of R. Yose bar Hanina. However, it is certainly substantiated by the *baraita* ". . . even if she is a *niddah,* even if she is ill," which assumes both types of *moredet* (*melakhah* as well as *tashmish*), as well as by the conclusion of bKet 63b. Nevertheless, Halivni distinguishes between *hova* (חובה) and *shibbud* (שיעבוד), "obligation" and "subservience," suggesting that she is subservient to him but has no (sexual) obligation to him (אבל, היא משעובדת לו, אין לה חובה), a suggestion I find difficult to accept.

4. This is not the position of the Babylonian Talmud, as we shall see in the next chapter.

5. See *Responsa Maharit,* note 5.

6. מכרא פרגנן is difficult. Cf. *Targum Yonatan* on Exod 22:15. מפרנא יפרין, which suggests "dowry."

R. David Frankel, in his commentary *Korban Ha-Edah* to the Jerusalem Talmud ad loc., explains מפרא פרגנן as "additions to the *ketubah,*" and R. Mosheh Margolit, in his commentary *Pnei Mosheh* to the Jerusalem Talmud ad loc., cites the Arukh, who defines מפרא פרגנן as the gifts which are given an engaged woman exclusive of the *ketubah.* The *Korban Ha-Edah* ad loc. adds: "there are those who interpret it as *nikhsei melog,* the property which she brings into the marriage and for which she retains responsibility, but the usufruct of which belongs to the husband. Indeed, according to the logic of the Jerusalem Talmud, since the *nikhsei melog* as well as the *nikhsei tzon barzel* were anticipated—and indeed received—at the time of the marriage, they are to be included in the penalty reduction."

What is unclear is the case of an inheritance which accrued to the woman after the marriage but before the rebellion. It would similarly appear that, since this sum is presently anticipated, it should be included in the reduction as well.

7. The statement in the Jerusalem Talmud comes after the following passage. Nevertheless, it fits much better within this context.

8. Deut 25:6.

9. Ibid., 7–10. The shoe has always been a symbol of material rootedness; cf. bBer 61a, where the daily blessing of thanksgiving to God for having provided the individual with all of his material needs is to be said when one puts on his shoe, as well as the law that when in mourning one removes one's shoe. Hence if the brother of the deceased refuses to provide his dead relative with a material presence in the world in the form of issue, and his widow with material sustenance, she removes his shoe; the act symbolizes his failure to provide her with material rootedness; may he lose your rootedness as well. Her spitting may symbolize her wish that his sperm fall on earth, since he refused to give her issue.

10. MBek 1:7. Nevertheless, it is not at all clear that this explicit and undisputed statement in the mishnah that nowadays *halitzah* takes precedence—is operative. Cf. bYeb 39b and 106a, as well as Maimonides' *Hilkhot Yibbum* 1:2; the commandment of *yibbum* takes precedence. Rabbenu Tam's view is in accord with the mishnah in Bekhorot; Cf. *Hagahot Maimuniyot,* ad. loc., n. 1.

11. Cf. Maimonides, op. cit. 2:10. A woman who refuses a levirate marriage must accept the penalty of a *moredet,* which is a forfeiture of her marriage contract. The brother is forced to give her *halitzah,* however, just as the husband would be forced to grant a divorce to a wife who finds him distasteful—*Shulhan Arukh* 165.

The *Maggid Mishnah* adds that if the brother is not fit for her—if he has apparent physical blemishes or is much older—she would not be given a letter of rebellion, despite the fact that Maimonides adjudicates that the commandment of *yibbum* takes precedence. (This is not in accord with R. Yose bar Bun.)

12. This difficult text has been subject to a number of possible interpretations. The *Korban Ha-Edah* explains: "Even that which R. Hiya taught can be explained in accordance with the latter mishnah, for it makes absolutely no difference legally, for now they do not write a letter of rebellion at all. (Now there is an immediate forfeiture of the alimony, in accordance with the *Tosefta*)."

The *Pnei Mosheh* explains: "You may even interpret both statements in accordance with the latter mishnah. The statement of Shmuel [that a letter of rebellion against a woman awaiting a levirate marriage is not written] deals with a case in which he wishes the levirate marriage . . . and she wishes *halitzah,* and the teaching of R. Yiya deals with the case in which she wishes neither *halitzah* nor a levirate marriage. [And the following citation in the Jerusalem Talmud regarding] the court which came later is a separate issue unto itself [with no relationship to the previous discussion]." Here the *Pnei Mosheh* paraphrases the passage rather than interpreting it. He interprets the case of her desire for *halitzah* and/or a levirate marriage, and therefore his understanding is unacceptable to me. (העיקר חסד מן הספר) The Ridbaz's (R. David Slutzker) interpretation is similar to my own.

13. *Jerusalem Talmud,* loc. cit.; cf. Deut 24:3.

14. Since the divorce must be in accordance with the husband's will, and a

"forced" divorce would conflict with this prerequisite, the Talmud provides that "he is struck [by an agent of the court] until he declares 'I will it'" (*Yev* 106a; *Kid* 50a; *B.B.* 48a); and Maimonides, *Hilkhot Gerushin* 2:20, explains:

מי שהדין נותן שכופין אותו לגרש את אשתו ולא רצה לגרש: בית דין של ישראל בכל מקום ובכל זמן מכין אותו עד שיאמר רוצה אני ויכתוב הגט והוא גט כשר. וכן אם הכוהו עכו"ם ואמרו לו עשה מה שישראל אומרים לך ולחצו ישראל ביד העכו"ם עד שיגרש הרי זה כשר ואם העכו"ם מעצמן אנסוהו עד שכתב, הואיל ודין נותן שיכתוב: הרי זה גט פסול. ולמה לא בטל גט זה שהרי הוא אנוס בין ביד עכו"ם בין ביד ישראל? שאין אומרים אנוס אלא למי שנלחץ ונדחק לעשות דבר שאינו מחוייב בו מן התורה כגון מי שהוכה עד שמכר או עד שנתן. אבל מי שתקפו יצרו הרע לבטל מצוה או לעשות עבירה והוכה עד שעשה דבר שחייב לעשותו או עד שנתרחק מדבר האסור לעשותו אין זה אנוס ממנו אלא הוא אנס עצמו בדעתו הרעה, לפיכך זה שאינו רוצה לגרש מאחר שהוא רוצה להיות מישראל ורוצה הוא לעשות כל המצות ולהתרחק מן העבירות ויצרו הוא שתקפו וכיון שהוכה עד שתשש יצרו ואמר רוצה אני כבר גרש מרצונו . . .

He whom the law provides that one forces him to divorce his wife, if he did not wish to divorce [her]: the Jewish court in all places and in all times beat him until he says: "I wish [to divorce her]; he will then write a bill of divorce, and it is a valid bill of divorce. Similarly, if the non-Jews beat him and said, "Do what the Jews tell you"; and the Jews pressed him into the hands of non-Jews until he will divorce [her], behold, this [bill of divorce] is valid. And if the non-Jews forced him on their own until he wrote [the bill of divorce]—since the law provides that he write [a bill of divorce], behold, it is an invalid bill of divorce [i.e., it still has some halakhic status, e.g., to invalidate the woman from marrying a *kohen*]. And why is such a bill of divorce [brought about by force] not null and void, since he is forced, either by Jews or by non-Jews? [The reason is] that one does not say "forced" except of one who is pressured and pushed to do a thing in which he is not obligated by the Torah, such as a person who was beaten until he sold or gave [property]. But one whose evil inclination overcame him to fail to perform a commandment or to do a transgression, and he was beaten until he did the thing which he was obligated to do, or distanced himself from a thing which is forbidden to do—he is not forced away from it, but he forces himself regarding his own evil intention. Therefore, this person who does not wish to divorce [his wife], since he wishes to be a Jew, and wishes to do all the commandments and to distance himself from transgressions, and it is his evil inclination which has overcome him, and when he is beaten until his [evil] inclination weakens and he says, "I wish [to divorce her]"—he has already divorced (her) willingly . . .

15. See B. Porten, *Archives from Elephantine* (Berkeley and Los Angeles, 1968), esp. pp. 208–210, p. 209, n. 37, for ancient Near Eastern parallels and pp. 261–262 for a passage from an unedited bill of divorcement. See also Y. Muffs, *Studies in the Aramaic Legal Papyri from Elephantine* (Leiden, 1969), pp. 3, 193, 194. The fact that

the marriage contract was drawn up after the birth of children would seem to indicate that we are not dealing with a normative halakhic community. Nevertheless, these contracts bear a remarkable resemblance to a rejected suggested in bGit 49b:

כי נקפא איהי, נמי ליתקני רבנן כתובה מינה

When she initiates the divorce, perhaps the Rabbis ought to mandate that he [receive] alimony from her?

See Lieberman, *Tosefta Ki-feshutah,* vol. VI, p. 371, and H. L. Ginsberg, "The Brooklyn Museum Aramaic Papyri," *Journal of the American Oriental Society* 74 (1954): 159.

16. For the readings adapted here, see especially S. Lieberman, *Hilkhot Ha-Yerushalmi Leha-Rambam* (New York, 1948), p. 61.

For use of the term *shutafut* ("partnership") for marriage in the seventh-century Nestorian church, see Z. W. Falk, *Jewish Matrimonial Law* (Oxford, 1966), p. 68, n. 1. For classical parallels, see S. Cohen, *Jewish and Roman Law* (New York 1966), ch. 1, p. 295. no. 72.

17. It may be assumed that the divorce was effectuated by the court's coercing the husband to give his wife a divorce. It is unlikely that the Jerusalem Talmud discarded the Biblical command: "He shall write her a bill of divorce and place it in her hand" (Deut 24:1).

CHAPTER III

1. Cf. L. Ginzberg, *A Commentary on the Palestinian Talmud,* pp. xlii–xlvi on the struggle between proponents of the two Talmuds.

2. Bket 63a, cf. The Babylonian Talmud with variant readings, *Makhon Ha-Talmud Ha-Yisraeli Ha-Shalem* (Jerusalem, 1977), ed. M. Herschler, vol. 2, pp. 83–85.

3. See pp. 21–23 f. above.

4. BKet 58b; Maimonides, *Hilkhot Ishut* 12:4; *Shulhan Arukh, Even Ha-Ezer,* 69:4.

Cf. *Tosafot,* bKet 63a, s.v. *Rav Huna says.*

5. The classical commentaries of the Jerusalem Talmud, the *Pnei Mosheh* and the *Korban Ha-Edah,* take the two Talmuds as if they were in perfect harmony on this issue, and utilize the "break in the basket" psychology to interpret the Jerusalem Talmud in accordance with the conclusion in the Babylonian Talmud. An objective analysis of the language, however, will confirm my interpretation.

6. There is, however, one aspect of the Talmud which emerges with beautiful logic from this interpretation. Rav Nahman bar Rav Yitzhak cites R. Yose b. R. Hanina as his "great man," who would agree with Rav Nahman bar Rav Hisha and disagree with Rava. Now, since R. Yose b. R. Hanina maintains that the wife can be a *moredet* if she refuses to perform her household duties—and not necessarily only if

she refuses sexual relations—he may very well not consider a public proclamation such an act of "boorishness." Rava, however, would most likely agree with Rav Huna (his predecessor in Sura) and would insist that a *moredet* must be a wife who refuses sexual relations. He has already read the provision of a "public proclamation" into the Tosefta, would most likely consider such an act "boorish," and would therefore be most likely to uphold the mishnah.

7. This view would read: "whose view, then are *they* following" (אינהו כמאן סברוה) rather than "whose view, then, is he following." Cf. *Tosafot* Ket 63b, "and so is it written in the old texts and in the *Halakhot Gedolot*." According to this reading, the redactor's question concerns the view upon which Rava and Rami bar Hama—who agree with each other—base their opinion. *Tosafot HaRosh,* and Rosh (Asheri), Alfasi, and Rabbenu Hananel (see *Tosafot* ad loc.), who agree with the reading of Rabbenu Tam, and the Rambam, Tur, and Karo who uphold the halakhah in accordance with the *Tosefta*. The Ri MiGash and the Rambam cite the reading of Rashi, and the Rasba (Ibn Adret) brings both readings. I believe that one can maintain the reading according to Rashi and still interpret the passage according to Rabbenu Tam, because Rava was still the main halakhic decisor of his generation. See the Ravad ad loc. for a third view: we maintain the reading in accordance with Rashi, and therefore the halakhah in accordance with the mishnah, but that Rav Sheshet teaches that the *moredet* is to be persuaded, which means that we ask her if she wishes to be judged like the mishnah or the *baraita*. See Hirschler, op. cit., p. 87, n. 22.

8. Rashi comments that she is not to be forced to remain with him, but he gives her the bill of divorcement and she leaves with her *ketubah*.

It is not clear from Rashi whether her husband is to be coerced into giving the divorce, but it is possible that that would be his contention. On the other hand, Rabbenu Tam ad loc. insists that the husband is not to be forced, and after bringing many proofs to his position maintains that Rashi agrees with this lack of coercion. Cf. Hirschler, Ket 63b, p. 88, n. 30. There is a variant which reads: "and *he* is not to be forced" (לא כייפינן ליה), and both the Ra'ah and Rashba (Ibn Adret) cite both readings. Cf. also *Responsa Rabbenu Tam*, Si 24 (pp. 40–41), the Ravad on the Rif, and the *Responsa* of the Sages of Provence, Si 72 (p. 258), who all cite such a reading. I would argue, however, that this other version is not consistent with the Talmud's citation of Mar Zutra, which would then logically have to be: "he is to be forced" (כייפינן ליה), nor is it consistent with the entire content of Amemar's remarks, which seem to contrast the wife who says "He is repulsive to me" with the wife who claims "I wish to remain married [to him], but I want to cause him pain."

9. See above, pp. 9 ff.

10. But this is not only because of the Talmudic comment ולא היא, which indicates that the *sugya*'s redactor(s) sided with Mar Zutra. Amemar was clearly the greater of the two: Cf. bShev 30b, Ber 50b, B.M. 22a.

11. This is the universally held case of *moredet,* and the previous passage would

appear to uphold the position of Amemar that a wife who claims "He is repulsive to me" is not to be termed a *moredet*. Rashi disagrees, perhaps because the grabbing of the silk garment would seem to indicate divorce; I would argue that her grabbing of the garment merely meant that it might not be included in the *ketubah* reduction. Rashi is probably influenced by the conclusion of the Rabbanan Sabborai, see below.

12. See B. M. 86a, and my discussion, pp. 69 ff. It may be dated somewhat earlier to the past–Rav Ashi authorities see Halivni, *Mekorot U-Mesorot*, Moed, 1982, Introduction.

13. MB.K. 3:11. המוציא מחברו עליו הראיה. One who wishes to take an object out of his fellow's possession (because he claims ownership) must being evidence to that effect. See also bB. K. 46a, where this principle is described as a "Major principle in judgment" (כלל גדול בדין).

14. See above, Chap. I, n. 33.

15. Rashi and Ritva so understand this case. Maimonides (*MT, Hilkhot Ishut* 14:8) interprets this case as *moredet* who wishes to remain married; he insists that a *moredet* who finds her husband repulsive is granted a divorce—even with compulsion—immediately, with no waiting period, in accordance with Amemar.

16. Whether or not the Rabbis have the right to coerce the husband to grant his wife a divorce when she claims "He is repulsive to me"—and by Talmudic (Rabbanan Sabborai) fiat—will be the basis for all future halakhic discussion on this issue. We have seen previously how it was Biblically and Mishnaically within the exclusive domain of the husband to decide whether to give his wife a divorce (Deut 24:1-2, mYeb 14:1). There were exceptions whereby the husband could be coerced by the Rabbis to give the divorce at the behest of the wife, but only if she brought objective reasons justifying her desire to be freed of the marriage (if, for example, the husband developed great blemishes, as in mKet 7:9-10): Maimonides, in *MT, Hilkhot Gerushin, 2:20*, explains how a person can be coerced to grant the divorce. See above, chap. II, n. 14. One can well understand that forcing such a divorce must be permissible and acceptable, otherwise it is invalidated. Hence it is a major issue whether the Talmud called for coercion or not. The Jerusalem Talmud avoided the entire issue of coercion by a stipulation in the marriage contract.

CHAPTER IV

1. With the clear exception of the opinion of Amemar as explained in the previous chapter.

2. Ch. Tykocinski, *Takanot Ha-Geonim*, ed. Havatzelet (Tel-Aviv and Jerusalem, 1959), pp. 11-12.

3. *Hemda Genuzah*, ed. Venice, 69a, cited in *Otzar Ha-Geonim*, ed. Lewin, vol. 8 (Jerusalem, 1938), pt. I, p. 194.

4. The "two academies" were the Academy of Sura, founded by the Amora Rav in 219 C.E., and the Academy of Pumbedita, which acquired significance after the destruction of the Academy of Nehardea (which had been founded by the Amora Shmuel at approximately the same time as Pumpedita) in 259 C.E. Pumbedita had as its head such halakhic luminaries as Rabba bar Nahmani, Abaye, Rava, and Rav Yosef; in Sura, R. Huna and Rav Ashi. The two Academies were the two most important centers of learning in Babylon in Talmudic times, and remained so throughout the period of the Geonim. (based on *Encyclopedia Judaica*, s.v. "Sura," "Pumbedita," and "Academies.")

5. *Hemda Genuzah*, 89; MS Simonson, 314; *Otzar Ha-Geonim*, p. 189.

6. Rami bar Hamah in our Talmudic texts.

7. We identified the Talmud's closing statement as having emanated from the Rabbanan Sabborai and the subsequent decree as having emanated from the Geonim. See p. 107.

8. We shall discuss this issue in far greater detail in the following section, where the exact meaning of *tarbut ra'ah* is explained by the Geonim.

9. *Responsa Maharam b. Barukh*, (Prague, [5] 368), n. 261, cited in *Otzar HaGeonim*, p. 190. See Tykocinski's discussion, op. cit., for exact dating.

10. This responsum was first cited in the collection *Halakhot Pesukot*, attributed to Rav Yehudai Gaon. It then appeared in a collection of responsa attributed by the collector to Rav Natronai Gaon, but contradicts his opinion, as can clearly be seen by its granting of the *ketubah* to the *moredet*. However, a portion of the responsum is cited by R. Yoel HaLevi in the name of Rav Amram Gaon, and it is similarly attributed to Rav Amram by *Hagahot Maimuniyot*, on Maimonides, *MT, Hilkhot Ishut*, chap. 14, n. 30. See *Responsa Maharam*, ed. Berlin, n. 261; Tykocinski, op. cit., p. 14.

11. Cf. Tykocinski, op. cit., pp. 14–15.

12. This responsum appears in a lengthy letter called "Yeshivatenu," and attributed by the collector to Rav Hananyah Gaon. Cf. [תקנת, טקוצינסקי, הגאונים pp. 15–17.

13. *Otzar Ha-Geonim*, vol. 8, pp. 191–192.

14. *Iggeret Rav Sherira Gaon*, ed. Lewin, pp. 99–102.

15. *Takanot Geonim Harkavy*, n. 230. This responsum is part of a collection of thirty-four other responsa which were sent to R. Yaakov b. Nissim of Kairwan. In *Siman* 252 a responsum speaks of "his academy" in contrast to the academy of Sura—so that apparently the responsa are from Pumbedita. Furthermore, three of the responsa are cited in another source in the name of Rav Hai Gaon. See Joel Müller, *Index to the Geonic Responsa* (New York, 1959), p. 43, as well as Tykocinski, op. cit., p. 18.

16. *Takkanot Geonim ed. Harkavy n.* 71. The Gaon who wrote this responsum could not have lived before the tenth century, since he cites Rav Tzemach Gaon. Cf. Tykocinski, loc. cit.

17. Responsa, Rav Shmuel ben Eli, in the *Responsa of Maharam ben Barukh,* Lemberg, n. 443; Berlin, p. 64, n. 494, and cf. Poznansky, *Babylonische Geonim im nachgaonäischen Zeitalter,* (Berlin, 1914), pp. 55–56.

18. See Baruch Levine, "Nikhsei Melug," *Journal of the American Oriental Society* 88 (1968): pp. 271–285.

19. Rif, Ket. 26b–27a.

20. The Raviyah, who died approximately 1265, lived one generation after Rabbenu Tam, whose dates are 1090–1171. From his writings it is clear that he was greatly influenced by the Rif.

21. Responsa Maharam ben Barukh, Berlin, p. 19. *Hagahot Maimuniyot* on Maimonides' *MT, Hilkhot Ishut* chap. 14:30.

22. *Ha-Ittur, Ot Mered,* 102, p. 4. (ed. print. MS Levov 59, pp. 72–73). See Tykocinski, op. cit.

23. See pp. 59–60 above. It would seem that Rabba (רבא) and not Rakia is the correct reading in the *Ittur* passage.

24. See above pp. 59–60.

25. *Ittur, Ot Mered,* loc. cit. "In the year 962 by the court of contracts," which is 651 C.E.

26. Jacob Efrati, *Tekufot Ha-Sabboraim Ve-Safrutah* (Petah Tikvah, 1973), p. 80.

27. B.B.M. 86a.

28. *Iggeret Rabbenu Sherira Gaon,* ed. Lewin, pp. 95 and 100.

29. Raavad, *Sefer Ha-Qabbalah,* ed. Cohen (Philadelphia, 1967), pp. 43–45.

30. Raavad himself gives both dates, and then numbers the years of their activity as 187. Apparently, he does not include either the year 500 or the year 689 in his calculation. See Efrati, op. cit., p. 35, n. 6.

31. See n. 19 above.

32. See n. 22 above.

33. Cf. Tykocinski, op. cit., pp. 17–18, and Efrati, op. cit., p. 80.

34. See above p. 00f.

35. Efrati, in *Tekufat Ha-Sabboraim Ve-Safrutah,* goes to great lengths to explain that there is really no dispute between the *Iggeret* of Rabbenu Sherira and the *Sefer Ha-Qabbalah* regarding the period of the Sabboraim. The Arab conquest of Babylon took place in the middle of the seventh century, after which the position and rights of the Exilarch were restored. This began the Gaonic period, at least from a political perspective, and is the date established by the Raavad for the new era. Since the term "gaon" had been in vogue close to one hundred years earlier, Rabbenu Sherira calculates the Gaonic period as having begun then in 589. See Efrati, op. cit., pp. 74–95. Rabbenu Sherira would also agree, however, that since the literary flowering of the Geonim did not take place until the latter half of the seventh century, in point of fact—from a literary perspective—the period of the Sabboraim extended for close to two hundred years. This is in agreement with the

reading of *Hemda Genuzah* that the immediate divorce decree dates from the period of the Sabboraim; see ibid., p. 80. I would still agree with Tykocinski's decision that the correct reading is not in accordance with *Hemda Genuzah* because Rabbenu Sherira is most precise about the dates for conclusion of the Amoraic period and the beginning of the Gaonic period.

36. A. Weiss, *Hithavut Ha-Talmud Be-Shlemuto,* (New York: *Kohut,* 1943), pp. 242–257. Weiss argues that Rav Ashi died, according to the *Iggeret* of Rabbenu Sherira, in the year 427 C.E., that is, seventy-three years before 500 C.E., the date given for "the conclusion of authoritative halakhic decision [*sof hora'ah*]." When the *Iggeret,* therefore, speaks of "Rav Ashi and Ravina," Rav Sherira is referring to Rav Asi, the last Amoraic head of the Academy of Pumpedita, who assumed his position in the year 476 C.E., and Ravina brei d'Rav Huna, who was the head of the Academy of Sura and died in the year 500. This represented a watershed in the history of the Oral Law, since the Exilarchate was removed and the subsequent Jewish leaders— until the Arab conquest in 589 C.E.—suffered a loss in authority and prestige. However, this does not mean that the Talmud itself was sealed. There is a great deal of Talmudic material which is post-Amoraic, as testified to by Rav Sherira himself and various Rishonim, as well as by the internal style of the Talmudic discussions. See Efrati, op. cit., pp. 50–63, and M. A. Tannenblatt, (*Ha-Talmud Ha-Bavli Be-Hithavuto Ha-Historit*) (Tel-Aviv: Devir, 1972), pp. 171–188.

37. *Iggeret Rav Sherira Gaon,* pp. 69–71, French Version. The original read as follows:

ובתר הכין אע"ג דהוראה לא הות איכא פירושי וסבארי קרובים להוראה ואיקרו הנהו רבואתא רבנן סבוראי וכל מאי דהות תלי פרשוה . . . וכמה סבארי קבעו בגמרא, אינין ורבנן דבתריהון נמי, כגון רב עינא ורב סימונא. ונקטינן מן ראשונים דגמארא דריש האשה נקנית עד בכסף מנא הני מילי, רבנן סבוראי בתרא תרצוהי וקבעוהי, ודעוד מינה נמי.

38. See Efrati, op. cit., chap. 2, pp. 1–13 for an analysis and history of this important work, and pp. 64–67 for an analysis of the following statement regarding the Rabbanan Sabborai, parallel to the Iggeret:

ואחרייהם (אחרי רב אשי ורבינא שהיו סוף הוראה) רבנן סבוראי, שבזכותן נמתחו השמים ונרקעה הארץ עד רב גיזא ורב סימנא, שהיו סוף סבוראיק, לא הוסיפו ולא הפליגו מדעתן כלום על דעת אחרייהם אלא תקנו פרקים שבכל תנויי כסדרן (מהדורא כהנא ע' 9)

And after them (Rav Ashi and Ravina, who concluded authoritative halakhic decisions) the Rabbanan Sabborai, whose merit the heavens were stretched and the earth was set firm, until Rav Giza and Rav Simana, who were the last of the Sabboraim. They neither added nor created anything on their own knowledge [on behalf of others], but they established chapters [halakhic analyses—*sugyot*] in all of the areas of their study in their proper order.

I believe Efrati correctly accepts the emendation—for the author of the *Seder*

Tannaim and Amoraim would hardly praise the Sabboraim as those in whose merit the heavens and earth were maintained only to describe their work as having no originality whatever—on the basis of which the meaning of the paragraph becomes eminently clear: the latter Sabboraim did not arrange and enlarge upon the words of the Amoraim (which the early Sabboraim did do), but they established, rather, new *sugyot* of their own throughout the Talmud, as the first *sugya* of Tractate Kiddushin.

39. See bKet, 63b–64a, *Dikdukei Soferim Ha-Shalem,* p. 90, n. 9. Cf. E. Z. Melamed, *An Introduction to Talmudic Literature* [*Pirkei Mavo Le Safrut Ha-Talmud*] (Jerusalem, 1973), p. 474, where this statement is also identified as Sabboraic.

40. See above, pp. 51–52.

41. See above, pp. 52-54.

42. See above, pp. 56-58 f.

43. See above, pp. 59-60 f.

44. H. Graetz, *History of the Jews,* vol. 3, p. 92.

45. I. H. Weiss, *Dor Dor Ve-Dorshav,* vol.? p. 8.

46. J. Mann, "The Responsa of the Babylonian Gaonim as a Source of Jewish History," *Jewish Quarterly Review,* 1919–20, p. 121.

47. Tykocinski, op. cit. pp. 25–26.

48. *Encyclopedia of Islam,* vol. IV (Leiden, 1934), pp. 636–640. See the fascinating study by M. Friedman, "The Governmental Involvement in Kairwan in the Divorce of a Betrothed Woman" (התערבות השלטון בקירואן בגירושי ארוסה, in Mikhael, *A Compilation of the History of Judaism: the Diaspora,* vol. 5 (Tel-Aviv, 1978), pp. 215–242. Friedman cites a Gaonic responsum, probably from the pen of Rav Sherira or Rav Hai, regarding a young betrothed couple in Kairwan. The girl's father does not wish his daughter to marry the young man (the *erusin*-[betrothal] has already taken place, but not the *nisuin–huppah* [marriage]), because the young man's father has suffered grave business reversals. He would prefer that his daughter marry her deceased sister's husband and thus raise his orphaned grandchildren. The *nate* (judge) orders the girl's father to go through with the marriage, insisting that no divorce may be issued without the expressed desire of the husband, and the girl's father maintains that the tradition in Kairwan is different. Friedman suggests that the judge was unaware of the Gaonic decree regarding *moredet;* I would argue that the judge was maintaining that, as long as the betrothed girl did not claim "He is repulsive to me," she had no right to demand a divorce. The judge even went so far as to say that if the young man divorced the girl, he ought to do it in front of the Sultan, which would render it invalid (translation of text, p. 230, line 7). The father of the girl then brought the case to a "great sage." There also appeared before the Sage messengers of the Sultan. Prior to the rendering of the decision, the father of the young man agrees to have his son give the divorce. The Sage exclaims in anger, "Why did you speak with us? Your view is not our view" (p. 234, line 18). The boy is then spoken to in a calm fashion by the elders, and informed how to give a proper

divorce. Friedman deduces from this source that Tykocinski is correct, and that there may have been some subtle pressure exerted in this fashion. I would argue the very opposite: despite the fact that it is apparent that the girl's father had a close connection with the Sultan, neither judge forces the divorce, and the young man, or rather his father, is ultimately convinced by the people to go through with the divorce.

49. S. I. Goitein, *The Mediterranean Society* (Berkeley and Los Angeles, 1978), vol. III, p. 264.

50. See above pp. 9–12; *Ketubot* 77a.

51. Reuben Levy, *The Social Structure of Islam* (Cambridge, 1962), pp. 122–123.

52. Deut 17:8–11; cf. the rabbinic dictum: "Jephthah in his generation is as Samuel in his generation" (R. H. 28b).

53. BGit 36a.

54. See MEd 1:5.

55. See bGit 6b, Ber 3b, Er 13b.

56. BKet 51a, 69b, 84a, 85a.

57. *Hemda Genuzah,* end of n. 10, 45, and Lewin, *Otzar Ha-Geonim* on Ketubot (vol. 8), p. 210, n. 9; cf. Tykocinski, op. cit., pp. 30–46.

58. Cf. BSan 3a; cf. *MT, Hilkhot Ishut* 18:11 regarding the Gaonic decree that a woman may collect her *ketubah* from movable property.

59. Cf. Tykocinski, op. cit., pp. 30–50, 126–127. On the Gaonic material in general, see I. Haut, *Divorce in Jewish Law and Life* (New York, 1983), pp. 51–53.

CHAPTER V

1. See above, pp. 29–30.

2. MKet 4:7–12.

3. For this entire chapter, I am greatly indebted to the work of Mordecai A. Friedman, "Termination of the Marriage Upon the Wife's Request: A Palestinian Ketubah Stipulation," *Proceedings of the American Academy for Jewish Research* 37 (1969): 37 f. Despite the fact that I disagree with his conclusion, as will be demonstrated below, he has drawn my attention to the wealth of material within the Genizah. I have also availed myself of his translation. (See now his *Jewish Marriage in Palestine: A Cairo Geniza Study* [Tel Aviv, 1981], esp. vol. II. The first text is now no. 3, p. 55).

4. אשוי means "agree." Cf. Lieberman, *Tarbiz* 5, p. 97, n. 4, and Friedman, op. cit., p. 87. n. 39.

5. Our usual phrase, "according to the law of Moses and Israel," is here written "and the Jews," so too in yYeb 15:3 (14d), and in yKet 4:8 (29a). See also L. Epstein, *Jewish Marriage Contract* (New York, 1927), p. 57, n. 9, and Friedman, op. cit. p. 37, n. 40.

6. Cf. bYeb 90b, with reference to the broad scope of rabbinic authority in general. See also Friedman, op. cit., p. 42, nn. 55a and 56. He cites the position of Rabbenu Asher, *Responsa* 43:8, that the Gaonic decree relied upon the principle of כל דמקדש אדעתא דרבנן מקדש (bKet 3a): "Everyone who marries, marries with the agreement of the Rabbis," i.e., the Rabbis have the authority retroactively to declare a marriage null and void, rather than on the principle of גט מעושה (compulsory divorce). The possibility exists that the divorce is granted solely by the court, but this is difficult in the light of the previous halakhic literature.

7. Friedman, *Jewish Marriage,* no. 2, p. 41: Only the last two digits, 84, are preserved in the MS, but, as Friedman proves in his penetrating analysis, it can only be 4784. Ibid., p. 38, n. 48.

8. As Friedman notes, "Life and death refers to the stipulation calling for the return of one-half the dowry if the wife dies childless." Ibid.

9. If the woman acted indecently, however, as expressed in mKet 72a, she would forfeit her *ketubah.*

10. *Mohar* is apparently the *ketubah* alimony sum. Cf. Exod. 22:16.

11. See Zev Falk, "Mutual Obligations in the Ketubah," *Journal of Jewish Studies* 8-9, (1957-58): 215-217, and cf. p. 216 n. 2, Friedman, op. cit., p. 40. n. 51.

12. MKid 1:1; but cf. bKid 2b, "acquisition" vs. "sanctification."

13. Friedman, op. cit., pp. 40-41.

14. See Jacob Katz, *Exclusiveness and Tolerance* (New York: Schocken, 1969), p. 114, n. 3.

15. *Bet Ha-Behirah Le-Ketubot,* ed. A. Schreiber (Jerusalem, 1946), pp. 269-270. Cited by S. Lieberman, *Hilkhot Yerushalmi,* p. 61, Comment 195, noted by Friedman, p. 34, n. 29.

16. The Meiri's primary master was Reuben b. Chaim; he also corresponded with Solomon b. Abraham (the Rashba) (*Encyclopaedia Judaica,* s.v. "Meiri").

17. Cf. 4:7-12.

18. It is interesting to note that the Meiri himself, although he cites this possibility, ultimately disagrees with it. He holds that the Geonim *permit* the husband to divorce his wife immediately, but do not necessarily force him to do so. Cf. *Bet Ha-Behirah, Ketubot,* p. 269, n. 4.

19. Friedman, op. cit., pp. 42-43. Friedman notes there, though, that we could be dealing with parallel developments. See also J. N. Epstein, "Notizem z.d. jüdisch-aramäischen Papyri von Assuan," *Jahrbuch der Jüdisch-literarischen Gesellschaft,* vol. VI, pp. 368-369. (See *Mehqarim Be-Safrut Ha-Talmud Uve-geshonot Shemiyot* [Jerusalem: Magnes, 1983], pp. 320-328).

CHAPTER VI

1. See *Encyclopaedia Judaica,* s.v. "Mordecai ben Hillel ha-Kohen." He (1240?-1298) was a descendant of Eliezer b. Joel ha-Levi, a relative of the Rosh,

and brother-in-law of Meir ha-Kohen, who was the author of the *Hagahot Mai-muniyot*. Usually referred to as "the Mordecai," for his halakhic work, which is appended in standard editions of the Talmud to that of the Rif, he was an outstanding student of the Maharam of Rothenburg and of Isaac b. Moses, author of the *Or Zarua*. The Mordecai was edited by his sons and students.

2. Mordecai in bKet 186; cf. in addition *Tosafot* Ket 64a. s.v. *aval amerah* that Rabbenu Hananel does not coerce him to grant a divorce, below pp. 96–97. Cf. Rif to bKet *ad loc.* However, the Rabbenu Nissim *ad loc.* insists that this enforced divorce is the decree of the Geonim, and was therefore nullified with their decree.

3. *Hidushei Ha-Ri Migash to Tractate Ketubot,* ed. M. Shapiro (Bnei Brak, 1976), p. 20b.

4. The purpose of this work is a matter of dispute between B. Z. Benedict and Y. Ta-Shema. The argument of the former is that the entire purpose of the *Sefer Ha-Maor* was to justify the Provencal tradition in the face of the different traditions of North Africa and Spain that were expressed by Alfasi. The proofs to this position are to be found in B. Z. Benedict, "Al Magamato Shel Rabbi Zerahia Ha-Levi Be-Sefer Ha-Maor" *Memorial Volume to Benjamin De Fris* (Jerusalem, 1969), esp. p. 160. On the other hand, Yisrael Ta-Shema, in his doctoral dissertation "The Parameters of *Sefer Ha-Maor* the Laws of the Rif" (Bar Ilan University, 1973), published in *Shnaton Ha-Mishpat Ha-Ivri* (Hebrew University, 1978), vol. V, pp. 361–406, attempts to demonstrate that the *Sefer Ha-Maor* is a separate work of commentary on the Talmud which merely cites certain positions of Alfasi during the course of its novellae. I believe that the arguments of Ta-Shema are the more compelling.

5. Baal Ha-Maor to the Rif, bKet 27a.

6. The first halakhist to cancel the Geonic decrees and prohibit a coerced divorce for a woman who claims her husband repulses her was Rabbenu Tam, as we shall see in detail below. Rabbenu Tam died in 1171, the year Rabbenu Zerahyah HaLevi began writing his *Sefer Ha-Maor*. It is clear that Rabbenu Tam, known as "the Frenchman" and probably the most authoritative decisor among the Franco-German Sages, was well known in Provence. R. Yitzhak ben R. Abba Mari of Marseilles, author of *Sefer Ha-Ittur* (written 1179), cites Rabbenu Tam and queries him on points of law. (see E. E. Urbach, *Ba'alei Ha-Tosafot,* p. 100 and esp. no. 62). Similarly, the Baal Ha-Maor quotes Rabbenu Tam, whom he evidently respected (see Y. Reifman, *Toldot Rabbenu Zerahyah,* [Prague, 1844], p. 61, and Urbach, op. cit., p. 100). It is therefore possible that Rabbenu Zerahyah HaLevi, who was a younger contemporary of Rabbenu Tam, was influenced on this matter by the French decisor.

7. MT, *Hilkhot Ishut* 14:8–14; see I. Haut, *Divorce in Jewish Law,* pp. 53–54.

8. See above, pp. 62–63.

9. BKet 63b.

10. Unlike Rashi, Rabbenu Tam, and Alfasi, who all interpret the case of Rav Zevid as dealing with a woman who finds her husband repulsive.

11. Maimonides adjudicates in accordance with the *baraita* ("like our rabbis" [*Rabbotenu*] as understood by Rami bar Hama—i.e., the court sends agents to her twice (before and after the proclamation), and Rava in the name of Rav Sheshet— i.e., they attempt to persuade her in addition to the double agents before she forfeits the entire *ketubah*. Thus Maimonides understands that Rava reacted—[it is "boorish"—to the notion that she would lose her alimony without an attempt at further persuasion. In this regard, Maimonides' position is similar to that of Alfasi. Cf. *Kesef Mishnah* to Maimonides' *Hilkhot Ishut* 14:9.

12. Cf. Maimonides' *Hilkhot Ishut* 3:19 rules that a father ought not to betroth his daughter who is still a minor, because she must first come of age and declare, "This one I want." Apparently, the presumption that "a woman would rather live with anyone than live alone" (bKid 41a) requires the assent of the woman in question, according to Maimonides.

13. See Shlomo Eidelberg, *Responsa of Rabbenu Gershom the Light of the Exile* (New York: Yeshiva University, 1955), p. 19. *Sefer Ravan,* pt. 1, Jerusalem, 1975), p. 121b, mentions that the decrees were instituted by the communities, which probably means that they were ratified by the communities. After all, "No decree is instituted for a community unless the majority of the community is able to accept it," teach our Sages (b.A.Z. 36a). See also I. Haut, *Divorce in Jewish Law,* pp. 55–56.

14. *Sefer Ravan,* pt. I (Jerusalem, 1975), p. 261b (Rabbenu Eliezer b. R. Natan, a contemporary of the Rashbam and Rabbenu Tam).

15. See *Sefer Ha-Yashar Le-Rabbenu Tam,* Ephraim Zalmen Margaliot, (New York, 1959), pp. 39–42, based on ed. of Shraga Fisch Rosenthal, *Sefer Ha-Yashar Le-Rabbenu Tam, Responsa* (Berlin, 1888), *Siman* 24, p. 39 and I. Haut, *Divorce in Jewish Law,* pp. 54–55, for further discussion.

16. BKet 63b, s.v. *v'inhu.*

17. Ibid., and 64a, s.v. *aval.*

18. Rabbenu Yehudah deLyon.

19. *Sefer Ha-Yashar, Hiddushim,* ed. Schlessinger, n. 4.

20. BKet 63b. See previous discussion, p. 52.

21. Maimonides' *Hilkhot Ishut* 14:8.

22. See above, p. 58 f.

23. Although his opening statement is a bit unclear, he asserts further on that there is no discussion of enforced divorce in the Talmud, and it is strange to assume that he would get so upset if he felt that the Geonim had merely moved up the time.

24. See above pp. 86–87.

25. Rabbenu Tam upholds a minority opinion in this regard. Rabbenu Aharon HaLevi and Ibn Adret (Ritva) both are of the opinion that every act of marriage-sanctification is in effect administered with a stipulation: on the condition that it be satisfactory to the Rabbis in Israel, "in accordance with the laws of Moses and Israel." (See *Shitah Mekubetzet* on bKet 3a and *Hidushei Ha-Ritva.*) If such is the case, the right to cancel *kiddushin* is granted to the Sages of every generation. Similarly,

the Meiri, the Rashba, the Rosh, and the Rivash and the Tashbetz would seem to hold that even in the post-Talmudic period there is such a right, and indeed was exercised. See Freiman, *Seder Kiddushin Ve-Nisuin* (Jerusalem, 1945), and Berkovits, *Stipulation in Marriage and Divorce* (Jerusalem, 1966), esp. pp. 119–150.

26. Although Rashi's position is never clearly stated, and there is an apparent contradiction in the way the Mordecai and Rabbenu Tam transmitted the views of Rabbenu Hananel on the question of *moredet*. Nevertheless, Rabbenu Tam could rely on his tradition.

27. See Urbach, *Baalei Ha-Tosafot* (Jerusalem 1980) vol. I, pp. 60–113. Cf. Rabbenu Tam's interpretation of mA.Z. 1:1) s.v. *Asur*. He suggests that businessmen are permitted to traffic with the Gentiles on their holidays (i.e., that only dealing in objects that will actually be used for idolatrous purposes is forbidden), and cf. his sharp polemics against Rabbenu Meshullam in defense of Rashi.

28. S. Albeck, "Yahaso shel Rabbenu Tam Le-Ve'ayot Zemano," *Zion* 19 (1954): 104–141.

29. Cf. Urbach, op. cit., pp. 67–77, for a discussion of the dispute.

30. Rabbenu Meshullam ben Natan of Melun was a contemporary of Rabbenu Tam. See Urbach, op. cit., pp. 62–77, for a discussion of their disagreements.

31. Rabbenu Tam, *Responsa* 101.

32. BR.H. 33a, *Tosafot*, s.v. *ha*. Interestingly enough, Maimonides, in the case of *moredet* the champion of woman's rights, disagrees, and forbids a woman to make the blessing (*MT, Hilkhot Tzitzit*, 3:3); halakhically speaking, however, they are two different issues.

33. Urbach, op. cit., p. 61. He married the sister of R. Shimshon the Elder of Falaise; and questions concerning Rabbenu Tam's practices were addressed to *G'veret Ishto* ("the Mistress, his wife") after his death. Women also did business at that time—Ravan 115, *Or Zarua*, Baba Kama 351, and *Tosafot* A.Z. 23a s.v. *tu*—allowing wives of priests to do business with Gentiles despite problem of *yihud*, since the women (unlike captives) may cry out for help. Cf. also Finkelstein, *Jewish Self-Government in Middle Ages* (1924), pp. 374–379, and Guidemann, *Torah and Life* (*Ha-Torah Veha-Hayim*) vol. 1, pp. 182–190.

34. H. Ben-Sasson, "Hanhagatah Shel Torah," *Behinot* 9 (1956): 39–53.

35. Deut 17:9; .cf. bR.H. 25a. This is especially interesting in light of the Talmudic principle "the generations are lessening in intellectual activity."

36. See *Enzyklopedia Talmudit*, s.v. *ha la khah ke-batrae*, where it is noted that this principle is not mentioned in the Talmud. It is first found in the early Geonim, e.g., *Seder Tannaim ve-Amoraim*, chaps. 25 and 50. For sources in the Rishonim, also cited by the *ET*, see e.g., Rif, end bAr; *Tosafot* bKid 45b, s.v. *hava uvda;* Rosh, bSanh, 4:6; Ran and Ritva in first chapter of bSuk, in the name of the Geonim.

37. Luke 16:15–18. Mark and Paul similarly prohibit divorce across the board, whereas Matthew permits it only in the case of adultery (Matt. 5:32).

38. When we also bear in mind that marriage to one woman was viewed as a

concession—"it is better to marry than to burn with passion" (1 Cor 7:1–8)—it is obvious that marriage to many women would be seen as a vice. Moreover, since precedents for monogamy were clearly to be found within the Bible—"therefore shall a man leave his father and mother, cling to his wife and they shall be one flesh" (Gen 2:24); the negative relationship between Sarah and Hagar; Rebecca and Leah's unseemly conduct during the incident of the mandrakes—and in light of the fact that the Sages of the Talmud were all monogamous. Rabbenu Gershom legislated the Jewish ideal of monogamy in an area which was intellectually ready to accept it.

39. Albeck, op. cit., p. 104.

40. *Hiddushei Ha-Ramban* to bPes 117, "I received from my teacher R. Yehudah, may the righteous be remembered for a blessing, who received from his teacher R. Yitzhak b. Avraham Ha-Tzarfati, that *hallel* on the nights of Pesach . . ." Cf. Chavel, *Rabbenu Mosheh ben Nahman* (Jerusalem, 1967), p. 38, n. 2; p. 40.

41. Cf. *Hiddushei Ha-Rambam* to b.S.B. 92b, bYeb 93a, bKid 22a.

42. Cf. *Hiddushei Ha-Rambam* to BShevu 37a; Chavel, *Kitvei Ramban,* vol. 1, p. 231; and idem *Rabbenu Mosheh ben Nahman,* p. 45, esp. n. 23.

43. *Milḥamot* of the Ramban, on the Rif, Ketubot, p. 27a.

44. I. H. Weiss, *Dor Dor Ve-Dorshav,* vol. 5 (Vilna, 1923/24), pp. 32–33, n. 2.

45. *Responsa of Rabbenu Shelomo Ibn Adret* (Bnei Brak, 1948), pt. 1, responsa 572, 573, p. 215.

46. *Hiddushei Ha-Rashba,* pt. 2 (Jerusalem, 1963), pp. 97–98.

47. Of course, he does not explain why a wife might not be required to learn to love even a husband with objective blemishes, although the Rashba would counter that when she had consented to marry him he did not have the blemishes, whereas in the case of our responsum, when she had consented to marry him, he had still been twenty years her senior. How very different is the position of Rabbenu Isaiah of Trani, the grandson of Rabbenu Isaiah of Trani the Elder, one of the thirteenth-century Italian Baalei Tosafot, who wrote in his commentary on our Talmudic text in bKet 63b (printed on 64a), that he refuses to allow an enforced divorce—because there always exists the possibility that she merely cast her eyes on another, unless there is objective proof on his unseemliness—but if the husband does divorce her, she receives her *ketubah* with the additions. His understanding of psychology is radically different from that of the Rashba.

אבל הרב פירש דאדרבה, להקל באו עליה ולא להחמיר, וכך הוא משמעות הדברים. ה"ד מורדת שכופין אותה על ידי הפסד כתובתה לרבנן כדאית להו ולרבותינו כדאית להו, דאמרה בעינא ליה ומצערנא ליה, שאין בעלה מאוס בעיניה, בין תובעת גירושין בין אינה תובעת גירושין הואיל ואין בעלה מאיס בעיניה ודאי כופין אותה ע"י הפסד כתובתה כדי שתתפייס עם בעלה, אבל אמרה מאיס עלי, שבעלה מאוס בעיניה, לא כיפינן לה ע"י הפסד כתובתה אלא מניחין אותה במרדה דכיון דבעלה מאיס בעיניה אנוסה היא בדבר ולא מדעתה עושה כן ואפילו אשה כשרה אי אפשר להבעל לשנואי לה ואע"פ שאין שום מום ניכר בו הרבה פעמים אשה מואסת בבעל אעפ"י שאין

שום מום ניכר בו וזה דומה לאדם שאין יכול לאכול מאכל השנאוי לו ונתעב עליו, ואין שום דרך
כאן לכפייה, כי אם לעשות דרך בקשה ולפתוחה אולי תחשוק בו. ואדרבה, אם היינו יודעים כודאי
שטעמה אמת שהוא מאוס מאוס בעיניה ולא נתנה עיניה כאחר היינו כופין הבעל להוציא כי הך דתנן
לקמן בפרק המדיר ואלו שכופין אותו להוציא מפני שהוא מאוס בעיניה, ואין האשה יכולה לסבול
שתבעל לו אלא אלא משום דהכא אנו מסופקים בטענתה שכין שאין אנו רואים בבעלה באותן המומים
י"ל שמא עיניה נתנה באחר ומשום זה שהיא אומרת כך לפיכך אין כופין הבעל להוציא אבל מ"מ
גם היא נמי אין כופין להפסיד כתובתה דשמא טענתה אמת דלב יודע מרת נפשו אלא מפתין אותה
שמא תחשוק בה ואם רואין שאינה מתרצה בדבר, אין ב"ד נזקקין לכופה דשמא אנוסה היא, ושמא
גם היא עצויבה בדבר שבעלה מאוס בעיניה ואי משום עיגון הבעל, יכול לישא אשה אחרת עד שלא
יפטור לזו ויוציא זו ויתן לה כתובתה שאין ב"ד יכולין לקונסה בכתובתה מאחר שהיא טוענת טענת
אונס וזה הפתרון הוא נכון ואין לזוז ממנו ולפי זה הפתרון היכא שאומרת מאיס עלי לא הוי מורדת
וא"כ כשבא לגרשה, נותן לה כתובה ותוספת שהרי התוספת כותב לאשתו בעבור חבת ביאה
וכבר בא עליה ואימתי אין לה תוספת? כשמגרשה משום מורדת שכך היא תקנות הגאונים,
שתוספת אין לה אבל כתובה יש לה אבל עכשיו שמגרשה משום טענתה ולא הוי מורדת, אפילו
תוספת יש לה, שהרי אינו מגרשה כתקנות הגאונים . . .

[That which the Gaon interpreted, so did the Rabbenu Tam and the other commentaries interpret, and according to their interpretation they are more stringent upon her when she says "He is distasteful to me" than when she says "I wish to stay married to him, but I wish to pain him."] But the Master interprets the opposite; they approach her [the *moredet* of "He is repulsive to me"] more leniently and not more stringently, and this is the meaning of the words:

What is the case of *moredet,* that they force her through a loss of the marriage contract, the Rabbis in accordance with their view [the mishnah] and our Rabbis in accordance with their view [the *baraita*], when she says: "I desire [to stay married to] him, but [I desire to] pain him," for her husband is not distasteful in her eyes.

Whether she claims a divorce or does not claim a divorce, they certainly force her through a loss of her marriage contract in order that she be reconciled with her husband.

But one who says "He is distasteful to me," that her husband is distasteful in her eyes, we do not force her through the loss of her marriage contract, but they allow her to remain in her rebellion, for since her husband is distasteful to her, she is forced [against her will] with regard to this matter, and not willingly does she do so.

And even a proper woman cannot have sexual relations with one she detests.

And even though there is no obvious defect in him, many times a woman will find a husband distasteful despite the lack of an obvious defect.

And this is similar to a person who is unable to eat a food which is detestable to him and it is an abomination for him. There is no room here for coercion, except by requesting and importuning that perhaps she will desire him.

And to the contrary, if we were to definitely know that her reason is true, that he is [indeed] distasteful to her, and that she has not cast her eyes on another, we would force the husband to let her go, as in those [instances] we learn in the Mishnah later on in Chapter Ha-Madir: "And these [cases] they force him to let her go," because he is distasteful in her eyes, and the woman cannot stand having sexual relations with him.

But here, since we are in doubt regarding her claim, for since we do not observe the husband with those defects [enumerated in the mishnah], it is possible that perhaps because she cast her eyes on another she says thus ["He is distasteful"]. Therefore we do not force the husband to let her go. However, neither do we force her to lose her marriage contract, for perhaps her claim is true, for a heart knows the bitterness of one's soul.

But they importune her—perhaps she will come to desire him. And if they see that she does not acquiesce in this matter, the court may not force her, for perhaps she is [as] one who is forced [against her will], and perhaps she too is saddened by the situation that her husband is distasteful in her eyes. And as far as the "chaining" of the husband [is concerned], [that he is deprived of sexual relations], so that he not be "chained," if he does not find another woman, before he is freed from this one, let him allow this one to leave, and give her the marriage contract.

For the Jewish court is unable to fine her regarding the marriage contract, since she claims to be [as] one forced [against her will].

And this resolution is correct, and no one is to depart from it. And according to this resolution, and whenever she says "He is distasteful to me," she is not a *moredet,* and so when he goes to divorce her, he gives her the marriage contract and the addition, for a man writes an addition for his wife because of his desire of sexual relations with her, and he has already had sexual relations with her. And when does she not receive the addition? When he divorces her because she was a *moredet,* for thus were the decrees of the Geonim [*sic*] that the addition she does not receive but the marriage contract she does receive. But now that he divorces her because of her claim and she is not a *moredet,* she even receives the addition, for he is not divorcing her in accord with the Geonic decrees.

Now I have identified this position as that of Rabbenu Isaiah of Trani the Younger (his grandfather assumes a new fundamental in line with Rabbenu Tam) in accord with the proofs of Abraham Liss, *Piskei Ha-Rid to Tractates Yevamot and Ketubot, Makhon Ha-Talmud Ha-Yisraeli Ha-Shalem* (Jerusalem, 1973), p. 10.

It is fascinating to note that in the generation following Rabbenu Tam and the

Rid, even a decisor who was sensitive to the psychological difficulties of a woman submitting to a husband she detests can no longer find it possible to interpret or legislate enforced divorce.

48. Rosh Commentary to bKet 63b, sec. 35.

49. *Responsa of the Rosh* (New York, 1954), 43:8, p. 40b.

50. Unlike Rabbenu Tam, who questions the Gaonic right to legislate regarding marriage in the first place. See above pp. 98-99.

It is interesting to compare this position of the Rosh with his statements in his commentary to bKid 29b, p. 41. After citing the lengthy Gaonic version of the blessing for the redemption of the firstborn, he writes:

ובצרפת ואשכנז לא נהגו לברך ברכה זו ולא מצינו שמברכים שום ברכה שלא הוזכרה במשנה או בתוספתא או בגמרא כי אחרי סדור רב אשי ורבינא לא מצינו שנתחדשה ברכה, וגם ראשית הברכה איני מבין . . .

In France and Germany they are not accustomed to make this blessing. And we do not find that we recite any blessing which is not mentioned in the Mishnah, Tosefta, or Gemara, for after the arrangement of Rav Ashi and Ravina [of the Talmud] we do not find the creation of a blessing, and also the beginning of the blessing I do not understand . . .

Perhaps we might argue (based on general rabbinic authority) that if the Geonim have the right to cancel *kiddushin* according to the Rosh, they may have the right to create a blessing. Nevertheless, in both instances the practical effect is a rejection of Geonic legislation. For the issue of canceling *kiddushin,* see also Elenson, *Nisuin Shelo Kedat Mosheh Ve-Yisrael* (Devir, 1975), pp. 108–113.

51. Despite the fact that R. Mordecai Yaffe's code, called the *Levush,* was contemporaneous with the *Shulhan Arukh,* and that Rav Shlomo Luria insisted that his code-commentary was more authoritative because it was closer to the original Talmud—see Weiss, *Dor Dor Ve-Dorshav,* vol. III, pp. 215 ff.; David Feldman, *Birth Control in Jewish Law* (New York and London, 1968), p. 13—the *Shulkhan Arukh* with the *Mappah* (glosses by R. Mosheh Isserles—the Rema), with its manifold commentaries, soon overcame all major opposition.

52. *Shulhan Arukh, Even Ha-Ezer* 77:2.

53. *Nikhsei melug* (lit., "Property of pecking") is property which the wife brings into the marriage with her; although her husband enjoys ("pecks at") profits from its "fruit" (as literally in the case of landed property), she retains full responsibility for the property itself, absorbing all profits and losses. *Nikhsei tzon barzel* (lit., "property of [the] iron flock"), on the other hand, is property for which the husband assumes full responsibility; the wife never loses, in normal circumstances, the value of the property (thus "iron": stable and enduring). Such property is specified in the *ketubah* as part of the husband's financial obligations to his wife. Cf. mYev 7:1, and Bertinoro there.

CHAPTER VII

1. See above, pp. 51-52.
2. See Rav Mosheh Isserles, *Shulhan Arukh, Even Ha-Ezer* 157:4.
3. *Ein Tenai Be-Nissuin,* ed. Rabbi Yehudah Lubetzki (Vilna, 1930).
4. BGit 33a.
5. The Maharam Elashkar, responsum no. 48, insists that only if the majority of the communities within one country agree to annul a marriage retroactively can that marriage be considered annulled. But Rabbi Solomon ben Adret in his Responsa, pt. I, no. 185, insists that in the post-Talmudic period, no Jewish court or even courts have the power to annul a marriage retroactively. For a full discussion of these issues, see A. H. Freiman, *Seder Qiddushin Ve-Nissuin* (Jerusalem: 1945); Rav Elyakim Elinson, "Seruv Latet Get," *Sinai* 69 (1971): 135 ff.; Rav Nisan Zaks, "Qiddushin Al Tenai," *Noam* 1 (1958): 52-68.
6. Eliezer Berkovits, *Tenai Be-Nissuin Uve-Get* (Jerusalem, 1967).
7. Isaac Klein, *A Guide to Jewish Religious Practice,* (New York, 1979), p. 393.
8. Lamm, "Recent Additions to the *Ketubah,*" *Tradition* 2, no. 1 (1959): 93-119.
9. A. Leo Levin and Meyer Kramer, *New Provisions in the Ketubah* (New York, 1955).

It is interesting to note that there have already been a number of secular court cases which have addressed themselves to the issues involved.

In 1973, in *Margulies* v. *Margulies,* 45A.D.2d517, the court decided that a husband could not be forced—via incarceration—to honor a *ketubah* stipulation to grant his wife a religious divorce. But in 1979, in *Stern* v. *Stern,* (*NLJL*Aug. 8, 1979 [Supreme Court, Kings County, p. 13, col. 5, Mr. Justice Held]; for further discussion, see I. Haut, *Divorce in Jewish Law and Life,* pp. 81-2. Judge Held ruled that a husband must give his wife a religious divorce. He maintained that the *ketubah* is not just a religious document; it is also a personal contract between two individuals, agreed upon by both. As in any case of voluntary arbitration, the secular courts must uphold the agreement.

10. *New York Law Journal,* Feb. 17, 1983, p. 4. See J. David Bleich, "Modern Day Agunot: A Proposed Remedy," *Jewish Law Annual* 4 (1981): 167-168, and idem, "A Suggested Ante-Nuptial Agreement: A Proposal in the Wake of *Avitzur,*" *Journal of Halachah and Contemporary Society* 7 (Spring 1984): 25-41, esp. 38-39. However, I believe it is most important that this agreement be tied to the *tenayim,* making it an aspect of the wedding ceremony itself and not a separate—and totally secular—antenuptial agreement. It should also stipulate the precise conditions under which the agreement is entered into, rather than merely an understanding to appear before a Beth Din. The formula I suggest is based on bKet 97b and has the approval of Rabbi J. B. Zolty, former Chief Rabbi of Jerusalem. The text of his letter appears in the Appendix.

1. Z. Falk, *The Divorce Action by the Wife in Jewish Law,* Institute for Legislative Research and Comparative Law, Jerusalem, 1973, pp. 41, 42.

2. *Piskei Din,* vol. 9, p. 94, Supreme Rabbinical Court, Jerusalem, 1973; ibid., vol. 7, pp. 201, 204, Supreme Rabbinical Court, Jerusalem, 1967.

3. *Piskei Din,* vol. 9, pp. 171, 182, Tel Aviv-Jaffa Rabbinical District Court, 1970; see also Irwin H. Haut, *Divorce in Jewish Law and Life,* Studies in Jewish Jurisprudence, vol. V, Sepher-Hermon Press, New York, 1983, esp. pp. 85–88.

4. Vol. 2, n. 112.

5. Vol. 4, n. 21 and vol. 5, n. 26.

6. *Hechal Yitzhak, Even Ha-Ezer,* vol. 1, n. 1, p. 11, col. 2.

7. No. 69, 23.

8. *Yabi, a Omer, Even Ha-Ezer,* vol. 3, n. 18, p. 287, and n. 19, p. 292.

BIBLIOGRAPHY

PRIMARY SOURCES

Abraham b. David (Baal Ha-Hasagot). In Moses Maimonides, *Mishneh Torah.*

Abraham of Montpellier (min Ha-Har). *Perush R. Avraham min Ha-Har al Sukkah, Megillah, Hagigah, Yoma, Rosh Ha-Shanah.* Ed. M. Y. Blau. New York, 1974/75.

Alfasi, Isaac b. Jacob (Rif). *Halakhot.* In Babylonian Talmud.

Asher b. R. Yehiel (Rosh). *Responsa.* Vilna, 1882.

————. *Sefer Rabbenu Asher.* In Babylonian Talmud.

Ashkenazi, Bezalel. *Shitah Mekubetzet: Ketubot.* Repr. Jerusalem, n.d.

Duran, Simon b. Zemah. *Tashbatz.* Repr. Jerusalem, n.d.

Eliezer b. R. Nathan (Ravan). *Sefer Ra'van.* Jerusalem, 1975.

Gerondi, Zerahia b. Isaac (Baal Ha-Maor). *Sefer Ha-Ma'or Ha-Gadol.* In Babylonian Talmud.

Gershom b. Judah (Rabbenu Gershom). *Responsa.* Ed. S. Eidelberg. New York, 1955.

Halakhot Pesuqot (Yehudai Gaon or Natronai Gaon). Jerusalem, 1966/67.

Ibn Adret, Solomon b. Abraham. *Hiddushim* on *Ketubot.* Repr. Jerusalem, n.d.

————. *Responsa.* Vol. I. Bnei Brak, 1981/82.

Ibn Daud, Abraham. *The Book of Tradition: Sefer Ha-Qabbalah.* Ed. Gerson Cohen, Philadelphia, 1967.

Isaac b. R. Abba Mari. *Sefer Ha-Ittur.* 2 vols., Repr. Jerusalem, 1969/70.

Isaac b. R. Moshe. *Or Zaru'a.* vol. I. Zhitomir, 1862. Vol. II. Jerusalem, 1891.

Isaac b. R. Sheshet (Rivash). *Responsa.* Vilna, 1881.

Isaiah of Trani (the Elder). *Pisqei Rid al Masekhtot Yevamot U-Ketubot.* Ed. A. Yia. Jerusalem, 1973.

Jacob b. R. Meir (Rabbenu Tam). *Sefer Ha-Yashar, Responsa.* Ed. S. R. Rosenthal. Berlin, 1898.

————. *Sefer Ha-Yashar, Hiddushim.* Ed. S. Schlessinger. Jerusalem, 1965.

Joseph mi-Trani (Maharit). *Responsa.* Lemberg, 1861.

Karo, Joseph. *Shulhan Arukh: Even Ha-Ezer.* Repr. New York, 1966/67.

———. *Kesef Mishneh.* In Moses Maimonides, *Mishneh Torah.*

Lewin, B. M. *Otzar Ha-Geonim.* Vol. 8. Jerusalem, 1938.

Luria, Solomon b. R. Yehiel. *Yam shel Shlomo.* Repr. New York, n.d.

Maimonides, Moses. *Mishneh Torah.* Repr. New York, 1948.

Malachi Ha-Kohen. *Yad Malakhi.* Repr. Jerusalem, 1953/54.

Meir b. R. Baruch. *Responsa.* Prague, 1609.

———. *Responsa.* Lemberg, 1860.

———. *Responsa.* Ed. N. N. Rabinowitz. Berlin, 1889.

Mekhilta de-Rabbi Ishmael. Ed. H. S. Horovitz, I. A. Rabin. Jerusalem: Bamberger and Wahrmann, 1960.

Mekhilta de-Rabbi Shim'on ben Yohai. Ed. J. N. Epstein, E. Z. Melamed. Jerusalem: Meqitze Nirdamim, 1955.

Menahem b. Solomon (Meiri). *Bet Ha-Behirah al Masekhet Ketubot.* Ed. A. Schreiber. Jerusalem, 1946.

Mordecai b. Hillel. *Halakhot.* In Babylonian Talmud.

Moses b. R. Yosef mi-Trani (Mabit). *Kiryat Sefer.* Vilna, 1900.

Nachmanides, Moses. *Hiddushim.* Repr. New York, 1966/67.

———. *Kitvei Ramban.* Ed. H. D. Chavel. Jerusalem, 1962/63.

———. *Milhamot Ha-Shem.* In Babylonian Talmud.

Sifra de-Vei Rav (Torat Kohanim), with commentaries. Jerusalem: Sifra, 1958/59.

Sifrei 'al Sefer Devarim. Ed. L. Finkelstein. New York: Jewish Theological Seminary, 1969.

Sifrei de-Vei Rav (Numbers). Ed. H. S. Horovitz. Jerusalem: Wahrmann, 1966.

Teshuvot Ha-Geonim Sha'arei Tzedek. Repr. Jerusalem, 1965/66.

Tykocinski, H. *Taqqanot Ha-Geonim.* Berlin, 1929.

SECONDARY SOURCES

Albeck, Ch. *Mavo La-Talmudim.* Tel Aviv: Devir, 1969.

———. *Mehqarim Ba-Baraita Ve-Tosefta Ve-Yahasan La-Talmud.* Jerusalem: Mosad Ha-Rav Kook, 1969.

Albeck, S. "Yahaso shel Rabbenu Tam Le-Ve'ayot Zemano." *Zion* 19 (1953/54): 104–41.

———. *Untersuchungen ueber die Redaktion der Mishna*. Berlin: C. A. Schwetzschke & Sohn, 1923.

Benedikt, B. Z. "Al Magamato shel Rabbi Zerahia Ha-Levi be-Sefer Ha-Ma'or." In *Sefer Zikaron Le-Binyamin DeVries*, pp. 160–67. Jerusalem: 1968.

Ben-Sasson, H. "Hanhagatah shel Torah." *Behinot* 9 (1956): 39–53.

Berkovits, E. *Tenai Be-Nissu'in Uve-Get*. Jerusalem: Mosad Ha-Rav Kook, 1967.

Bleich, J. D. "A Suggested Ante-Nuptial Agreement: A Proposal in the Wake of *Avitzur*." *Journal of Halachah and Contemporary Society* 7 (Spring 1984): 25–41.

———. "Modern-Day Agunot: A proposed Remedy." *Jewish Law Annual* 4 (1981): 167–187.

Chavel, C. *Rabbenu Moshe ben Nahman*. Jerusalem: Mosad Ha-Rav Kook, 1967.

Cohen, B. *Jewish and Roman Law*. New York: Burning Bush Press, 1966.

Elinson, E. *Nissu'in shelo Ke-Dat Moshe Ve-Yisrael*. Tel Aviv: Devir, 1975.

———. "Seruv Latet Get." *Sinai* 69 (1971): 135–58.

Encyclopaedia Judaica. 16 vols. Jerusalem: Keter 1971–72.

Ephrati, J. E. *Tequfat Ha-Saboraim Ve-Sifrutah Be-Vavel Uve-Eretz Yisrael*. Petah Tiqvah: Hotza'at Agudat Benei Asher, 1973.

Epstein, J. N. *Mavo La-Mishnah*. 2 vols. Jerusalem: J. L. Magnes, 1963/64.

———. *Mevo'ot Le-Sifrut Ha-Amoraim: Bavli Vi-Yrushalmi*. Ed. E. Z. Melamed. Jerusalem: J. L. Magnes, 1962.

———. *Mevo'ot Le-Sifrut Ha-Tannaim: Mishnah, Tosefta U-Midreshei Halakhah*. Ed. E. Z. Melamed. Jerusalem: J. L. Magnes, 1957.

———. "Notizen z. d. jüdisch-aramäischen Papyri von Assuan," *Jahrbuch der juedisch-literarischen Gesellschaft* 6 (1909): 361–73.

Epstein, L. *The Jewish Marriage Contract*. New York: Jewish Theological Seminary, 1927.

Falk, Y. Y. *Penei Yehoshu'a*. 3 vols. New York: Sentry Press, 1951/52.

Falk, Z. W. *Jewish Matrimonial Law*. Oxford: Clarendon Press, 1966.

———. "Mutual Obligations in the Ketubah." *Journal of Jewish Studies* 8–9 (1957–58): 215–17.

Feldblum, M. S. *Perushim U-Mehqarim Ba-Talmud: Masekhet Gittin*. New York: Yeshiva University Press, 1969.

———. "Professor Abraham Weiss: His Approach and Contribution to

Talmudic Scholarship." In *Abraham Weiss Jubilee Volume*, ed. M. S. Feldblum, pp. 7–80. New York: Feldheim, 1965.

Feldman, D. *Birth Control in Jewish Law*. New York: NYU Press, 1968.

Finkelstein, L. *Jewish Self-Government in the Middle Ages*. New York: Jewish Theological Seminary of America, 1924.

Freiman, A. H. *Seder Qiddushin Ve-Nissu'in*. Jerusalem: Mosad Ha-Rav Kook, 1945.

Friedman, M. "Hit'arvut Ha-Shilton Be-Qairwan." *Mikhael* 5 (1978): 215–42.

Friedman, M. A. "Termination of the Marriage Upon the Wife's Request: A Palestinian Ketubah Stipulation." *Proceedings of the American Academy for Jewish Research* 37 (1969): 29–55.

———. *Jewish Marriage in Palestine: A Cairo Genizah Study*. Tel Aviv: University of Tel Aviv, 1981.

Ginsberg, H. L. "The Brooklyn Museum Aramaic Papyri." *Journal of the American Oriental Society* 74 (1954): 153–62.

Goitein, S. I. *A Mediterranean Society*. Vol. I, Berkeley and Los Angeles: University of California, 1978.

Graetz, H. *History of the Jews*. 6 vols. Philadelphia: Jewish Publication Society, 1891–98.

Guedemann, M. *Ha-Torah Veha-Hayyim*. 3 vols. Warsaw, 1911.

Halivni, D. W. *Meqorot U-Mesorot: Be'urim Ba-Talmud Le-Seder Nashim*. Tel Aviv: Devir, 1968.

Haut, I., *Divorce in Jewish Law and Life,* New York: Sefer Hermon, 1983.

Hyman, A. *Toledot Tannaim va-Amoraim*. Vols. I–III. Jerusalem: Kiryah Ne'emanah, 1963–64.

Kaplan, J. *The Redaction of the Babylonian Talmud*. New York: Bloch, 1933.

Karl, Z. *Mehqarim Be-Sifrei: Nissayon Maqif Le-Tefisat Derashot Hazal tokh Gishah Hadashah*. Tel Aviv: Devir, 1953/54.

Katz, J. *Exclusiveness and Tolerance*. New York: Schocken, 1969.

Klein, I. *A Guide to Jewish Religious Practice*. New York: Jewish Theological Seminary, 1979.

Krauss, S. *Talmudische Archaeologie*. 3 vols. Repr. Hildesheim: Georg Olms, 1966.

Lamm, N. "Recent Additions to the *Ketubah*." *Tradition* 2 (1959): 93–119.

Levin, A. L., and M. Kramer. *New Provisions in the Ketubah*. New York: Yeshiva University, 1955.

Levine, B. "Nikhsei Melug." *Journal of the American Oriental Society* 88 (1968): 271–85.

Lewin, B. M. *Iggeret Rav Sherira Gaon.* Repr. Jerusalem: Makor, 1971/72.

Lieberman, S. "Torotan shel Ge'onim Ve-Rishonim me'et Simhah Asaf" (Review). *Tarbiz* 5 (1933/34): 395–400.

———. *Tosefta 'al pi ketav yad Vina ve-Shinuyei Nusha'ot mi-Ketav Yad Erfurt, Qeta'im min Ha-Genizah u-Defus Venezia 1521.* New York: Jewish Theological Seminary, 1955–.

———. *Tosefta Ke-Feshutah: Be'ur Arokh le-Tosefta.* New York: Jewish Theological Seminary, 1955–.

Lubetzki, Y., ed. *Ein Tenai Be-Nissu'in.* Vilna, 1929/30.

Mann, J. "The Responsa of the Babylonian Geonim as a Source of Jewish History." *Jewish Quarterly Review,* n.s. 10 (1919–20): 121–51, 309–65.

Melamed, E. Z. *Pirqei Mavo' Le-Sifrut Ha-Talmud.* Jerusalem: privately printed, 1973.

Morell, S. "An Equal or a Ward: How Independent Is a Married Woman." Unpublished paper.

Muffs, Y. *Studies in the Aramaic Legal Papyri from Elephantine.* Leiden: E. J. Brill, 1969.

Neusner, J. *A History of the Jews in Babylonia. Vol. I, The Parthian Period.* 3d ed. Chico, Calif.: Scholars Press, 1984.

———. *The Rabbinic Traditions About the Pharisees Before 70.* 3 vols. Leiden: E. J. Brill, 1971.

Porten, B. *Archives from Elephantine.* Berkeley and Los Angeles: University of California Press, 1968.

Posnanski, S. *Babylonische Gaonim im nachgaonaeischen Zeitalter . . . nach handschriftlichen und gedruckten Quellen.* Berlin: Mayer & Muller, 1914.

Rabinovicz, R. *Diqduqei Soferim.* 12 vols. Repr. Brooklyn: Jerusalem Bookstore, 1959/60.

Rackover, N. "Coercion in Marital Relations." In *Jewish Law and Current Legal Problems,* pp. 137–60. Jerusalem: Jewish Legal Heritage Society, 1984.

Reifman, Y. *Toldot Rabbenu Zerahiyah Ba'al Ha-Ma'or.* Prague, 1842/43.

Tannenblatt, M. A. *Ha-Talmud Ha-Bavli Be-Hithavuto Ha-Historit.* Tel Aviv: Devir, 1972.

———. *Peraqim Hadashim Le-Toldot Eretz Yisrael Bi-Tequfat Ha-Talmud.* Tel Aviv: Dvir, 1976.

Ta Shema, Y. "Gedarav shel Sefer Ha-Ma'or al Hilkhot Ha-Rif." *Ha-Mishpat Ha-'Ivri* 5 (1978).

Weiss, A. *'Al Ha-Yetzirah Ha-Sifrutit shel Ha-Amoraim.* New York: Horeb, 1961/62.

————. *Ha-Yetzirah shel Ha-Saboraim.* Jerusalem: Magnes, 1952/53.

————. *Hithavvut Ha-Talmud Be-Shelemuto.* New York: Kohut Foundation, 1943.

————. *Le-Heqer Ha-Talmud.* New York: Feldheim, 1954.

————. *Le-Qorot Hithavvut Ha-Bavli.* Warsaw, 1929.

Weiss, I. H. *Dor Dor Ve-Doreshov.* 4th ed. Vilna, 1923/24.

Zaks, N. "Qiddushin al Tenai." *No'am* 1 (1957/58): 52–68.

Zevin, S. Y. *Entsyqlopedia Talmudit.* 18 vols. 1947–.

Zuckermandel, M. S. *Tosefta 'al pi Kitvei Yad Erfurt U-Vina.* Rev. ed. Jerusalem: Wahrmann Books, 1970.

Index

Index to Biblical and Talmudic References